INTERNATIONAL ASSOCIATION FOR THE EVALUATION

OF EDUCATIONAL ACHIEVEMENT (IEA)

International Studies
in Evaluation VIII

D0300747

An Empirical Study of Education in Twenty-One Countries: A Technical Report

Gilbert F. Peaker

With Contributions by
T. Neville Postlethwaite
Roy. W. Phillipps
Bruce H. Choppin

and a Foreword by
Torsten Husén

Almqvist & Wiksell International
Stockholm, Sweden

A Halsted Press Book
John Wiley & Sons
New York – London – Sydney – Toronto

7305

Library of Congress Catalog Card Number

Halsted Press ISBN
Almqvist & Wiksell
ISBN 91-2200025-9

Design Dick Hallström

Printed in Sweden by
Almqvist & Wiksell, Uppsala 1975

Library of Congress Cataloging in Publication Data
Peaker, Gilbert Fawscett.
An empirical study of education in twenty one countries.
(International studies in evaluation; 8) "A Halsted Press book".
At head of title: International Association for the Evaluation
of Educational Achievement.
Includes bibliographical references.
1. Comparative education. 2. Educational surveys—Mathematical
models. I. International Association for the Evaluation of
Educational Achievement. II. Title. III. Series.
LA132.P33   370   75-30533
ISBN 0-470-67456-3 (Wiley)

Contents

Foreword

Technically the IEA Six Subject Survey has been a formidable task. When the project was launched one could not, apart from the IEA Mathematics Study, draw upon experiences from any similar large-scale research endeavors. Coleman and his co-workers had at that time not yet published their survey on equality of educational opportunity. We were therefore fortunate to enlist the expertise represented by Gilbert F. Peaker, who had been responsible for the statistical analysis of the survey on 11-year-old school children in England sponsored by the Plowden Commission.

The—one is tempted to say—courageous ambition that the team of researchers who designed the Six Subject Survey held, was to analyze what accounted for between-student and between-school differences in scholastic achievements in a series of key subject areas. With that purpose in mind we started by attempting to develop an input–output model which we intended to apply in a great variety of national systems of education. Two international conferences, one at the UNESCO Institute for Education in Hamburg and the other one at the Lake Mohonk conference center close to New York were held. Researchers representing a great variety of the social sciences, such as economics, sociology, psychology and anthropology, at these meetings suggested a large number of independent variables that seemed to hold explanatory promise in accounting for differences in achievement criteria. The information relevant to these variables could only be collected (considering the size and the nature of the enterprise) by means of questionnaires completed by school principals, teachers, and students. Thus, the original list had to be considerably pruned but even so finally consisted of several hundred variables. Apart from certain home background variables, the bulk of those which were kept pertained to school resources and, particularly, to the teaching process. As far as the latter is concerned, we had for financial reasons no direct access to observational data on the teaching–learning process that went on in the classroom. Our measures were what in the educational research jargon are referred to as "proxies."

The limitations of the model that has been employed in the statistical analysis of the IEA data have in detail been spelled out in this book by Mr. Peaker. We had, for instance, access to cross-sectional data only which confronted us with problems in ordering the variables in temporal sequence. Although one might question the adequacy of the model, the variables which were supposed to measure the teaching process and the methodology employed seemed to be consistent with the IEA research strategy. I think it is fair to say, and this is also emphasized by Mr. Peaker, the "efforts to subdivide the quantity of teaching into different aspects or elements were rather unrewarding." On the other hand, the replication of the analyses in widely different countries and at different levels of the educational systems has been helpful in arriving at conclusions which could be generalized.

It would be preposterous to try here to present within the confines of a paragraph or two some generalizations from a study of this magnitude and diversification. But one cannot avoid making the point that due to the strong institutionalization of the educational systems in countries with a long tradition of universal primary education, the variation between countries in student competence is strikingly limited, in spite of large differences in formal characteristics of the school systems. Furthermore, I think it ought to be emphasized, considering the debate that has been going on in recent years in the wake of research in the United States reported by, for instance, Coleman and Jencks, that schools, indeed, make differences with regard to learning. The IEA analyses of widely different subject areas lend little support to the pessimistic conclusions that have been floating around in recent debates on the worthwhileness of schooling. The proportion of the variance in achievements accounted for by the school in the IEA research is, due to a better coverage of the relevant variables, on the whole larger than in previous surveys. Thus amount of teaching is throughout positively related to outcomes. It is true, however, that home background tends consistently to account for more of the variance than do the school and teaching variables. To what extent this depends on the lack of good measures of "process variables" (possibly accessible only by direct classroom observation) is, of course, an important and still open question.

The Data Bank covering the Six Subject Survey consists of some quarter of a billion of pieces of information which have been entered onto 10 different types of merged files and cover all the items and scores obtained in the subject areas that have been investigated. Each student has been assigned the responses pertaining to his school.

This information was obtained from the questionnaire completed by the school principal. The information on teaching was obtained from the teacher questionnaires. The responses by the teachers on a particular stage have been aggregated to the level of the school. For each type of merged file a codebook has been prepared as follows:

Science, Reading and Literature (Population I, 10-year-olds)
Science, Reading and Literature (Population II, 14-year-olds)
Science, Reading and Literature (Population IV, students in the pre-university grade)
English as a Foreign Language (Population II)
English as a Foreign Language (Population IV)
French as a Foreign Language (Population II)
French as a Foreign Language (Population IV)
Civic Education (Population I)
Civic Education (Population II)
Civic Education (Population IV).

I have considered it important to present this nutshell information about the Data Bank because of its value for cross-national research in education. Those of us who have spent years in collecting this unique set of data on national systems of education hope that the international research community in education will avail itself. of the Data Bank. It should certainly be of great potential value for those who want to conduct empirical investigations in comparative education.

*

It remains for me to acknowledge the contributions of those who made the work, which is reported in this volume, possible. In the first place, we are highly indebted to Mr Peaker who began his association with IEA in the role of what he preferred to call a "sampling referee" and soon became our statistical advisor. His long and varied experience in the field of survey research, not least his experience from the Plowden studies, has been brought to bear upon the research reported by IEA. His humane wisdom seasoned by many years of association with schools, together with his inclination to quote what other wise men have said on pedagogical matters, lend, as the reader will discover, a particular flavor to his writings. We are, indeed, grateful for his committed contribution to our work and for writing up the present volume.

As applies to the other volumes in the series "International Studies in Evaluation," the research reported in this book is the outcome of a complex cooperative endeavor. I would in the first place like to thank those who in various technical capacities have been instrumental in bringing the Six Subject Survey to a completion. We are grateful to those who had to coordinate the project, Dr T. Neville Postlethwaite, and his successor, Mr Roy W. Phillipps. Dr Douglas A. Pidgeon and Professor Robert L. Thorndike served on a Technical Committee, which had to consider and take action on major technical problems. Thanks are also due to the data processing units at Teachers College, Columbia University and at the University of Stockholm, respectively. Mr John Hall who for the major portion of the time was in charge of the former unit, had to carry the main responsibility for the editing, filing and the univariate and item analyses of the data. He was ably assisted by Mr Paul Barbuto and Mr Kevin Doyle. The major portion of the multivariate analyses has been conducted at the Stockholm data processing unit where Mr Mats Carlid, Miss Birgitta Cedheim and Mr Krister Widén have had to carry the heavy load conducting the analyses and in the data processing connected with them. It is hoped that in the future a detailed report on the whole of the data processing activities can be published separately. The Executive Directors have at times been assisted with the planning and the coordination of the analyses of the six subjects by many colleagues. However, the contribution made by Dr John P. Keeves at a critical point of the Stage 2 processing deserves particular mention.

In recent years Dr John R. Schwille, together with the Stockholm Data Processing Unit, has been responsible for the setting up of a Data Bank.

Thanks are also due to the Office of the Chancellor of the Swedish Universities which by providing data processing time has enabled us to complete the extensive analyses.

The Bank of Sweden Tercentenary Fund has by a generous grant supported the publication of the present volume.

Stockholm, Institute for the Study of
International Problems in Education, 1975

Torsten Husén
Chairman of IEA

Author's Preface

The IEA enterprise was a large cooperative undertaking carried out over the course of several years by many workers in a score of countries. It is being reported in a series of nine volumes, of which this is one, as well as in several monographs on particular topics. This volume, despite its title, does not by any means purport to be a complete account of the technical problems of the whole enterprise, with some parts of which the author has no more than a nodding acquaintance. The ensuing pages are about those aspects of the undertaking with which the author has been more closely concerned. Even with this limitation he has found the writing a daunting task, and no one can be more aware of the many imperfections in its accomplishment, although a large part of his waking hours during the last ten years has been spent in wrestling with the problems.

The problems are of two kinds, closely interconnected. There are the problems of data reduction, which are large but manageable, and the problems of interpretation, which are more difficult and doubtful. Any interpretation of the equations obtained from the reduction must, in the nature of the case, rest upon some prior notion about what goes on in schools. The conclusions are bound to be in the form "*If* this is how the thing works then here are some relevant quantifying equations."

We do not start from scratch. Systems of universal compulsory education have now existed in many countries for about a hundred years. Every lesson is an educational experiment, so that there is a very large mass of prior evidence about how schools actually work. Traditional practices are based on this mass of evidence, which can be described as common experience and common sense, and successful innovations have been developed from it. The most advanced sciences, such as physics, have made great progress by always retaining as much of the common sense world as is possible without intolerable complication. This suggests that more rudimentary sciences would do well to follow their example in this respect, and stick to common sense unless forced to depart from it. On the other hand the social sciences can hardly follow the example of physics in the design of experiments. In education, as in medicine, the part that can be played by experiment is limited by ethical considerations. This makes attention to experience and common sense all the more important.

Common sense tells us that what we can learn today depends on what we learned yesterday and on all our earlier yesterdays; early experiences condition later experiences, and consequently, while it is never too late to mend, it becomes harder as we grow older and habits tend to become fixed. The teacher's function is to strengthen good habits and to convert bad habits into better ones, the first object being more easily attainable than the second, for the latter demands a high level of teaching skill. Teaching skill is easily recognized from its effects but hard to describe otherwise; consequently it is only weakly represented among the instructional group of variables in the study. Here is one reason for the rather small effects attributed in the study to this group of variables. Another is that in comparison with the family group they are short term variables operating over only a brief interval before the time of survey. Yet another is that success in running a school depends on balancing many factors; too much of one thing may imply too little of another. This is well recognized, and consequently the range of variation for some factors is small, and the response surface may be near an optimal point. If so the best linear approximation may be nearly flat, as at the top of a hill. This would explain not only the small coefficients but also the fact that different variables emerge in different countries.

It will be plain to the reader that many of the measured variables in the study are merely surrogates; thus the group of family background variables are rather weak surrogates for the child's natural predispositions (except that they exclude inter-sibling variation) and their modification by upbringing. The surrogates serve their purpose up to a point because they are correlated with the genuine variables. If we had more of the latter they would both improve the prediction and diminish the apparent effects of the surrogates.

The total prediction is quite considerable, particularly between schools. But even when the prediction rises to 80 % there is still a residual of 20 %. In other words there are some schools that are doing decidedly better than the measured variables predict, and others that are doing worse. Part of the original plan was to single out from each sample the ten schools with the largest positive residuals, for further inquiry in the hope of identifying some of the reasons that made them outstanding. Unfortunately funds ran out before this stage was reached in the general study, but the inquiry is being pursued in Australia, and this example may be followed in other countries. In a limited sense the answer can be foreseen. When so much else has been covered by the measured variables it is highly probable that the main reason is better teaching, but the question is whether the better teaching can be effectively described.

The object of this preamble has been to indicate briefly the kind of assumptions on which the interpretations advocated in the volume finally rest. The critical reader may find them hard to accept. If so the author can only reply that *some* assumptions based on experience are needed as a foundation, and that if he rejects this set it is incumbent on the critic to supply a better set, unless he is content to be merely agnostic.

In conclusion it is the author's pleasant duty to acknowledge his debt to all his colleagues in IEA, and in particular to Dr T. Neville Postlethwaite, whose unflagging energy over the years kept the whole unwieldy enterprise in motion, to the National Technical Officers for their exemplary patience in the lengthy correspondence, frequently in what was to them a foreign tongue, about the sampling designs and the problems associated with their execution, and to the Data Processors in New York and Stockholm and to his fellow authors.

Looking back over ten years of international cooperation one sees the project gradually taking shape with all bearing a hand to overcome the difficulties as they arose, under the genial lead of Professor Torsten Husén. In the final stages, when the grasshopper tended to become a burden and desire to fail, Mr Roy Phillipps and the first group of Spencer Foundation Fellows lent new impetus. It is perhaps needless to repeat, that although the writer has done his best there is much that he has omitted and not all his colleagues would subscribe to the interpretation he advocates in its entirety.

Chapter 1

A Reader's Guide

Two themes run through this book. In the first place it is about the mathematical models used to describe the evidence collected in the IEA Six Subject Survey. Secondly it is about the interpretation of that evidence. In principle the mathematical theme is simple; the operations traverse the well worn ground of regression analysis, and such complexities as there are stem from the sheer size of the study. The interpretation advocated is also simple in principle. Some readers indeed may take the view that it is simple-minded—a view that was shared by some of those who collaborated in the study.

The reception of the reports already published has made it plain that interest and criticism are likely to focus mainly on this question of interpretation. It may not therefore be out of place to begin with a brief account of the reasons for and against the choice of interpretation. Most of them can be found in the preface to *The Doctor's Dilemma* (G. B. Shaw, 1906). "Thus it is easy to prove that the wearing of tall hats and the carrying of umbrellas enlarges the chest, prolongs life and confers comparative immunity from disease, for the statistics show that the classes which use these articles are bigger, healthier, and live longer than the class which never dreams of possessing such things. It does not take much perspicacity to see that what really makes this difference is not the tall hat and the umbrella, but the wealth and nourishment of which they are evidence, and that a gold watch or membership of a club in Pall Mall might be shown in the same way to have the like sovereign virtues. A university degree, a daily bath, the owning of thirty pairs of trousers, a knowledge of Wagner's music, a pew in church, anything in short, that implied more means and better nurture than the mass of labourers enjoy, can be statistically palmed off as a magic-spell conferring all sorts of privileges."

What holds for simple correlations also holds for manipulations of them. Thus if the correlation between x and y is 0.5 then x can "explain," in the mathematical sense, 25 % of the variation of y, and similarly, if the multiple correlation between y and a set of x is 0.9 then the set can "explain," in the same sense, 81 % of the variation.

These are mathematical facts, but perspicacity and a knowledge of the background are needed to see what more they can be. "Background," in this context, means all the previous evidence, which should be taken into account along with the immediate evidence from the study.

To say that all the previous evidence should be taken into account is a counsel of perfection, both because it is unlikely that all the previous evidence is known to any one person and also because it is partly formulated and partly vaguely perceived. Thus anyone who, like the writer, has spent most of a long life in schools will be aware that children who begin as fast learners, or slow, tend to continue as fast, or slow. Exceptions to this rule certainly exist, but are rather rare. Unusually good teaching is one of the causes producing the exceptions, but this again is rather rare. Moreover, while the unusually good teachers are easily recognized in the daily life of a school it is not the case that they conform to an easily specifiable pattern. Unusually effective teachers are seen to be so because they have an unusual effect, but they come in many shapes and sizes. This makes it easier to judge the merit of a teacher than to give reasons for the judgment; the case fits the advice that the Earl of Mansfield, Lord Chief Justice in the eighteenth century, gave to his colleagues— "Never give your reasons, for your judgment will probably be right, but your reasons will certainly be wrong." This vagueness about the reasons does not destroy the validity of the judgment, but it means that the effect of variation in teaching skill is likely to be underrated in any formal study of variation among students. The judgment itself cannot be used, for that would make the argument circular. It must be replaced by independently assessed characteristics, which are likely to be only weakly related, and therefore to make rather poor surrogates.

The general point illustrated by the preceding paragraph is that we are aware of much more about human behavior than can be brought within the compass of a formal scheme, and that what we know, or at any rate believe, from common experience and common sense, is not to be ignored in interpreting the results of a formal study. The instances in which common sense and the lessons of experience have been shown to be mistaken form a favorite theme with the historians of science, but this does not alter the fact that such instances are extremely rare in comparison with those on which we rely from minute to minute in the conduct of daily life. There is a very strong balance of probability in favor of a cautious interpretation of new evidence in cases where more than one interpretation is possible. This is the foundation for the interpretation advocated here.

THE SEQUENCE OF VARIABLES

The variables observed in the IEA study can be divided into several groups. In the first place we have the long-term group of family or home variables which have operated throughout the student's life up to the time of survey. Secondly we have a middle-term group, which has operated for an interval shorter than that during which the long-term variables have been at work, but longer than that for the third group. This third, or short-term, group comprises the current instructional variables, representing conditions of learning operating at the time of survey and for a brief interval preceding it. In a fourth group are what we have called the kindred variables, which can be thought of as concomitants rather than causes of learning. The fifth group contained a single variable—the score in the short test of Word Knowledge, which was taken by all students. The sixth group also contained a single variable, the score in the test of Reading Comprehension for those students who had taken this test.

The composition of the groups and the details of the analyses form the subject of the ensuing chapters. Here we are concerned with the general principle of the procedure, which was to form a series of regression equations for each subject by regressing the criterion variables first on the long-term group of independent variables, then on the long-term and the middle-term groups, and so on until all the groups were included. The extensive tables in Chapter 4 exemplify this procedure. In these tables it will be seen that the observed variables account for a large fraction of the variation between students—a fraction that varies from subject to subject and from country to country, that may be as large as three-quarters and that is never less than substantial. Consequently we may say that in the mathematical sense of the third paragraph in this chapter much of the variation is "explained." But what can this mean? How is the mathematical fact to be interpreted? In itself it is essentially ambiguous. Thus if we regress a variable x_0 on three others, $x_1, x_2,$ and x_3, the resulting equation can be written as either

$$(1)\quad x_0 = b_{01.23}x_1 \qquad +b_{02.13}x_2 \qquad +b_{03.12}x_3 \qquad +x_{0.123}$$
$$\text{or } (2)\quad x_0 = b_{01}x_1 \qquad +b_{02.1}x_{2.1} \qquad +b_{03.12}x_{3.12} \qquad +x_{0.123}$$
$$\text{or } (3)\quad x_0 = b_{01.23}x_{1.23} \qquad +b_{02.3}x_{2.3} \qquad +b_{03}x_3 \qquad +x_{0.123}$$

18

The three equations are algebraically identical (and so are other permuted forms). Mathematically there is nothing to choose between them. The choice must depend on the genesis of the variables. If x_1 is a long-term, x_2 a middle-term, and x_3 a short-term variable it becomes reasonable to say that (2) corresponds to reckoning forwards, from early to late, (3) to reckoning backwards, from late to early, and (1) to ignoring early and late. In (2) we let x_1 account for as much of the variation as it can, before bringing in x_2, and then let x_2 account for as much as it can, before bringing in x_3. In (3) the procedure is reversed; we give the late variable the first bite at the apple. In (1) we are impartial. Impartial, that is to say, mathematically. But should we be impartial in face of the full facts?

The full facts in the IEA survey include those that are briefly sketched in the third paragraph above. Children who are fast learners when they begin their schooling tend to continue as fast learners, and similarly for slow learners. This suggests that it is reasonable to let the long-term family variables have the first bite. Although exceptions to the rule are rather rare they certainly do occur, and occur continuously as the children go through the successive stages of their schooling. This suggests that the second group—the middle-term group—which contains all that has been observed in the study about the middle stage, should have the second bite. If so the third bite, taken by the short-term group, will be rather small, because the first two groups are correlated with the third. Since the short-term group includes all the observations made on the current conditions of learning, this interpretation says that the variation induced by the variation in the current conditions of learning is rather small in comparison with the variation that ensues from earlier conditions. It is plain from the reception of the earlier reports that some readers feel that this is a meagre and disappointing interpretation, which ought to be resisted. This amounts to saying that equation (1), or perhaps (3), or some other permutation, is to be preferred to equation (2). The formal difference between (1) and (2) is that the variables on the right hand side of (1), namely x_1, x_2, x_3, are correlated, whereas those on the right hand side of (2), namely x_1, $x_{2.1}, x_{3.12}$, are not. If we convert (2) into an incremental account of the explained variation of x_0 the successive increments of R^2 are b_{01}^2, $b_{02.1}^2 \, s_{2.1}^2$, and $b_{03.12}^2 \, s_{3.12}^2$. From (1), on the other hand, we do not get a clear cut incremental account, owing to the correlation between x_1, x_2 and x_3. This formal difference, however, is merely the correspondence between the two mathematical statements and the two interpretations and throws no light on the question of which statement, or which interpretation, is to be preferred. The choice must rest on other grounds.

The strong point in favor of the interpretation advocated in this chapter is that it corresponds to what actually happens in the course of schooling. Against this it can be argued that what actually happens need not happen, and that the purpose of the study should be to describe what might happen rather than what does happen. This is certainly a more ambitious aim, and therefore tempting. How far is it practicable? Can we infer, from the observations actually made, what would be the case if the later variables were not correlated with (i.e., conditioned by) the earlier ones? If the question relates to the evidence in the study from a particular national system it is hard to see how this could be done. The correlations, and therefore the regression coefficients that stem from them, are all derived from the system in being. If the system were quite different the correlations and coefficients would also be different. If the system were slightly different it is unlikely that the correlations would be greatly changed, and this seems to offer some possibility of inferring the probable effects of small changes by using the regression equations. But further reflection suggests that such inferences would remain doubtful until they were confirmed or confuted by experiment. For example students who have been fast learners during their early schooling are often taught in a different way, by teachers with different characteristics during the later stages. Would the slower students benefit by being treated in the same way? If a student is to learn something of the calculus, or of matrices, it is an advantage to him to have a teacher who knows something of these matters. But would having such a teacher also be an advantage to a backward student struggling with the rudiments of arithmetic? A university professor facing a nursery class is likely to be at a loss; if he is not it is more probably because he is a good family man than because of his academic prowess.

If the recent conditions of learning are not discounted too much by being taken third in the regression are they discounted enough? Ought they to have a still lower place? Or, what comes to the same thing, should the result of the reading tests be included in the preceding middle-term group? The middle-term group is intended to serve as a surrogate for the progress before the variables in the short-term group come into operation. As it stands it is not a very good surrogate, because it comprises only two variables, namely

Type of program and Type of school, and takes no account of the variation of students within these types. In a longitudinal survey it could be supplemented, and indeed largely replaced, by a pretest, which would include the variation within types. Is it reasonable to let the reading tests play the part of a pretest for all subjects but reading? The argument against this is that these tests were taken at the same time as the tests in the other subjects. The argument in favor of it is that their results would have been highly correlated with those of earlier reading tests. The effect of including them in the middle-term group is clearer than the case for doing so. The effect is twofold, as may be seen in Chapters 4 and 6. In the first place, more of the variation between students in the other subjects is explained. Secondly, the amount of this variation that is attributed to the recent conditions of learning in the third group is reduced. If we refrain from putting the reading tests in the regression we have a larger residual variation that is unexplained. Unexplained, that is to say, by any of the measured variables, though we may have a strong conviction that much of it is explained in another sense by the general activity or lethargy of the mental process. If so we could represent this by a hypothetical variable, called IQ, for want of a better name, and bring this hypothetical variable into the equations, where it would play much the same part as the reading tests. In particular it would reduce the amount of variation attributable to the third group, besides increasing the total amount of explained variation.

Even when the Reading Comprehension tests are included in the regression the explained variation never exceeds 80 %. This is hardly surprising, since it is plain that much is omitted from the measured variables, but it is another reason for caution in the interpretation. Had it been possible to measure some of the missing variables they would have been correlated not only with the criteria but also with the existing independent variables, and would therefore have reduced the estimates of the effects of the latter. This makes it all the more important that the interpretation, as far as it goes, should be consonant with all the external evidence as well as with the immediate evidence from the study itself. For example, the external evidence, in the shape of common observation of the daily life of schools, and in the memory of former students, suggests that variation in teaching skill plays a larger part than is suggested by the immediate evidence of the study, but this apparent conflict of evidence disappears when we consider the nature of the variables actually observed in the study. In the first place, no direct measure of this variation could be included without circularity, and the teacher characteristics that were included in the short-term group are rather poor surrogates. Secondly, the two surrogate variables, Type of program and Type of school, that comprise the middle-term block and represent progress made in the earlier stages of schooling, are surrogates for many factors, including the variation in teaching skill experienced by the student during this interval. In the third place, students commonly change their teacher at the end of the school year, so that there is a rather small chance of the same student having a succession of outstanding teachers. The teacher characteristics directly represented in the short-term block were school averages; this takes account, as it should, of the small chance of the same student having a succession of outstanding teachers, although it does not represent the full variation of these characteristics.

HOME AND SCHOOL

The immediate evidence and the external evidence agree in attributing more variation in student achievement to the family background than to the school factors. The reason is not far to seek. It is that parents vary much more than schools. Teaching is a profession, with standards of entry, whereas parenthood is open to all. Very bad schools are not allowed to exist. This point, which is plain enough, appears to have been overlooked in some of the comment on the volumes already published. If a variable has little variation its variation cannot explain much, but to say this is very different from saying that the variable is unimportant in itself. For example, the variation in the length of teacher education is small, and therefore does not explain much of the variation in student achievement. But it would be merely ludicrous to infer from this that teacher education is unimportant. It would be even more ludicrous to infer that teachers are unimportant. It is because the importance of teachers is generally recognized that the standards of admission to the profession have a rather small variation, in comparison with the variation in the home background of the students.

What applies to teacher qualifications applies also to other variables in the third group. It is not that these variables are thought to be unimportant and therefore neglected in the daily life of schools. It is rather that there is a consensus about their importance, and therefore a rather small range of variation. Schools exist for the good of their students, and not to make life easy for the inquirer in search of findings that are at once novel and clear-cut. Existing practices rest on a solid foundation of effort, experience, and human nature; this is what is meant when they are described as traditional. There is no reason to suppose that they are incapable of improvement, and indeed the example of the great innovators shows that this is not the case, but equally there is no reason to suppose that successful innovation can be easy, rapid, or widespread. Because education is a slow and cumulative process, changes that bring gains in one direction tend to bring losses in others, and it is hard to single out features of prime importance, other than those already generally recognized. This is perhaps the main reason why, as will be seen in the ensuing chapters, few of the variables in the third group emerge consistently from country to country. These variables comprised the answers to a large number of questions on teacher qualifications, methods, materials and time spent on the subject. The questionnaires were most carefully devised by the subject committees, and the variables so defined passed the operational test in the sense that they turned out to be correlated with the achievements of the students. But they were also correlated with the variables in the earlier groups, and with each other. Because they were correlated with the earlier groups the total variation that they explained was rather small, and because they were correlated with each other the unique variation associated with any one of them was very small indeed. The first fact reflects the cumulative nature of learning; skill and knowledge are accumulated gradually, and what happens during a short interval is bound to have only a rather small effect. The second fact reflects the protean and intuitive nature of teaching, which eludes categorization. Taken together the variables in the short-term group account for a larger proportion of the variation in foreign languages than in the other subjects. This is to be expected. In the first place, these subjects are not taken by all students so that the variation attributable to the first two groups of variables is reduced by selection. Secondly, the work is begun rather late in school life, so that the interval during which the short-term variables are operative is relatively longer. In the third place, the skill is acquired mainly in school. Reading comprehension, in the mother tongue, is at the opposite pole. All students are concerned; there is no selection. We begin to acquire skill in the use of the mother tongue from earliest childhood. Much of the skill is gained out of school.

The influence of selection also accounts for the larger part played by the short-term variables in the final stage of school life among those members of the age group who are still attending school. The United States form the exception that proves the rule, because a much larger proportion of the population is still in attendance, and the early variables have almost their full range. In some countries at this stage the curriculum is no longer common; students specialize in different subjects and the short-term variables play a larger part, because of this specialization as well as because of selection.

All this supports the view that where, as is usually the case, the instructional variables in the short-term group do not account for very much of the variation in achievement it is because (1) they *are* short term, and (2) their range of variation is slight, owing to the consensus, and also owing to the fact that they do not cover the most important aspects of teaching. None of the evidence provides any support for the view that schools and teachers do not matter.

SUMMARIES OF THE ENSUING CHAPTERS

At this point the reader who is mainly interested in the analyses and their interpretation may like to turn to Chapter 4. In this chapter and those that follow he will find the detailed application of the interpretation sketched in broad outline in these opening remarks, and he will be able to reach his own conclusion, as to whether the interpretation advocated is reasonable or whether some other interpretation is to be preferred.

If he is interested in the problem of securing representative samples of schools, students, parents and teachers he should turn to Chapter 2, which is about the recommended sampling designs, the extent to which the achieved samples fell short of the designed samples and the use of weights to repair as far as possible the damage caused by this shortfall. Because the sampling designs had to be multi-stage the simple random sampling formulae for standard errors are inapplicable. The standard errors have to be calculated indirectly by estimating the design effects, and a section of the chapter describes how this was done.

Chapter 3 is about why and how the variables were organized into groups. The reasons for the grouping have been given in outline in the preceding pages; in Chapter 3 they are set out in more detail and reinforced by arguments drawn from longitudinal studies. The third group contained a very large number of variables describing the current conditions of learning, and the steps taken to reduce this assembly to a manageable size are described. The first step was to

24

combine category variables into scales, the second to combine some clusters of related variables into single compounds, and the third to apply a screening process to divide the variables into those that could be discarded without any serious loss of information and those that ought to be retained for the subsequent analyses.

Chapter 4 is about the regression analyses between students, in the developed countries. It contains extensive tables presenting in full some of the regression equations that were presented in summary form in the subject volumes. These long tables are for Science in Population II, but the relation exemplified applies to the other subjects and populations which are treated more briefly. There is a section on the effects of retentivity in Population IV.

In Chapter 5 we pass from the analyses between-students to the analyses between-schools. In the samples the average number of students per school was 26, so that if each school contained a random sample of the whole population we should expect the variance of the school means to be about 4 % of the variance between students. In fact of course the distribution is very far from random, and the average variance ratio is 25 %. Israel and Italy have the highest ratios, and Sweden the lowest, in all three populations. Between-countries the variance ratio is correlated with the achievement scores; a large variance ratio implies that there must be some schools fed mainly by deprived areas which find it hard to get off the ground in reading and hence in other subjects, and this drags down the average achievement by more than the amount by which it is raised by schools at the other end of the scale. Tables are given showing the amount of the variation in achievement that is explained by the measured variables when (1) the unit is the school, (2) the unit is the individual student, and (3) the account between schools is rescaled by multiplying by the variance ratio. The measured variables account for a larger proportion of that part of the total variation that lies between-schools, mainly because the home background plays an even more predominant role when the evidence is aggregated by schools. A consequence of this predominance is that comparatively few variables appear in the equations. The amount of variation explained by the current learning condition is small, except for Population IV, and of course it becomes even smaller if the reading tests are included as intervening variables for the other subjects. In Population IV the current learning conditions play a larger part because the curriculum is no longer so uniform.

Chapter 6 explores the effects of varying the order in which the groups of variables are put into the regression, by using the commonality analysis devised by Newton and Spurrell. For n groups there are $n!$ possible orders, and the corresponding increments of R^2 could be obtained by making $n!$ regression runs. Newton and Spurrell (1967) showed that this can be greatly shortened by obtaining their $2^n - 1$ "elements" instead. Once these elements have been obtained all possible increments can be produced by suitable additions. Table 6.1 gives the Newton and Spurrell elements for the Civic Education cognitive score for Population II, country by country. In Table 6.2 the results in Table 6.1 are used to obtain the block (i.e., the group) increments when the order is varied. In the first section of the table we have the preferred order; the second section is focused on the assessment of the third group—the recent conditions of learning—in all possible orders. The mean assessment for all countries varies from 25 % when the group is taken first down to 9 % when it is taken last. In the preferred (third) position it is 11 %. The object of this part of the chapter is to enable the reader to see for himself the extent to which the assessment turns on the order adopted.

In the second part of Chapter 6 the Newton and Spurrell procedure is applied to some earlier work by the present author, reported in *The Plowden Children Four Years Later* (Peaker, 1971). The Plowden study surveyed an English national sample in 1964 and again in 1968, so that in it we have a longitudinal study in which the chronological order is free from the doubt in the IEA study, in which all the variables were measured at the same time. In the IEA study we have no pretest, and the argument for letting the Reading Comprehension tests serve as a surrogate for a pretest is weakened by the fact that the Reading Comprehension tests were given at the same time as the other tests. In Plowden the 1964 tests can serve as the pretest for 1968. The effect, illustrated in Tables 6.3 through 6.7, is to increase the proportion of the variation that is explained but to diminish the amount explained by the current learning conditions, which is what happens when the reading tests are used as intervening variables in the IEA study.

Chapter 7 explores some relations between the mean scores for countries. When we were dealing with the scores for individual students, or with their scores aggregated for schools, we had no pretest. But when the scores are aggregated over countries it is reasonable to take the score for Population I as a pretest for Population II, since it is unlikely that there will have been much change in the country mean during the interval extending back to the time when the present Population II was Population I. The two populations are aged 10 and 14, and there is a prior expectation that their scores will be in the ratio of their ages if the two sets of tests are on the same scale. At first sight the proviso seems to make the proposition a mere tautology, and of course it would be so if we looked merely at the ratio of the means aggregated over all countries and rescaled one set of tests until we obtained the expected result. The interest lies in seeing how far the ratios for the individual countries depart from the general average. In fact they do not depart much (see Table 7.1). Between countries as between individual students the pace of learning tends to stay constant; those who begin as fast learners or slow tend to continue as fast or slow. The country means for Population II can in fact be closely predicted by those for Population I. For Reading Comprehension and Science in Population II 93% of the variation in Reading Comprehension and 88% of the variation in Science is predicted by the Population I scores (see Table 7.2). If the grouping variable dividing the developed from the developing countries is omitted these estimates fall to 85% and 78%. Within the groups the estimates are of course much lower (7% and 51%), owing to the wide separation of the groups. With countries as with individuals the amount of overtaking is rather small. Over widely separated groups the correlations between initial and final orders are therefore high, but within groups they are small. It is common to gain or lose a few places, but rare to gain or lose many.

Even from this preliminary sketch it will be plain to the reader who has seen some of the other reports in the series that there is much in them that is not touched on here. In this report attention is focused on the regression analyses. There are two reasons for this choice. In the first place much of the computational effort went into these analyses. Secondly they display the problem of interpretation in its most acute form. Each variable is correlated with all the others; everything depends on everything else. This is indisputable, but does not take us very far. To go beyond this rudimentary stage, we have to organize the variables in some way, e.g., by factor analysis or by regression analysis, and so reach weighted clusters more highly correlated than the individual variables. This can be done in many ways, among which we have to choose. The reasons for our choice are to be found not in the immediate evidence of the survey itself, but in what we have in the way of external evidence about how educational systems work. From a Bayesian standpoint this external evidence furnishes the prior probabilities. Allied with the immediate evidence it gives the posterior probabilities. At the outset we are not sure whether the revised version will differ much from the original. In the upshot it did not; the prior probabilities have been only slightly modified. From one standpoint this is satisfactory; it would have been disquieting to have evidence that much educational effort was misdirected. From another standpoint it is disappointing, in that little in the way of recommendation emerges. These two are of course opposite sides of the same coin.

In considering the analyses one should keep in mind that they are necessarily analyses of the observations, and that what was not observed can play no part in the analyses themselves, though it may play an important part in the interpretation. The observations are observations of symptoms rather than of causes; thus the family variables are not direct measures of the teaching that takes place at home, but they serve as partial surrogates for it because they are correlated with it. Similarly the middle-term variables are not direct measures of the teaching, at home and at school, that has taken place in the early years of schooling, but again they are partial surrogates for it. Because these variables are surrogates for teaching, and also for aptitude in the student, they account for some of the variation in achievement. Because they are only partial surrogates they underestimate the part played by teaching, at home and at school, and by aptitude; if they were better surrogates they would account for more. The short-term variables in the third group, of current conditions of learning, play a rather small part, mainly because they have not operated for very long. They also are surrogates, but for them the surrogate argument works both ways. If they were better surrogates themselves they would account for more of the variation unless this increase were wiped out by more efficiency in the earlier variables; on the existing evidence it is not clear whether there would be a net gain or a net loss. What is clear is that the analyses underestimate the effects of teaching, at home and through the course of schooling.

A related point is that the observations can only represent the range of variation that actually occurs. In practice, class sizes and staffing ratios do not vary much, and this is merely one example of a consensus that restricts the range of most of the variables in the study.

The arguments for the interpretation advocated in this chapter are set out at greater length, and in varied forms, in the ensuing chapters, and are reconsidered, under the heading "Retrospect," in the final Chapter 8. The author's aim has been to express the arguments with as much clarity as he can command. It is for the reader to say whether he finds them convincing. It is open to him to rebut them either by using the evidence in the published reports or by resort to the data bank in which all the evidence of the study has been preserved in full. In either case the major problem for him, as for the IEA authors, will be to combine the internal evidence of the study with all the external evidence of which he is aware. Underlying any interpretation is the general proviso—"*If* this is how the thing works then *these* equations are the most relevant. But if not, not."

THE DATA BANK

There are many ways in which the Data Bank might be explored. For example, it might be used to replace the published equations, which are in standard form, by their metric versions. It is conceivable that there might be a closer resemblance between the metric versions of the same coefficient in different countries than between the standardized. Another way of using the bank would be to look for evidence of curved response surfaces. The first degree surface $z=a+bx+cy$ may be only a rough approximation to a better fitting second degree surface $z=d+ex+fy+gx^2+hy^2$. In some contexts the roughness of the approximation might be important. For example, if the contours of the curved surface were ellipses, as they could, but need not be, z would have a maximum (or a minimum), though not necessarily in the range actually covered by x and y. Since the successful running of a school depends on balancing many factors there are grounds for supposing that such optima exist; Marie Lloyd used to sing "A *little* of what you fancy does you good" (with the implied proviso that a lot might do you harm), and there are instances of schools where damage has been caused when a new practice has been overdone, or where old ones have grown out of balance. However it seems unlikely that the squared terms would extend so far in the ground covered by the IEA variables. The product or xy term, if found to exist, would indicate an interaction between x and y, which might be interpreted in various ways.

Another line that might be followed would be to carry out the organizing, discarding and combining of the available variables in a different way—for example, with the object of enabling the path analyses to emerge more clearly from the relations between only a few combined variables. The justification of any such process would depend, like that of the process already used, on an interpretation of the external evidence.

It is plain that many alternative ways of using the data bank are possible. One test of their success would be the size of the consequent residuals. An alternative that could account for markedly more of the variation than its competitors would have a strong argument in its favor. But the work already done gives rather strong grounds for believing that this is unlikely to happen. To say this is not to imply that exploration of the bank cannot be profitable. It is rather to say that the profit is more likely to come by critical discussion and the comparison of the alternatives with each other and with the external evidence. The external evidence includes the history of educational systems, the unformalized but massive experimental work that goes on in schools—every lesson is an educational experiment—and what is known of beliefs about the purpose of education. As to the last it seems plain that beliefs currently held are hard to reconcile. For example, does equality mean equality of opportunity (implying a more equal chance to become unequal) or of outcome (implying submission to a common experience or culture)? It does not need much perspicacity to see that these beliefs are incompatible, in the same way that "keep to the right" and "keep to the left" are incompatible as rules of the road. In the case of the rule of the road one side or the other must be converted. It will not do to argue that there is much to be said on both sides, and that therefore the best course is to drive straight down the middle and hope for the best. Is the educational case like this? Or is it a case where the response surface has an optimum somewhere between the two extremes? And if so, where? The tenacity with which the opposing beliefs are held suggests that conversion need not be considered, any more than in Cyprus or Ulster. If so, can a compromise be found under which the two sides can live together, or is separation needed, and practicable? One thing at least can be said in favor of discussion. So long as it continues a breakdown is avoided. These questions may seem somewhat remote from the uses of the data bank, but they are not really so. As has been remarked above there is, underlying any interpretation of the data, the general proviso "*If* this is how the thing works then *these* equations are the most relevant. But if not, not." In the social though not in the physical sciences how the thing works depends to quite a large extent on how people think it ought to work. In economics the problem of inflation furnishes a good example, but instances are to be found everywhere. Politics is the art of the possible.

Chapter 2

Sampling

This chapter is about (1) the populations to be sampled, (2) the sampling designs, (3) the execution of the designs and (4) the accuracy of the resulting estimates.

POPULATIONS

For the international study three populations of students were specified. Population I comprised the 10-year-olds, Population II the 14-year-olds and Population IV the students in the pre-university year of secondary education. There were two other populations that could be included if the National Center so wished. Population III was a group at a major terminal point in a national system somewhere between Populations II and IV, and Population IVS was a subset of Population IV specializing in the particular subject being tested. It was agreed at the outset that the populations were to be limited to those individuals who were actually in school at the time of the survey, and that no effort should be made to test members of an age group who for one reason or another had never been in or had fallen out of schooling. It was also agreed that children who were in special schools because of severe mental or physical handicap should be excluded.

Populations I and II were defined by age rather than grade because age is a uniform attribute from country to country, whereas the meaning of grade varies; in some countries grade is a synonym for age, but in others it is a standard of achievement. In the latter case, Populations I and II are spread through several grades. Sampling them is a troublesome enterprise for the schools and a fruitless one where it entails testing severely retarded children. This consideration led five countries to redefine the populations by excluding certain groups. The five were Chile, Hungary, India, Israel and Italy. The following exclusions were made:

1. In Chile; 34 % of 10-year-olds who were more than one year retarded or not attending school, and 43 % of 14-year-olds not attending school.

2. In Hungary; 5 % of 10-year-olds who were more than one year retarded, and 11 % of 14-year-olds either retarded or not in attendance.

3. In India; an unspecified proportion of 10-year-olds in the first and second grades, and of 14-year-olds in the fifth and lower grades, and all students in English-speaking private schools.

4. In Israel; 16 % of 14-year-olds no longer attending school, and all Arabic-speaking students.

5. In Italy; 60 % of 10-year-olds below the fifth grade, and a small proportion of 14-year-olds who were two years retarded. On rather similar grounds, vocational schools were excluded from Population II in Belgium. It is plain that the mean scores for countries where the population was redefined to exclude retarded children must be higher than they would have been had the normal definition been adopted.

Population IV comprised a grade group, determined in each country by the length of the full school course, so that, for example, it is an older group in Sweden than in Scotland. There is also a very wide range in the proportion of students who are still at school at this stage. Some of these details are given in Chapter 4.

In India all populations were limited to the six Hindi-speaking States, and in Thailand some disturbed parts of the country had to be excluded.

THE SAMPLING DESIGNS

Each National Center was asked to draw up a plan of sampling the specified populations in its country. It was recommended that

1. The plan should be such that every student in the population should have the same chance of appearing in the sample.

2. There should be two stages for the selection of students, the first stage being the selection of schools, and the second the selection of students within selected schools.

3. Schools should be stratified by size, sex, type and region.

4. For each population in each country at least 100 schools, and preferably more, should be selected.

5. In each stratum the two sampling fractions (for the selection of schools and for the selection of students within selected schools) should be so adjusted that about 30 students would be selected from each selected school. This adjustment was subject to the condition implied by (1) above, that the product of the two sampling fractions

should be constant. If, for example, this constant product were 1/120 then for a stratum in which each school contained on the average 60 members of the population the sampling fraction for students within selected schools would be $30/60=\frac{1}{2}$, and the sampling fraction for schools would be 1/60. For a stratum where the schools contained on the average 120 members of the population the sampling fraction for students within selected schools would be $30/120=1/4$, and the sampling fraction for schools would be 1/30. Thus large schools would have more chance of selection than small ones, but this would be counterbalanced by their being represented in the sample by a smaller proportion of their population.

These recommendations were designed with two objects in view. On the one hand, the total amount of work had to be kept within the resources of the project. On the other, the samples selected had to be such that they would yield reliable estimates. Because something like a third of the variation lies between schools it was essential that the samples should contain enough schools. But it was also essential that the sample drawn from each selected school should contain enough students to represent it fairly. The recommendations were based on the experience of Phase 1 in the IEA project—the Mathematics Study—where similar suggestions had proved satisfactory (Husén, 1967, Vol. I, Ch. 9).

Within this general framework, discussions were held with each National Center about the modifications needed to adapt the design to local circumstances. There was much variation between countries in the resources available for the project, and in the amount of preliminary information contained in the countries' central statistics. Where resources were scanty the samples had to be smaller than the recommended minimum of 100 schools. Where the central statistics were inadequate for the draw to be made in two stages, with the selection of schools as the first stage, another stage had to be brought in. In these cases the first stage had to be the selection of administrative districts, the second the selection of schools from selected districts, and the third the selection of students from selected schools. The advantage of this plan is that it is only necessary to canvass the selected districts, instead of the whole country, before selecting the schools. The disadvantage is that the variation between districts now forms part of the sampling fluctuation of the estimates. Three stage sampling was applied in Iran and the United States.

Three stage sampling, in which every district, and therefore every school and every student, has a chance of being selected, must be distinguished from partial sampling, which is restricted to pre-designated parts of the country. Partial sampling was applied in India and Thailand. In India the sampling was limited to the six Hindi-speaking states, in which Hindi is the language of instruction, and English-speaking schools were excluded even within these states. In Thailand, owing to the disturbed state of the country, the sampling was mainly limited to Bangkok and its neighbourhood but with some schools as far away as Chiengmai and Songkla.

With these exceptions the recommended design was adopted, and National Centers proceeded to define their strata and to make the draw. The next step was to communicate with the selected schools, to find out which of them were prepared to take part. Cooperation could by no means be taken for granted. The study was a voluntary exercise, and participation involved a school in a considerable amount of work—much more than had been needed for the earlier Mathematics Study. For this reason it was to be expected that the refusal rate would be quite high, and it was recommended that National Centers should make the draw for schools in duplicate, so that within any stratum replacements should be available for schools that could not be persuaded to take part. In the upshot the refusal rate turned out to vary considerably from country to country. Among the countries with high rates were England and the United States, perhaps because these countries have been much exposed to various forms of educational surveys and the consequent interruptions of school routine. Australia, Hungary and New Zealand had low rates. The use of replacements in a sample means that it is no longer a probability sample, and that some allowance for possible bias must be superimposed on the estimates of possible error made on the assumption that it can be treated as a probability sample. On the other hand the work done on the comparison of probability samples with quota samples, which do not even initially purport to be probability samples, suggests that given adequate stratification the amount of bias may be quite small.

After a selected school had agreed to take part the next step was to designate the students who should represent it. Two alternative methods were recommended. In the first the school listed all students who fell within the population, and the National Center selected the needed number from this list systematically with a random start. Where this was impracticable, e.g. owing to difficulties of communication or lack of time, students whose birthdays fell on randomly or systematically selected days of the month were chosen.

A special problem arose in countries where a large part of a population was contained in a great number of very small schools. For such strata it would have wasted effort to preserve the rule that the product of the two sampling fractions should be constant. Since the number of students per school was very small, a very large number of schools would have had to be selected to preserve the rule. Consequently, it was recommended that for such strata the overall sampling fraction should be reduced and compensation made by weighting.

Another special problem arose over the testing of English and French as Foreign Languages, at Stage 3. Civic Education, like the Stage 2 subjects (Science, Reading Comprehension and Literature) is taken in all schools, so that the Stage 2 procedure described above was applicable. But English and French are taken as foreign languages only in some schools. In countries where these schools are identified in the central statistics all that was needed to redefine the population to be sampled to include the schools offering these subjects and exclude the others. Where this was not the case the procedure recommended was to begin by drawing an adequate sample of all schools and then to discard from this sample the schools which on inquiry turned out not to be offering English (or French). The decision as to what was an adequate size for the initial sample turned on what was known about the proportion of schools teaching the foreign language. If this were thought to be one in three then the initial sample would need to be three times the size of the final sample desired. The best plan was plainly to make the initial selection in successive cycles covering all strata, so that a representative sample would be obtained if the correspondence with schools ceased as soon as the requisite number for the final sample had appeared. But if, as in Population I in the United States, the proportion of schools where French is taken is very small even this would be a tedious and wasteful procedure, so that in this case a judgment sample was selected from schools known initially to be teaching French.

THE EXECUTION OF THE DESIGNS

After the field work had been completed it was possible to compare the achieved with the designed samples. The comparison is summarized in Table 2.1. In this table the (*a*) columns give the number of schools that took part, and that persevered to the end, as a percentage of the designed number of schools, for each country and

Table 2.1. *Stage 2 Sampling—Losses in Execution.*

Country	Population I			Population II			Population IV			
	(a)	(b)	(c)	(a)	(b)	(c)	(a)	(b)	(c)	(d)
Australia	–	–	–	99	97	96	99	93	92	94
Belgium (Fl)	58	73	42	53	73	39	34	80	27	36
Belgium (Fr)	77	91	70	34	66	22	63	93	59	50
Chile	82	98	80	75	96	72	76	98	74	75
England	79	92	73	66	91	60	32	83	27	53
Finland	99	98	97	100	98	98	100	82	82	93
FRG	49	94	46	59	95	56	80	89	71	58
France	–	–	–	–	–	–	90	97	87	87
Hungary	99	96	95	100	94	94	100	98	98	96
India	50	93	46	44	92	40	31	90	28	38
Iran[a]	–	–	–	–	–	–	–	–	–	
Israel	97	95	92	91	88	80	84	97	81	84
Italy	73	67	49	86	97	83	70	87	61	64
Japan	100	100	100	98	100	98	–	–	–	99
Netherlands	66	98	65	52	94	49	39	95	37	50
New Zealand	–	–	–	100	91	91	100	83	83	87
Scotland	98	94	92	95	89	85	88	91	80	86
Sweden	99	97	96	96	95	91	95	95	90	92
Thailand	94	87	82	90	90	81	95	69	66	76
United States	68	94	64	57	80	46	43	81	35	48
Mean	81	92	74	78	90	71	74	89	65	70[b] 72[c]

Note: Column (a): Schools achieved/Schools designed, percent.
Column (b): Students achieved/Students designed, within achieved Schools, percent.
Column (c): Students achieved/Students designed, percent (i.e. Col. (a)×Col. (b)).
Column (d): Mean of Columns (c) for the populations sampled.

[a] Iran did not provide sampling information.
[b] Row Mean.
[c] Column Mean.

population. It will be seen that the percentage ranged from 100 to 31, with an average of 78. The (b) columns give the number of students who actually took the tests and questionnaires as a percentage of the designed number within the schools that actually took part. Here the percentages ranged from 100 to 66, with an average of 90. As might be expected the loss was much less in the (b) than in the (a) column. The (c) column gives the product of the entries in the two previous columns—in other words, the number of students who actually took the tests and questionnaires as a

Table 2.2. *Size of Achieved Samples for Stage 2 Subjects.*

Country	Population I			Population II			Population IV		
	Schools	Teachers	Students	Schools	Teachers	Students	Schools	Teachers	Students
Australia	–	–	–	221	1 638	5 301	194	1 600	4 197
Belgium (Fl)	31	222	717	31	237	699	18	183	472
Belgium (Fr)	33	158	767	21	83	564	42	308	1 231
Chile	81	352	1 470	103	593	1 311	73	492	2 052
England	162	1 301	3 573	146	1 498	3 256	70	867	2 274
FRG	68	397	1 741	83	443	2 233	80	714	1 988
Finland	97	350	1 305	77	496	2 325	77	630	1 807
France	–	–	–	–	–	–	141	633	3 582
Hungary	152	846	4 858	210	1 520	7 026	39	451	2 855
India	176	251	2 704	155	311	2 931	124	339	3 153
Iran	53	47	1 640	33	42	1 336	34	45	1 435
Israel	110	664	1 887	125	334	1 958	71	238	863
Italy	298	373	4 503	343	1 152	7 383	253	1 538	16 437
Japan	250	1 552	2 467	196	752	1 945	–	–	–
Netherlands	60	166	1 629	50	267	1 236	38	179	1 164
New Zealand	–	–	–	74	1 134	1 974	69	1 071	1 714
Scotland	105	1 129	2 169	70	819	1 982	69	978	1 328
Sweden	98	665	2 009	95	1 157	2 475	142	2 131	2 988
Thailand	31	–	1 810	29	–	1 932	13	–	724
United States	239	1 632	5 479	142	992	6 870[a]	114	816	5 200[a]

[a] Split half and half between Science and Mother Tongue.

percentage of the whole designed number, including that part of it that lay within the schools that fell out. The percentages ranged from 100 to 27, with an average of 70. Finally the (d) column gives the average of the (c) columns in each row, and so represents for each country the degree of success, or lack of it, in carrying out its sampling design. The percentages ranged from 99 to 36, with an average of 70 (or 72, according to whether the row mean or the column mean is taken). Japan (99), Hungary (96), Australia (94), Finland (93) and Sweden (92) had the smallest losses. At the other extreme with the highest losses were Belgium (Fl.) and India. This was understandable. In Belgium, after the original plan for the survey had been made, the Flemish and the French speaking parts of the country decided that the two parts should each have its own survey. This late decision made the process of persuading schools to participate even more difficult than usual. In India the size of the

Table 2.2. (continued). *Size of Achieved Samples for Stage 3 Subjects.*

Country	Population I			Population II			Population IV		
	Schools	Teach-ers	Stu-dents	Schools	Teach-ers	Stu-dents	Schools	Teach-ers	Stu-dent
Civic Education									
FRG	36	178	1 083	45	218	1 317	–	–	
Finland	–	–	–	72	302	2 401	73	333	2 35
Iran	–	–	–	54	56	2 222	52	56	2 18
Ireland	–	–	–	43	270	848	38	259	80
Israel	16	33	433	47	106	1 043	–	–	
Italy	127	535	2 423	67	320	939	–	–	
Netherlands	78	151	1 762	74	162	1 696	46	69	1 31
New Zealand	–	–	–	76	582	2 010	68	565	1 69
Sweden	–	–	–	–	–	–	87	418	1 86
United States	–	–	–	127	317	3 207	120	285	3 04
English as a Foreign Language									
Belgium (Fr)	–	–	–	42	105	725	54	174	1 48
Chile	–	–	–	–	–	–	80	265	2 31
FRG	–	–	–	47	248	1 110	59	360	1 37
Finland	–	–	–	70	187	2 164	73	299	2 36
Hungary	–	–	–	–	–	–	46	118	1 06
Israel	–	–	–	44	70	1 096	20	52	6 1
Italy	–	–	–	52	126	809	18	37	32
Netherlands	–	–	–	91	146	2 098	52	64	1 56
Sweden	–	–	–	97	492	2 488	81	403	1 76
Thailand	–	–	–	40	310	1 957	15	142	93
French as a Foreign Language									
Chile	–	–	–	–	–	–	60	155	1 52
England	–	–	–	138	437	2 101	73	311	72
Netherlands	–	–	–	70	128	1 546	59	75	1 76
New Zealand	–	–	–	74	255	1 818	68	221	1 69
Rumania	–	–	–	74	84	2 278	76	76	2 26
Scotland	–	–	–	51	235	839	51	275	97
Sweden	–	–	–	–	–	–	70	316	1 96
United States	9	0	207	190	238	4 420	175	222	3 29

country and the novelty of the enterprise meant that the National Center was working under a severe handicap. In England (53) and the United States (48) it was not the novelty of the enterprise, but rather the opposite, that made it hard to secure participation. In both countries the schools had been rather heavily exposed to re-

Table 2.2 (continued). *Size of Achieved Samples—Summary.*

Subject	Population	Number of Countries	Mean of Schools per County	Mean of Teachers per School	Mean of Students per School
Stage 2 Subjects	I	17	120	5	20
	II	19	116	6	23
	IV	19	87	8	32
Civic Education	I	4	64	4	22
	II	9	67	4	26
	IV	7	69	4	27
English as a Foreign Language	II	8	60	3	26
	IV	10	50	4	28
French as a Foreign Language	II	6	100	2	22
	IV	8	79	3	22
Weighted Mean[a]			91	5	25

[a] Counting each Stage 2 row three times.

search enterprises of various kinds, and now tended to look askance at new requests, particularly when, as in the IEA case, these would make rather formidable demands on their time.

The actual sizes of the achieved sample are set out in Table 2.2. For each population the first column in the first two sections of the table gives the number of schools, the second the number of teachers and the third the number of students. The first section of the table covers the Stage 2 subjects, the second the Stage 3 subjects, and the third section presents a summary by giving the mean numbers of schools per country, teachers per school and students per school throughout the samples. It will be seen that the number of schools frequently fails to attain the recommended minimum of 100, and indeed that the mean number was only 108 for Stage 2, 70 for Stage 3, and 91 for the two stages taken together. This short-fall stems mainly from the fact that some countries found that their resources for the project were too small, although the losses shown in Table 2.1 were partly responsible. On the other hand the schools are adequately represented in the samples in respect of students and teachers. The average number of students per school is 25, which is not far short of the recommended 30. The average number of teachers per school is five. The teachers who were drawn into the sample were those who were currently teaching the students in the sample except in large schools where a sample of the teachers could be taken. It was decided at the outset that any attempt to link particular teachers to particular students was likely to break down from sheer complication. Instead teacher characteristics were averaged for the school, and it was these averages that entered into the regressions.

WEIGHTING

The percentage of loss varied from stratum to stratum. Adjustments for this were made by weighting. If there were N students in the whole population, and N_i in the population of the ith stratum, and if the sample contained n students altogether, of whom n_i were from the ith stratum, then the general sampling fraction was $f=n/N$, the sampling fraction for the ith stratum was $f_i=n_i/N_i$, and the weight given to each student in the ith stratum of the sample was f/f_i. The sum of the weights for the stratum was therefore $n_i(f/f_i)=N_if$, which is the weight the stratum would have had if the losses had been evenly spread. Over the whole sample the sum of the weights is $Nf=n$, the number of students in the whole sample.

If, as occasionally happened, a small stratum was not represented at all in the sample then it was also excluded from the population in the weighting calculation, so that the sum of the weights was still equal to the number of students in the whole sample.

The variation of the weights is displayed in Table 2.3, from which it will be seen that three quarters of them lay in the range from 0.8 to 1.4, with 7% exceeding 2.0, and 2% falling below 0.3. The more extreme values all relate to very small strata in countries where the number of students was large.

A special feature of the compact column of Australian weights should be mentioned. In Australia it was agreed that the States should each be represented by samples of the same size to enable them to be treated separately in the National Reports. Since 35% of the Commonwealth population lies in New South Wales, 28% in Victoria, 15% in Queensland, 10% in South Australia, 8% in Western Australia and 4% in Tasmania the weights for the Commonwealth calculation varied considerably from State to State. In the table an adjustment has been made for this, by quoting the State, not the Commonwealth weights.

Weighting the strata was important, because the stratifying factors were size, type, sex and region. Of these, type of school and sex of

Table 2.3. *Distribution of Stratum Weights by Country for Stage 2 Subjects—Populations I, II and IV.*

Weights	Australia	Belgium (Fl)	Belgium (Fr)	Chile	England	FRG	Finland	France	Hungary	Israel	Italy	Japan	Netherlands	New Zealand	Scotland	Sweden	United States	Total	%
Population I																			
2.2+	–			2	1	7		–	1					–			3	14	9
2.0–1.8	–			1		1		–			1			–			2	4	7
1.7–1.5	–	1				3		–			1			–	1	1		7	
1.4–1.2	–		1	1	1	3	1	–		2	2			–	1	2	5	18	
1.1–0.9	–			7	2		1	–	1	5	3	14	3	–	2	3	15	56	77
0.8–0.6	–	1	2	6	3	6	4	–	3	2	5		1	–		1	4	38	
0.5–0.3	–					4		–			2			–	1	1		8	7
0.2–0.1	–				2	1		–						–				3	
Total	–	2	3	15	9	24	7	–	5	9	14	14	4	–	5	8	29	148	100
Population II																			
2.1+				1	8	1		–	2	1					1	1		15	5
1.9				2	3	3	2	–						1		1		12	
1.6				1	5			–		2			1			1		10	8
1.3	6	1	2	7	11	3	5	–	3	1	1	1		1	3	4	3	52	
1.0	14	2	1	8	4	7	4	–	2	2	3	12	2	6	7	4	8	86	77
0.7	11	1	1	12	14	8		–	5	4	2		2	4	3	2	12	81	
0.4				2	3	7	4	–	2	1				2	1	3	1	26	10
0.1				2				–										2	
Total	31	4	4	33	28	42	24	–	14	11	6	13	5	14	14	14	27	284	100
Population IV																			
2.1+				4	2	2	1				7	–		1	2		2	21	7
1.9		1		1	2	2	2			1	3	–	1				1	14	12
1.6	1		1	3	3	1	1			2	3	–			1		2	18	
1.3	2		1	1	3	3	1	2	1	1	10	–	1	1	1		1	29	
1.0	25	3	1	8	8	1	4	4	1		19	–	3	7	7	6	2	99	72
0.7	4		1	2	5	5	4	4	1	2	20	–	2	1	1		13	65	
0.4				1	4	4	1			2	2	–			2		6	22	9
0.1								1			1	–						2	
Total	32	4	4	16	21	25	13	11	6	9	65	–	4	13	12	8	27	270	100

school are major sources of variation, and region is sometimes so. Size is a minor source; it was made a stratifying factor mainly to enable the two designed sampling fractions, for schools and for students within selected schools, to be adjusted within the constant product condition to produce about 30 students per school. Because the population statistics were not available to distinguish among sex-types, sex of school was not used as a stratifying factor in the calculation of the English weights. This was unfortunate since the highest refusal rate was for high-scoring schools for boys. Because no adjustment was made for the undersampling of this group the mean score was underestimated. The problem was not detected until it was noticed, in the work for the English National Report, that in Science the girls appeared to be doing better than the boys, a result that contradicted common experience.

The sum of its student's weights was the weight for a school, and also for its teacher characteristics, since it was the mean value of a characteristic that entered into the calculations. It should be noted that the influence of teachers is almost certainly underrated in the study. A minor reason for this is that teacher characteristics entered only as averages, but the major reason is that the evidence related only to what was done in the classroom, and not to how well it was done. In later life many of us recognize that at least one of our teachers has had a marked effect on our subsequent history, but it is hard to bring this recognition into a systematic study because the relation of teacher and student is strongly idiosyncratic, like the relation of husband and wife.

ESTIMATING THE DESIGN EFFECT

This section is about the design effect, commonly called DEFF, that arises from the sampling design when the sampling is done in two or more stages, as in the IEA study. DEFF is the square of the ratio of the assessed standard error of an estimate to the expected standard error for a simple random sample of the same size. But how is the assessment to be made? For simple statistics like means and proportions it is possible to make formulae that take account of the stages of the design and the stratifications, but for more complicated statistics such as correlations and regression coefficients the formulae soon become hopelessly lengthy. A practicable alternative is to compare the estimates obtained from a number of independent samples following the same design. With due precautions this comes to the same thing as dividing the whole sample into subsamples, and comparing the estimates from subsamples. "*With due precautions*" means that the division into subsamples must follow the stages and the stratifications of the design, to keep the subsamples fluctuation independent, and to keep the variation between strata out of the estimate of sampling. The drawback to this method is that unless the samples are very large the subsamples must be either few or small, and in particular too small for stable estimates of regression coefficients. To overcome this the complementary samples can be used instead of the subsamples, each complementary sample being obtained by leaving one of the subsamples out of the whole sample. From each complementary sample there can be obtained what Tukey, (see Mosteller and Tukey, 1968) under the heading of "jackknifing," calls a pseudo-value. The pseudo-value is $y_j^* = cy_{all} - (c-1)y_{(j)}$, where c is the number of subsamples, and therefore of complementary samples, y_{all} is the estimate for the whole sample, and $y_{(j)}$ the estimate for the jth complementary sample. The pseudo-values then play the part that would be played by independent estimates of y, to give the assessment on $c-1$ degrees of freedom.

For this part of the study, attention was concentrated on Stage 2, Population II. A group of 30 variables could be handled by the program devised. The 30 comprised the 4 criteria, for Word Knowledge, Science, Reading Comprehension and Literature, and 26 independent variables that had been prominent in the regression equations that are described in subsequent chapters. The whole sample for each country was divided into ten subsamples, following the sampling structure, and the complementary samples were obtained by leaving out, from the whole sample, each subsample in turn. The complete calculation, for regressing each criterion on the relevant independent variables, was then carried out on each complementary sample. In the output the results were summarized by showing six numbers in a row for each statistic calculated. The statistics were the means, standard deviations, correlations and regression coefficients with b^2/c and R^2. The six numbers for each statistic were (1) the whole sample value, (2) the mean of the pseudo-values, (3) the standard error calculated by the formula for simple random sampling, ignoring the stratifications, (4) the standard error calculated from the ten pseudo-values, (5) the ratio (4)/(3), which is DEFF[1], (6) the square of (5), which is DEFF.

This is a formidable operation, and it would have taken too much time and money to apply it to more than a few samples. Fortunately the evidence obtained from the few, suggested some simple general rules that could be applied to other samples in the study without much risk of serious error. These rules can be inferred from the summaries displayed in Table 2.4, where it is shown that simple

Table 2.4. *Values of DEFF$^{\frac{1}{2}}$.*[a]

	k						
p	5	10	15	20	25	30	35
.20	1.3	1.7	1.9	2.2	2.4	2.6	2.8
.10	1.2	1.4	1.6	1.7	1.8	2.0	2.1
.06	1.1	1.2	1.3	1.5	1.6	1.7	1.7
.04	1.1	1.2	1.2	1.3	1.4	1.5	1.5

[a] Given by DEFF$=p(k-1)+1$, where k is the average number of students per school in the sample and p is the proportion of the variance that lies between schools.

forecasting formulae give good approximations to the values of DEFF$^{\frac{1}{2}}$ obtained from the ten complementary samples in each case analysed.

The clue to these forecasts is to be found in the simplest case—the estimation of the standard error of a mean. If a two stage sample contains n schools and k students per school, and if a proportion p of the student variance lies between schools, and the standard deviation is taken as unity, the variance of the mean is $p/n+(1-p)/nk$, so that

Table 2.5. *DEFF$^{\frac{1}{2}}$ for Criterion Means for Population II.*[a]

Country	DEFF$^{\frac{1}{2}}$ for:					Forecast		
	Word Knowl- edge	Science	Reading Compre- hension	Litera- ture	Mean	k	(a) p=0.1	(b) p=0.2
Australia	2.5	2.4	–	–	2.4	24	1.8	2.4
Chile	2.0	2.1	3.2	3.1	2.6	13	1.5	1.8
Finland	1.9	1.6	2.4	2.8	2.2	30	2.0	2.6
Hungary	2.8	3.5	3.2	–	3.2	33	2.1	2.7
New Zealand	2.2	1.8	1.7	1.9	1.9	27	1.9	2.5
Scotland	2.2	2.6	2.3	–	2.4	28	1.9	2.5
Sweden	1.9	1.6	1.6	2.0	1.8	26	1.9	2.4
Mean	2.3	2.2	2.4	2.4	2.3	26	1.9	2.4

[a] DEFF$^{\frac{1}{2}}$ is estimated from the comparison of ten complementary samples in each case, and compared with forecasts based on DEFF$=p(k-1)+1$, for (a) $p=0.1$ and (b) $p=0.2$.
Note: k is the average number of students per school in the sample. The Mean is that of the subjects taken in each country.

untry	Word Knowl- edge	Science	Reading Compre- hension	Litera- ture	(a) Mean	(b) n	(c) nk	Fore- cast	Mean minus Fore- cast
			Standard Errors for:						
stralia	3.5	3.4	–	–	3.4	225	5 301	3.2	0.2
ile	5.7	5.8	9.3	9.7	7.6	103	1 311	5.0	2.6
ıland	4.0	3.3	5.1	5.8	4.5	77	2 325	5.4	−0.9
ıngary	3.4	4.2	3.9	–	3.8	210	7 026	3.2	0.6
·w Zealand	5.0	4.0	3.9	4.4	4.3	74	1 974	5.6	−1.3
ɔtland	4.8	5.9	5.3	–	5.3	70	1 982	5.7	−0.4
·eden	3.8	3.4	3.3	4.3	3.7	95	2 475	4.9	−1.2
·an	4.3	4.3	4.4	6.0	4.7	122	3 199	4.7	0.0

te: These standard errors, in hundredths of a standard deviation, are estimated from the ·mparison of ten complementary samples, and are compared with the forecast $(p/n)+(1-p)/nk$, ·th $p=0.2$.
) Over the four subjects.
) n=number of schools per country.
) nk=number of schools per country times average number of students per school.

DEFF is $pk+(1-p)$, or $p(k-1)+1$. Table 2.4 shows the values of the square root of this expression for various values of p and k. The values shown for k cover the range encountered in the study, and the p values are those needed in what follows. The initial guess was that good forecasts would be obtained in all cases by choosing a suitable value for p.

Table 2.5 gives on the left the values of DEFF[1] obtained from the comparison of the ten complementary samples for the four criterion means in seven countries and on the right two forecasts, for $p=0.1$ and for $p=0.2$. It will be seen that the second column of forecasts gives quite a good fit. This is examined further in Table 2.6, where the estimated standard errors for the means are compared with the forecasts of $p=0.2$. The best fit is for Australia, and the worst for Chile, the differences being 0.2 and 2.6.

In Table 2.7 we turn from means to correlations. The first column gives c, the number of variables correlated in each country. This is 17 in Australia, where only one subject was taken, 25 in Hungary and Scotland, with two subjects, and 30 in the other four countries, with three subjects. With 30 variables there are 435 correlations, each with

Table 2.7. *DEFF$^{1/2}$ for Correlations ^{a} from Stage 2, Population II.*

Country	Number of Variables (c)	Percent:^{b} Below	Within	Above	Median DEFF$^{1/2}$	Fore-cast^c	Differ-ence	k
Australia	17	5	75	20	1.7	1.6	0.2	2₄
Chile	30	5	85	10	1.6	1.3	0.3	1₃
Finland	30	5	77	18	1.7	1.7	0.0	3₀
Hungary	25	4	78	18	1.9	1.7	0.2	3₃
New Zealand	30	4	80	16	1.4	1.6	−0.2	2₇
Scotland	25	6	76	18	1.5	1.6	−0.1	2₈
Sweden	30	5	82	13	1.2	1.6	−0.4	2₀
Mean	27	5	79	16	1.6	1.6	0.0	2₀

Note: These DEFF$^{1/2}$ for correlations have been estimated from the comparisons of ten comple mentary samples.

^{a} Between the (c) variables shown for each country. The number of correlations $=c(c-1)/2$.

^{b} Refers to the percentages of estimated values of DEFF$^{1/2}$ below, within and above what wou be the one percent limits if all the variation in DEFF$^{1/2}$ were merely sampling fluctuation fro a fixed value for all pairs of variables.

^{c} The forecast is DEFF$=p(k-1)+1$, for $p=0.06$.

its own DEFF. The table gives the median value of DEFF$^{1/2}$ in the fifth column, and a forecast, with $p=0.06$, in the sixth. It will be seen that the forecast gives a good fit, the mean difference being only 0.2. This is for the medians. But there are also hundreds of individual values scattered round the medians, and their distribution is shown in the previous columns headed "Below," "Within" and "Above." If the true value of DEFF were the same for all correlations in a given country the estimates would still be scattered because of sampling fluctuation. The actual scatter of the estimates is somewhat greater than this sampling scatter, but not very much, as may be seen from the table, which shows the proportion of the estimates below the lower 1 % and above the upper 1 % sampling limits. Thus for Australia 5 % of the estimates are below, 75 % within, and 20 % above these limits. Averaged over all the countries the proportions are 5 %, 79 %, and 16 %. It is plain that much of the variation in DEFF or DEFF$^{1/2}$ must be mere sampling fluctuation in the estimates, though some of it reflects differences in true values. The conclusion that seems to follow is that in other similar cases in the study there is little risk in using the forecast value with $p=0.06$, or indeed in using DEFF$^{1/2}=1.6$ everywhere.

In the same way we see that in Table 2.8 the forecast value $p=0.04$

Table 2.8. $DEFF^{\frac{1}{2}}$ for Regression Coefficients, from Stage 2, Population II.

Country	Science	Reading Comprehension	Literature	Median[b] $DEFF^{\frac{1}{2}}$	Forecast[c]	Difference	k
Australia	1.3 (15)[d]	–	–	1.3	1.4	−0.1	24
Chile	1.4 (16)	1.8 (15)	1.7 (13)	1.6	1.2	0.4	13
Finland	1.1 (17)	1.4 (16)	1.4 (14)	1.3	1.5	−0.2	30
Hungary	1.7 (17)	1.4 (15)	–	1.5	1.5	0.0	33
New Zealand	1.3 (17)	1.5 (15)	1.3 (14)	1.4	1.4	0.0	27
Scotland	1.3 (17)	1.2 (16)	–	1.2	1.4	−0.2	28
Sweden	1.3 (16)	1.3 (15)	1.3 (13)	1.3	1.4	−0.1	26
Mean	1.3 (16)	1.4 (16)	1.4 (14)	1.4	1.4	0.0	26

Note: These $DEFF^{\frac{1}{2}}$ for Regression Coefficients have been estimated from the comparison of ten complementary samples.

[a] $DEFF^{\frac{1}{2}}$ is based on the coefficients that arise when each criterion variable is regressed on the number of variables shown in brackets in each case. The values shown are the medians; thus 1.3 is the median of the 15 estimates of $DEFF^{\frac{1}{2}}$ obtained for Science in Australia.

[b] Median over the three subjects.

[c] The forecast shown is $DEFF = p(k-1)+1$, with $p = 0.04$ and k = the average number of students per school in the sample.

[d] The numbers in brackets add to 261, which is the total number of estimates from which the table is summarized.

gives an even better fit for regression coefficients. The number of coefficients in the equation varies slightly from case to case, as shown. Altogether there are 261, with 2 % below, 91 % within and 7 % above what would be the one per cent limits if all the variation were merely sampling fluctuation, within each country and subject. If all the 261 estimates are pooled these proportions become 3 %, 88 % and 9 %, so that there seems to be a good case for taking $DEFF^{\frac{1}{2}}$ as 1.4, or $DEFF = 2$, as applicable to regression coefficients in other similar cases.

This evidence from seven countries may be compared with that from twelve countries in the earlier Mathematics study. Here $DEFF^{\frac{1}{2}}$ for correlations was estimated at 2.0. The estimates were made from the comparison of four subsamples, selected locally, and it was noted at the time (Husén, 1967) that in some countries the subsampling had failed to follow the sampling structure, and that this would exaggerate the estimate of the design effect. This was for students aged 13. For the terminal students (i.e., Population IV in the present study) $DEFF^{1/2}$ was estimated at 1.4, again for correlations. There was no time to obtain estimates for regression coefficients, but some reflection on this aspect suggested that the subsamples if used directly would have been too small for stability, and this led to the decision to use the complementary samples in the next round, and also to the decision to have the subsampling done centrally instead of locally. It seems reasonable to think that the discrepancy between the two values obtained for $DEFF^{1/2}$ for correlations in Population II (i.e., between 2.0 in 1967 and 1.6 currently) may arise mainly from the greater attention given to the stratifications and from the use of ten complementary samples in the current study rather than four subsamples, and that therefore the later result is to be preferred, or should at any rate have more weight.

It will be seen from Table 2.2 that the average number of students per school was much the same for all subjects and for all populations, which makes it reasonable, in the absence of more direct evidence, to use everywhere the values of $DEFF^{1/2}$, obtained in seven countries for the Stage 2 subjects in Population II. The fact that in 1967 $DEFF^{1/2}$ for correlations was estimated at 2.0 for Population II and at 1.4 for Population IV might be invoked as a reason for applying a factor of 0.7 in Population IV, where owing to the selection or fall-out the schools are more homogeneous, but it seems more likely that the difference stems from imperfect use of stratification in 1967, which would exaggerate the Population II value much more than the Population IV. If the two results in 1967 are pooled we get 1.7—very close to the 1970 1.6.

The best suggestion therefore seems to be to use throughout the values of $DEFF^{1/2}$ shown in Table 2.4, with the first row $(p=0.20)$ for criterion means, the third row $(p=0.06)$ for correlations, and the fourth row $(p=0.04)$ for regression coefficients. The factors in the modal column, for $k=25$, can easily be remembered, in terms of DEFF, not $DEFF^{1/2}$, as 6 for criterion means, $2\frac{1}{2}$ for correlations, and 2 for regression coefficients.

It was originally planned to do similar work on the analyses between schools, but time ran out before this could be done. The small amount of exploration that was carried out threw no doubt on the expectation that when the unit of analysis was the school the design effects would be less than unity, owing to the stratifications. The simple random formulae can therefore be applied with the comfortable feeling that the estimated standard errors are on the large side.

SUMMARY

1. The specified populations were sampled in all the participating countries except India and Thailand. In India the study was limited to the six states in which Hindi is the language of instruction, and students in English-speaking private schools were excluded. In Thailand the study excluded the disturbed border areas.

2. Two stage sampling, with the selection of schools as the first stage, was used everywhere except in the United States and Iran, where districts were selected as the first stage.

3. Schools were stratified by size, sex, type and region, and it was recommended that (a) the overall sampling fraction for students should be kept constant, and (b) subject to (a) the number of students per school in the samples should be about 30, with a minimum of 100 schools.

4. The main difficulty experienced by National Centers in carrying out their designs was that many schools drawn by the sampling procedure declined to take part in the study. When this happened replacements were drawn from the same stratum, in some cases several times, until a consenting school was reached, but sometimes no replacement could be made. The risk of bias was reduced, yet plainly not altogether avoided, by making replacements from the same stratum.

5. The percentage of loss varied from stratum to stratum, but the balance between strata was restored by giving each student a stratum weight. Three quarters of the weights lay in the range from 0.8 to 1.4, with 7 % exceeding 2.0, and 2 % falling below 0.3. The more extreme values all relate to very small strata in countries where the number of strata was large. Altogether the samples contained about 10 000 schools, 50 000 teachers and 250 000 students.

6. Design effects for the analyses between students were calculated by dividing seven of the samples each into ten subsamples, with the division following the sampling structure, replicating the calculation of the regression equations on each of the corresponding complementary samples, and comparing the resulting estimates. This evidence was combined with the evidence from the Mathematics Study in 1967, and suggested that appropriate values for DEFF[1] were 2.4 for criterion means, 1.6 for correlations, and 1.4 for regression coefficients.

Chapter 3

Organizing the Variables

The IEA survey measured certain skills possessed by the students who took part and some of the factors that may have influenced the development of these skills. But by the time his skill was observed many things had happened to the student. He had been conceived, born, brought up by his parents in a certain neighborhood and passed through various stages of schooling. Throughout this progress he had been subject to a great variety of influences, of which only a few were fully represented in the survey evidence. In assessing the effects of the influences that were represented in the immediate evidence a major difficulty was to make due allowance for those that were not.

Besides the immediate evidence of the survey there is of course a great mass of other evidence. Some of this is contained in the proverbial wisdom of mankind: "The child is father to the man," or "As the twig is bent so grows the tree" are old saws that lay stress on the importance of beginnings. It is the common experience of teachers that students who begin as fast or slow learners tend to continue as such—for each student there is a tendency for the pace of learning to be roughly constant, in this resembling the rate of physical growth. But in physical growth as in the acquisition of skill the individual's tendency towards his own ordinary pace is to some extent at the mercy of outside circumstances; unusually propitious circumstances may accelerate growth, and unpropitious circumstances retard it. The factors measured by the IEA variables are in the nature of such propitious or unpropitious circumstances, but they by no means comprise an exhaustive list, and in assessing their effects we must try to allow for omitted external circumstances as well as for natural growth.

If the process at work were simply that each student acquired skill steadily, at his own pace, then the results of successive tests would be perfectly correlated; the student who was in the pth position at the beginning would be in the same position at the end of the sequence, and at all intermediate points. If in addition to the regular growth there were additional, and uncorrelated, increments between each pair of tests each test would be as well predicted by its immediate predecessor as by the whole sequence of preceding tests. In other words, if the nth test were regressed on the preceding $(n-1)$ tests the first $(n-2)$ coefficients would all be zero. This however would not alter the fact that the skill represented by the nth test had been gradually acquired throughout the whole interval. To bring out this fact we could use the second form of the regression equation, in terms of the residual variables and the successive increments of R^2. If the growth element predominates over the external increments the first increment of R^2 will predominate over the later ones.

EVIDENCE FROM LONGITUDINAL STUDIES

If the external increments are mildly correlated among themselves, the early coefficients, in the first form of the regression equation, will no longer be zero, but they will be small. This appears to be what happens in practice (Acland, 1972, Jencks *et al.*, 1972). The Acland study deals *inter alia* with the cohort of children who passed through 609 schools in New York, from Grade 2 in 1967 to Grade 6 in 1971, and for whom Metropolitan Reading Achievement Test scores are available at the end of each of these grades. *The unit of analysis is the school mean.* If we write x_{1j}, x_{2j}, x_{4j}, x_{5j} for the mean scores of the jth school in the successive tests from Grade 2 through Grade 6, and regress x_5 on the others, we obtain:

(i) $x_5 = 0.08x_1 - 0.08x_2 + 0.21x_3 + 0.72x_4 + x_{5.1234}$ $\qquad$ $R^2 = 0.84$

(ii) $x_5 = 0.78x_1 + 0.53x_{2.1} + 0.72x_{3.12} + 0.72x_{4.123} + x_{5.1234}$ $\quad$ Increment R^2

$s^2 = 1.00$	0.20	0.16	0.16	0.16	1	0.62
$b^2s^2 = 0.62$	0.06	0.08	0.08		2	0.06
					3	0.08
					4	0.08
					R^2	0.84

From (i) we see that the external increments are pretty small; in fact r^2_{45} is 0.83, and the omission of first three tests from the regression reduces the explained variance by only 1 %. From (ii) we see that the first test will explain 62 %, and that the later tests add only 22 %. The two forms of the regression equation are algebraically identical, as can be seen by replacing the residual variables in the second form by their values in terms of the original variables, but they stress different aspects of the situation.

The equations above have been worked out from a typical correlation matrix given in the Acland (1972) paper. Acland himself proceeds by using each test to predict its immediate successor and so obtaining the increment (i.e., the deviation from prediction) for each school, year by year. He then shows that successive increments for the same school are almost independent. "Some schools," he says, "are unusually effective in a given year, but these schools are unlikely to repeat themselves." He continues "The findings reported in this section suggest two things, both of considerable practical importance. The first is that there exist some unidentified characteristics of the school, either physical, social or organisational, that make a small impact on achievement. However the second finding is that this impact does not appear to be especially consistent. The implication for policy makers who plan long term programs for schools is both clear and discouraging. The implication for researchers is that school effects, if found, are likely to be complex."

Other longitudinal studies have given very much the same results. For the English national sample studied in *The Plowden Children Four Years Later* (Peaker, 1971) the correlations *(for individual pupils, not schools)* between the tests in 1964 and 1968 were 0.76, 0.76 and 0.72 for the cohorts aged ten, seven and six in 1964. In the very large *Project Talent* (Flanagan, 1966) study in the United States, performance at the twelfth grade was even more accurately predicted by the ninth grade scores. Similar results were obtained from the numerous long term studies carried out in England in connection with the transfer procedure form primary to selective secondary schools.

In short, detailed studies confirm what is a matter of common observation in schools, that there is a strong tendency for the individual student's pace of learning to stay constant; those who begin as fast learners generally continue as fast learners, and similarly for slow learners. There are deviations from this general rule, but large deviations are rather rare, particularly with increasing age. It is never too late to mend, but it becomes harder as one grows older. Habit is powerful, and becomes stronger with age, as septuagenarians like the writer can testify. It is perhaps worth remark that but for habit civilized life would be impossible, since no man would know what to expect of his neighbor.

LONG, MIDDLE AND SHORT-TERM VARIABLES

The recognition of the power of habit does not however dispose of the question of how habits come to be formed in the first instance, and subsequently changed, when they do change. What it does suggest is that they are only likely to be changed much by influences that are either very strong, or very prolonged, or both. The duration of an influence, as well as its magnitude, is important. This provides the clue to the organization of the IEA variables, where we can distinguish between long-lasting influences and those that are more transient. At the one extreme we have the student's home background, including his genetic endowment, which influences his entire life, and at the other those recent conditions of learning, assessed in the survey, which have only influenced him during a fairly short interval immediately preceding the survey. It would be a mistake to attribute to these influences effects that have an earlier origin, in his home background or in his earlier schooling. Our concern is to assess the differential effects of those recent conditions that we have measured, and in doing this we must do our best to make a due discount for the effects of earlier conditions, whether at home or at school. It is important to be clear about the nature of this enterprise. We are not saying that these differential effects of the variables that come under the head of recent conditions of learning are the only school effects. On the contrary, we recognize them as both recent and differential. In saying that they are recent we recognize that there are earlier school influences of which we have no record. In saying that they are differential we recognize that even if there were no differential effects schools would still be the main source of learning in the community.

With these provisos in mind the variables were sorted into a long-term, a middle-term and a short-term group. The long-term group contained the variables relating to the student's home background, together with sex and age. The middle-term group would have contained the pretest at the point where the short-term group began to operate, had such a pretest been available. In the absence of such a pretest the middle-term group contained the best available surrogates, these being Type of school and Type of program. In countries where secondary schools are selective there is a large difference between the average performances of pupils in different Types of school, but this often holds in other countries as well. Similarly for Types of program. Both variables were regarded as evidence of the learning conditions that operated before the recent conditions came into effect. They are clearly not so useful as a pretest would have been, since they do not discriminate among students in the same Type of school and Type of program, but they were the best evidence available. There was some debate as to whether grade should also be included in the middle-term group. This debate was confused by the fact that "grade" means different things in different countries. In some it indicates a standard of work, so that the question of repeating grades arises. In others it merely indicates an age, all students of the same age being the same grade, though they may be in different programs (streams, sets or tracks). In retrospect it seems clear that where "grade" indicates a standard of work there was something to be said for including it in the middle group, but in fact it was put in the third, or short-term group.

The third, or short-term group was very large, since it included all the variables that could reasonably be regarded as instructional or quasi-instructional, as distinct from those which it seemed preferable to think of as concomitants rather than causes of learning, these latter being placed in a fourth group. In the subject reports (and in the later chapters of this report) these four groups of variables are usually called blocks. Thus Block 1 contains the long-term variables, Block 2 the middle-term, and Block 3 the short-term instructional variables, with the concomitants or kindreds in Block 4. Beyond Block 4 there were also Blocks 5 and 6, and the criterion variables. Block 5 consisted of a single variable, the test of Word Knowledge. Block 6 also consisted of a single variable, the test of Reading Comprehension.

It will be seen that this organization of the variables is linked with the results of sequential testing in studies covering several years of school life. Thus in the Acland study cited above it is said that "The findings suggest that ... there exist some unidentified characteristics of the school, either physical, social or organizational, that make a small impact on achievement." The existence of these unidentified characteristics is inferred from the fact that although the test at the beginning of each interval is a good predictor of the test at the end of that interval, it is not a perfect predictor, so that some perturbing elements must be at work during the interval. Our purpose is to identify some of these elements, by regressing our criterion tests on the short-term group of variables, and on the middle- and long-term groups. The two latter groups are to play the part of the missing test at the beginning of the interval during which the short-term group operate. This is their primary function, though we recognize that they are also at work during the short term. They are not very satisfactory surrogates for the test, as may be seen from the Plowden study, where we have both the long-term and middle-term groups and the pretest. It is shown in Chapter 6 of this report that the pretest is decidedly more effective in discounting the short-term group. It is for this reason that the two Reading tests are brought into the picture, as Blocks 5 and 6, as alternative surrogates for the pretest. As surrogates they suffer from the opposite defect; Blocks 1 and 2 underplay this part, but Blocks 5 and 6 overplay it, since they were not pretests but simultaneous tests (and the Reading Comprehension test of Block 6 is itself the criterion for one part of the study). So we have a kind of bracketing process; the extent to which variables in the short-term group should be discounted is underestimated by Blocks 1 and 2, and overestimated by Blocks 5 and 6 (where the last is applicable). Fortunately, as will be seen in the upshot, the underestimate and the overestimate do not differ much in respect of the *relative* size of the parts that they assign to the separate variables that comprise Block 3.

SORTING AND COMBINING THE SHORT-TERM VARIABLES

The total number of short-term variables generated by the questionnaires was greater than the number of schools in any sample for any country, and was quite a large fraction of the number of students. Within this group therefore, some sorting and sifting was needed to reduce the assembly to a manageable size. In this reduction three kinds of process were employed, namely:

1. Combining categories into scales.
2. Combining scales into weighted composites.
3. Discarding variables.

For example, in the original record there were up to 10 categories for Father's occupation. Each student had been asked to state his father's occupation and give a short account of the work involved, and the answers were classified by the National Centers into not more than 10 categories on the basis:

Categories 9, 8, 7: Professional and Managerial occupations.
Categories 6, 5, 4: Skilled workers' occupations.
Categories 3, 2, 1: Unskilled workers' occupations.
Category 0: Unclassified or missing.

The scale value assigned to each category was obtained by first finding the mean criterion score for the category, and then rounding the means so obtained to the nearest integer on a 1–9 scale.

The same process of criterion scaling was applied to the middle-term variables Type of school and Type of program. One advantage of this kind of scaling is that it avoids the need for discarding from the subsequent analyses students whose replies are unclassifiable or missing. In some countries this category was quite substantial.

After Father's occupation had been scaled it was combined with five other variables to make a weighted composite to represent Home background by a single variable. We sometimes referred to this variable as the School Handicap Score (SHS). The other variables were Father's education, Mother's education, Number of books in the home, Use of dictionary and Family size (with reversed sign). These five were selected because they usually had substantial simple correlations with the criterion. The weights were obtained by regressing the Reading Comprehension score on the six, when it existed. When it did not the Word Knowledge score was used, or, failing that, the Science score. The weights varied considerably from country to country, so that the original intention of forming an international set of weights was abandoned, and the weights were determined country by country. To give them as much stability as possible the three criteria available at the time of the operation, namely Reading Comprehension, Science and Literature, were all regressed on the six, and the coefficients were rounded to integral values after averaging. The operation was carried out for Population II, but the weights obtained were used for all three populations.

SCREENING THE SHORT-TERM VARIABLES

After the composite variable for Home background and the scaled variables for Type of school and Type of program had been obtained it was possible to proceed to the next step of testing the great assembly of short-term variables to see which of them might safely be discarded. It was plainly impracticable to form a vast correlation matrix including all these variables, but it was possible to obtain the correlations of each of them, and of the Home background compound and the Type of school and Type of program variables, with the criteria, and then to obtain the regression coefficients for the short-term variables after the long and middle-term variables had been partialled out. This operation was performed in two stages, by first regressing on the Home background variable, and discarding most of the short-term variables on the results of this step, and then regressing with the survivors on both the long and the middle-term variables. To aid the selection process a computer program was made, to produce a visual record of the partial regression coefficients. In this record there was a row for each short-term variable in which the value for each country was indicated by its initial letter on a number scale. Since Sweden pre-empted the letter S the values for Scotland were indicated by W, the initial letter of that country's most valuable export. Down these arrays, which occupied several sheets of computer print, two pairs of confidence lines were drawn to indicate which variables should be retained. To be retained a variable needed either a median coefficient for all countries that was numerically greater than 0.1, or a coefficient in at least one country that was numerically greater than 0.2. The reason for the double standard was that the sampling fluctuation for the median is clearly less than the sampling fluctuation for a single country. Both standards are very lenient, because the object at this stage was merely to reduce the number of survivors enough to make it practicable to include them all in a correlation matrix where they would undergo the final test, in which their correlations with each other, as well as their correlations with the long- and middle-term variables, would play a part.

Scrutiny of the survivors sometimes suggested that two or more of them were conceptually linked and formed a natural cluster. In these cases the cluster was made into a compound, using as weights integral approximations to the partial regression coefficients already obtained after the long- and middle-term variables had been partialled out. As may be seen from the next chapter, the net result of all these operations was to produce about 20 variables for the final correlation matrices. Some of these variables were common to all countries, some to two or more countries, and some appeared in one country only. There were minor variations from subject to subject, according to the wishes of the subject panels, but the same general principles, as described above, were applied throughout.

Why did so few of the short-term variables survive the screening process, and why did the survivors, as will be seen in the ensuing chapters, account for no more than a small part of the variation in achievement among the students? The main reason beyond the fact that they *are* short term, is that the variation in school characteristics within a well established educational system is itself very small, in comparison with the variation in home background and natural talent. Teaching is a profession, with standards of entry, whereas parentage is open to all. Staffing ratios do not vary much. The range in books and buildings is not enormous. And so on, for all the very numerous variables in the group. If the study had included children outside the educational system it would have been possible to estimate the total effects of schools and teaching, at any rate roughly, from the immediate evidence. As it is, the immediate evidence is confined to the differential effects within well established systems, and we must look at external evidence to see what happens without the systems. The immediate evidence derived from an established system, whether by a cross-sectional or a longitudinal study, is evidence about how the system works. It is not evidence about how the absence of a system, or a radically different system, would work.

Another reason is that the short-term variables are by no means a complete account of the influence of teachers. For example, they say little about what actually happens in the classroom. To take one instance, it is plainly part of the teacher's task to endeavor both to confirm an earlier favorable judgment of a student and to confute an unfavorable one. The second part of this task is much harder than the first, and while some teachers are markedly successful in it others are less so. More generally, neither the ambition to teach well nor actual skill in teaching is directly represented among the variables in the study. Nor is the aptitude of the student, nor his ambition to master the subject.

THE RESIDUAL VARIANCE

It will be seen in the next chapter that on the average, over all subjects, about 56 % of the variation in student achievement can be accounted for by the whole array of variables, including the kindred group and the reading tests (except for Reading Comprehension itself). The inclusion of the Kindred group could perhaps be justified by the argument that these variables are a surrogate for student ambition, and similarly the reading tests might be regarded as a surrogate for aptitude. But even so 44 % of the variation remains unaccounted for. This amount summarizes the extent to which the model fails to cover the facts, whether by defects in the measurement of the variables (dependent and independent) that have been included or by the omission of variables that ought to have been included, and that are only imperfectly covered by their surrogates. As an illustration, the unexplained residue for Population II in England shown in the next chapter averages 35%, compared with 28% in the Plowden study with a pretest. Since the surrogates for the pretest were more sharply defined in England than in most countries, the average loss from not having a pretest may have been more than the 7% suggested by the English case.

Since the unmeasured variables and errors whose existence is indicated by the unexplained variation may be correlated with the measured variables, all the estimates obtained are tentative, in the sense that they might be altered if the model could be extended. They are also subject to sampling fluctuation, but that is a different point. In screening the short-term variables we were able to average out much of the sampling fluctuation by attending to the medians of the coefficients over countries. The analogue for bias in the model lies in comparing the results of studies with different designs, including common observation and proverbial wisdom. All sociological studies contain a large unexplained residue, and are to that extent untrustworthy, just as common observation may be partial and proverbial wisdom mistaken. But when the results concur they deserve some confidence.

Chapter 4

The Regression Analyses Between-Students in the Developed Countries

The IEA tests show a very wide variation, increasing with age, between the achievements of individual students. This variation can be divided into the variation of country means and the variation within each country about that country's mean. The variation between-country means lies mainly in the difference between the developed and the developing countries, and the evidence about it and the interpretation will be considered later. In this chapter our concern is with the variation in each developed country about the country mean. How far does the IEA evidence, considered in the light of the previous evidence, enable us to offer an explanation of this variation? It is plain at the outset that factors outside the control of the educational system, falling into the broad categories of heredity and environment, must account for much of it. But how much? Or, conversely, how much of the variation arises from variation in what is done by teachers and schools? Does our evidence show that the practices of teachers and schools vary so much that a great deal of the variation in student achievement can be attributed to this variation in practices? Or are these practices, so far as the evidence in our study goes, so relatively uniform in their effects that they can account for no more than a small part of the variation in student achievement? It should be noted that to say that practices are relatively uniform is by no means to say that they are in need of radical change. Mankind, and indeed the whole animal world, has relatively uniform habits of eating and drinking, but this does not show that these habits are in need of amendment. What it does show is that if the supply of food and drink were cut off the consequences would be serious. Similarly the consequences of cutting off the supply of schools and teachers would be serious, irrespective of whether, given the educational system and the consequent student achievement, much or little of the variation of that achievement is to be attributed to variation in schools and teachers.

The broad outline of the analysis is that for each country, and for each population and subject within that country, we form a series of regression equations. This is done by pivotal condensation of the collapsed correlation matrix described in the previous chapter, taking the blocks of variables in the order 1, 2, 3, etc. Within each block the variables are taken in the order of descending partials, with a lenient cut-off at $F=2$. At the end of each block a summary is printed, giving the value of R^2 and the increment of R^2 as each variable enters the regression, the regression coefficient for each variable at the end of the block, the first order correlation, and the "unique" variance b^2/c for each variable at that stage. At the end of the first block, and again at the end of the third, the complete matrix, or rather the diagonal and the part below it, is printed, giving the inverse matrix for the variables already in the regression, the matrix of regression coefficients for the variables not yet in the regression on those that are, and the matrix of residual variances and covariances for the variables not yet in the regression. The advantage of having the complete matrix printed is that supplementary calculations can be made by hand from it without too much labor; the disadvantage is that printing is a relatively slow process in the computer, so that much more ground can be covered if the printing is restricted. In the later stages of the study more printing was done to reduce the burden of hand calculation. This was decided upon when it had become plain that lack of time and money would make it impossible to carry out the second runs in the original plan. The rather tentative analyses for the subjects in Stage 2 were expanded for those in Stage 3, but time and funds ran out before these later analyses could be applied in second runs on Stage 2. The main development was that the whole matrix was printed after more blocks, and that Newton and Spurrell analyses were included to show the effect of varying the order in which the blocks were taken. These analyses are considered in a later chapter.

In any study which purports to be representative the question of sampling fluctuations cannot be ignored. In this study the primary sampling unit was the school and not the individual student. This means that the sampling fluctuations will be greater than they would be for samples of the same kind in which each student was drawn independently from the whole population. On the other hand the samples were stratified, which reduces the amount of sampling fluctuation. Working together these two factors produce the design effect, which Kish (1964), who has worked extensively on this matter, calls DEFF. For any statistic DEFF is an estimate of the ratio of the actual sampling variation to the sampling variation of the same statistic on the evidence of a simple random sample (srs) of the same size— that is to say an unstratified random sample containing the same number of units of analysis drawn independently. In our case these units are students in the present chapter, and schools in the later chapter where the analysis is between-schools. A large number of values of DEFF were calculated by a jack-knifing method described in Chapter 2. Here it will be enough to say that for regression coefficients in the analyses between-students the average value of DEFF[1] was about 1.4. In other words if the reader is interested in the standard error of one of the regression coefficients in the ensuing tables he will not be far out if he refers to the number of students in the sample, calculates the srs standard error for a sample of that size by the elementary formula, and takes the actual standard error as half as much again. For example, in judging significance, where he would say $t=2$ for a simple sample he will say $t=3$ for these complex samples. This is for the analyses between-students. For the analyses between-schools DEFF is less than unity, owing to the stratification.

It was said above that the cut-off in the regression runs was at the very lenient value of $F=2$, and it is likely to occur to the reader at this point that DEFF makes this value still more lenient. This is certainly the case. In the choice of the cut-off level there was the usual dilemma. The opposing risks are the risk of following false clues and the risk of failing to follow genuine clues. In the IEA study the choice was made harder because we had evidence from a score of countries, and because most of the effects being studied could be expected to be small. To take a severe cut-off would reduce the number of false clues; to be more lenient would admit more genuine clues as well as more false ones. With the severe choice more of the genuine clues would not appear at all, and that would be the end of the matter. With the lenient choice more genuine clues would appear, along with more false ones, and a further stage of sorting the false from the true could be undertaken, because a clue that appeared in several countries would have a higher probability of being genuine than one that appeared only in a single country. The two-stage process, of beginning with a lenient cut-off and following with a second stage of purifying the alloy of truth and falsehood, was judged likely to sacrifice less of the genuine metal than the alternative of beginning with a severe cut-off. Examples will be seen in what follows.

In the ensuing sections the evidence from Populations II, I and IV is considered in that order. Population II is taken first because it presents the fullest spectrum. In Population I the effect of the second block of variables is very small; in Population IV the range is restricted by selection. The evidence considered is drawn from the developed countries; the developing countries are covered separately. Where Belgium has been excluded from the tables the reason is that the late decision to treat the Flemish and French speaking parts separately meant that there were so few schools in the samples that the estimates were unstable. The purpose of the chapter is not to recapitulate all that can be found in the subject reports. It is to give enough detail to illustrate and clarify what has already been said about the interpretation of the analyses, and to give the reader enough evidence on which to make his own interpretation, if he disagrees with the interpretation suggested. With this end in view Science in Population II is treated rather fully in both text and tables. Since the analyses follow the same principles throughout the other subjects for Population II, and all subjects for the other populations, are then reviewed more briefly, and in particular without printing the analogues of the very long Table 4.1, which sets out in full all the regression equations for Science in Population II.

POPULATION II.
BETWEEN-STUDENT REGRESSION EQUATIONS

Science

Each of the first 12 sections (A–L) of Table 4.1 (pp. 106–117) sets out the successive regression equations for Science in one of the developed countries. The column headed 0 gives the first order correlations with the criterion variable, and the columns headed 1, 2, 3 etc. give the regression coefficients for the first, second, third etc. equation as successive blocks of variables are brought into the regression. Above the arrays of regression coefficients the second row of the table gives the value of R^2 for each equation. The third row gives the increment of R^2. It is arguable that Grade ought really to be included in the second rather than in the third block, and the effect on the increments of making this change is shown in the fourth row, in cases where it is not negligible.

It will be seen that the entries in the rows of regression coefficients tend to diminish from left to right; thus in the Australian section the regression coefficient for SHS is 0.35, 0.27, 0.18, 0.12 and 0.07 for equations 1, 2, 3, 4 and 5. One can think of the 0.35 as an index of the total effect of SHS and of the 0.27 as indicating the residual or direct effect of SHS if part of the total effect is thought of as transmitted by the intervening variables of Block 2. The intervention of Block 3 reduces the direct effect again, to 0.18. This shrinkage from left to right is less in the lower part of the tables, and in the upper part a conspicuous exception to the general rule is Sex. The extent of the shrinkage for any variable depends on the size of the partial correlations of that variable with the variables in the new intervening block; negative partials produce the increases that can be seen in a few cases scattered throughout the tables.

The last section (M) of Table 4.1 gives the regression coefficients in Equation 3 of the nine variables in Block 3 that appear with some consistency, and with consistent signs. Only four variables—Grade, Homework, Currently taking science, and Percentage of science teachers appear in a majority (seven or more) of the 12 countries. This is a disappointing result. It was clear enough in advance that the total contribution of these Recent conditions of learning would be quite small, but it was hoped that there would be more that appeared consistently.

There were two main reasons for expecting that the total contribution from this block would be small. In the first place the variables in the block describe *recent* conditions of learning. For these 14-year-old students much of the process had taken place before the Recent learning conditions described by the measures began to operate. In the second place the description is of what is done rather than of how well it is done; the variables do not give any *direct* indication of what is happening in the classroom. It can reasonably be inferred, from the fact that they are not wholly ineffective, that they do give an *indirect* indication; but this relation is rather vague and uncertain, which may account partly for the facts that each country has its own set of surviving variables in this block and that there is not a great deal in common between these sets. This distinction, between what is done and how well it is done, did not escape the attention of the members of the subject committee who devised the variables. The difficulty about devising measures of how well teaching is done is to avoid circularity. This difficulty is always present, but it is much increased in any wide inquiry extending over many schools. Within a single school it sometimes becomes plain that some members of the staff teach more effectively than others. But the evidence for this is simply that their students learn more rapidly, other things being equal. It is

64

not that more effective teachers conform to one pattern of behavior and less effective teachers to another. The proof of the pudding is in the eating, which is another way of saying that the difficulty is to avoid circularity. The IEA measures do avoid circularity, but the price to be paid for this is that they fail to give a full account of the effects of variation in teaching quality. What they leave out of the account goes into the residual variation, where it mingles with other unknown factors.

The argument of the second part of preceding paragraph is that if the estimate of the effects of the variables in Block 3 is correct it is an underestimate of the effects of variation in teaching quality. But is it correct? In other words, has full allowance been made for the initial variation among the students on whom the recent conditions of learning came to operate? The allowance has been made by partialling out the variables in the first two blocks, on the ground that these variables are the best surrogate for a pretest available on the evidence. But is this discount enough? Some light is thrown on this question by another variable, namely the Word Knowledge test, though this light is more diffuse than could be wished, for two reasons. In the first place the Word Knowledge test was not a pretest; it was given at the same time as the criterion tests, after the recent conditions of learning had operated, so that only the assumption that it was relatively immune from their influence can justify its use as a discount. Secondly, although it was originally intended to make additional regression runs with Block 5 (Word Knowledge) before Block 3 this was one of the many parts of the program that had to be abandoned when time and money ran out.

The "Unique" Variances. It is, however, possible to extract from the existing output the unique variances for Block 3 in Equations 3, 4, 5 and 6, and these are set out in Table 4.2, along with the increment of R^2 in the last column. (Throughout this table Grade is regarded as part of Block 2. If it were included in Block 3 the mean increment of R^2 would rise from 0.054 to 0.081. The effect for individual countries can be seen in Table 4.1.)

It will be seen that in the mean row the unique variance in Equation 3 is 0.048, not much less than the increment of 0.054. In Equations 4, 5 and 6 the unique variance for Block 3 falls to 0.036, 0.026 and 0.017. Thus the intervention of the Word Knowledge test *after* the intervention of the kindred variables in Block 4 produces a decline of 0.010 in the unique variance of Block 3. This suggests that

Table 4.2. *Population II, Science. Unique variance of Block 3 in Equations 3, 4, 5 and 6, compared with the Block Increment.*

Country	Equation				
	3	4	5	6	Inc. R^2
Australia	.045	.032	.015	–	.053
England	.042	.025	.014	.008	.067
FRG	.088	.082	.058	–	.095
Finland	.070	.033	.027	.021	.034
Hungary	.054	.036	.026	.013	.051
Italy	.047	.044	.031	.022	.051
Japan	.034	.016	–	–	.037
Netherlands	.056	.059	.057	.048	.074
New Zealand	.024	.016	.010	.004	.021
Scotland	.045	.028	.020	.015	.081
Sweden	.040	.035	.018	.004	.036
United States	.034	.024	.016	–	.048
Mean	.048	.036	.026	.017	.054

Note: Throughout this table Grade is regarded as part of Block 2.

without the intervention of Block 4 the decline would be somewhat greater, in the neighborhood of 0.015, and the corresponding decline in the increment of R^2 (between the value for Block 3 after Blocks 1 and 2 and its value after Blocks 1, 2 and 5) somewhat more. In other words, the fact that Blocks 1 and 2 together make only a rather inadequate surrogate for a pretest leads to a somewhat exaggerated estimate for Block 3.

This suggestion is supported by the English national survey described in *The Plowden Children Four Years Later* (Peaker, 1971). This was a longitudinal study, with the same children surveyed in 1964 and again in 1968. There were three age groups in the survey, the oldest group being 14 years of age on the second occasion, and therefore corresponding to the IEA Population II. For them the correlation between test and pretest was 0.761, and the increment of R^2 for Block 3, taken after home background, pretest, and type of secondary (i.e., later) school, was 0.050. This would be increased if the pretest were omitted, since the correlation between the final test and type of school was only 0.605 (because the value of this variable is the same for all children in the same type of school, and thus ignores the variation between children in the same type, which the pretest takes into account).

The youngest Plowden group were aged 10 on the second occasion, and had not yet made the transition from primary to secondary school, so that for them the Type of school variable does not exist, though the pretest does. For them the increment of R^2 for the recent conditions of learning, after Home background and pretest, is 0.056, rather more than the 0.050 for the group who were four years older, and therefore less malleable. This is in accord with the common observation that with increasing age it becomes harder to change one's habits; it is never too late to mend them, but it becomes harder as one grows older. As remarked above, septuagenarians like the writer can bear witness to the truth of this aphorism in the long run, and it is reasonable to think that what holds in the long run is also likely to hold in the short runs that together make up the long. An illustration for young children is the well known fact that between the ages of 5 and 11 the covariances of annual reasoning tests can be well represented by the ratio of the chronological age on the first occasion to the chronological age on the second, together with a reliability factor.

Taken together these considerations suggest that the effect of the specified recent conditions of learning on the variation in achievement is somewhat over-estimated by the increments of R^2 shown for Block 3 in Table 4.1. On the other hand, it is plain that there is much in the teaching process that is not represented in the specified conditions, so that although the increments overestimate the effects of the specified conditions they may well under-estimate the total effect of recent teaching.

The comparison with longitudinal studies like Plowden brings out another point. The Plowden study was initially a cross-sectional study in 1964. It was converted into a longitudinal study by the second survey in 1968. What was the final test in 1964 became the pretest for 1968. The 1964 achievement had to be analyzed in the same way as the IEA achievement, with a simulated pretest derived from what was known of the antecedent circumstances, but in 1968 the most important of the known antecedent circumstances was the 1964 achievement. Had there been a 1960 survey the most important known antecedent circumstance for 1964 would have been the 1960 achievement. What the student can learn during any interval depends very largely upon what he knows at the beginning of that interval. This holds throughout life. One gains little from attempting to read an advanced book on some subject with which one has not even an elementary acquaintance, or from attending a meeting without reading the previous papers. What one can do today depends on what one did yesterday. But equally what one could do yesterday depends on what one did the day before. When one discounts the effect of recent conditions of learning to allow for the past history of the learner one should not overlook the fact that this past history included conditions of learning that were once recent. When one attempts to assess the effect of recent teaching on the variation in current achievement it is right to make due discount for past history. But it would be wrong to ignore the fact that this past history itself includes the effect of earlier teaching. If the effect of teaching during a four year interval is assessed at, say 10 %, the total effect of teaching during school life must be more. But how much more is hard to say. It would certainly be wrong to say that if the effect over four years is 10 % the effect over a school life of eight years must be 20 %, since this would assume that those who had better teaching in the first interval also had it in the second, whereas the evidence (e.g., Acland, 1972) points to a relation that is nearly random. Although the effect on variation of recent teaching should not be confused with the total effect of teaching, none the less it seems likely that most of the variation in achievement is due to other causes.

A misunderstanding that would not be worth attention if it were less common is the argument that there can be little value in teaching if its effect on the individual variation in achievement is rather small. This argument overlooks the fact that the variation in question is variation within a system of education—that is to say within a system of teaching—and that without the system there would be no achievement. This point is illustrated in the IEA study by the very large difference between the scores of the developed and the developing countries. In the one case the teaching systems have existed for several generations; in the other they are comparatively recent. More is said on this point later, when the evidence from the developing countries is set out in more detail.

Reading Comprehension, Literature and Civic Education

Table 4.1 sets out in full the regression equations for Science in Population II in the developed countries that had enough schools in their samples to give trustworthy estimates. In the summary Table 4.3 the rows giving the increments of R^2 are extracted from Table 4.1. Tables 4.4, 4.5 and 4.6 give the corresponding summaries for Reading Comprehension, Literature, and Civic Education (with the Cognitive Score as the criterion). The definition of the blocks is the

Table 4.3. *Population II, Science. Increment of R^2 by Blocks, with Grade in Block 2.*

Block ...	1 Home Background[b]	2 Type of School	3 Learning Conditions	1+2+3	4 Kindred Variables	5 Word Knowledge	6 Reading Comprehension	4+5+6 Total
Australia	.160	.115	.053	.339	.053	.112	–	.165	.504
England	.231	.168	.067	.466	.053	.076	.079	.208	.674
FRG	.181	.069	.095	.345	.033	.085	–	.118	.463
Finland	.220	.121	.034	.375	.061	.052	.060	.173	.548
Hungary	.139	.030	.051	.220	.088	.064	.117	.269	.489
Italy	.103	.046	.051	.200	.043	.078	.070	.191	.391
Japan	.234	.001	.037	.272	.125	–	–	.125	.588
Netherlands	.193	.176	.074	.443	.048	.049	.048	.145	.588
New Zealand	.169	.185	.021	.375	.071	.084	.100	.255	.630
Scotland	.289	.116	.081	.486	.064	.075	.063	.202	.688
Sweden	.175	.031	.036	.242	.116	.102	.117	.335	.577
United States	.217	.037	.048	.302	.061	.158	–	.219	.521
Mean	.193	.091	.054	.338	.068	.085	.082	.235	.573[a]

[a] The column means are reckoned on the number of items, and the two last entries obtained by adding along the mean row.
[b] Block 1 also contains Sex and Age.

same throughout these four tables. Block 1 contains the Home background variables together with Sex and Age; Block 2 Type of school and Type of program, and also Grade; Block 3 the Recent conditions of learning; Block 4 the Kindred or concomitant variables. Block 5 consists of the single variable Word Knowledge, and Block 6 of the single variable Reading Comprehension. Block 6 does not appear in Table 4.4, since for this subject it was itself the criterion.

Tables 4.7 through 4.12 contain the corresponding summaries for the two remaining subjects—English and French as Foreign Languages. In each case the first table relates to Reading as the criterion, and the second to Listening. Not all the countries that took the Reading test also took the Listening test. In the third table in each set the Reading and Listening results are put down side by side for the countries that took both tests. As is shown in Chapter 2, the degree of selection is higher for French than for English—in other words English is a more popular subject. Because the subjects often are optional there is variation in the Number of years of study up to the time of the survey, and this variable, together with Age and Grade, is

Table 4.4. *Population II, Reading Comprehension. Increment of R^2 by Blocks, with Grade in Block 2.*

Block ...	1	2	3	1+2+3	4	5	4+5	
Country	Home Back- ground[a]	Type of School	Learning Conditions		Kindred Variables	Word Knowledge		Total
England	.273	.138	.025	.436	.073	.113	.186	.622
Finland	.202	.170	.008	.380	.088	.101	.189	.569
Hungary	.186	.039	.041	.266	.097	.094	.191	.457
Israel	.104	.124	.032	.260	.076	.117	.193	.453
Italy	.252	.145	.037	.434	.049	.116	.165	.599
Netherlands	.125	.232	.014	.371	.087	.085	.172	.543
New Zealand	.135	.234	.024	.393	.075	.121	.196	.589
Scotland	.261	.129	.033	.423	.086	.124	.210	.633
Sweden	.161	.014	.015	.190	.147	.146	.293	.483
United States	.221	.067	.032	.320	.107	.154	.261	.581
Mean	.192	.129	.026	.347	.089	.117	.206	.553

[a] Block 1 also contains Sex and Age.

put into a new Block 3, the other Recent conditions of learning now comprising a new Block 4. The Kindreds now comprise Block 5, and the Word Knowledge test is Block 6. To emphasize the fact that the definitions of the blocks have been changed, the arrangement of

Table 4.5. *Population II, Literature. Increment of R^2 by Blocks, with Grade in Block 2.*

Block ...	1	2	3	1+2+3	4	5	6	4+5+6	
Country	Home Back- ground	Type of School	Learning Conditions		Kindred Variables	Word Knowledge	Reading Compre- hension		Total
England	.252	.119	.039	.410	.062	.071	.118	.251	.661
Finland	.181	.097	.055	.333	.042	.072	.111	.225	.558
Italy	.106	.087	.030	.223	.050	.054	.111	.215	.438
New Zealand	.152	.139	.087	.378	.049	.077	.130	.256	.634
Sweden	.152	.000	.061	.213	.103	.096	.165	.364	.577
United States	.185	.024	.077	.286	.092	.100	.137	.329	.615
Mean	.171	.078	.058	.307	.066	.078	.129	.273	.580

[a] Block 1 also contains Sex and Age.

Table 4.6. *Population II, Civic Education (Cognitive Score). Increment of R^2 by Blocks, with Grade in Block 2.*

Block ...	1	2	3	1+2+3	4	5	4+5	
Country	Home Background	Type of School	Learning Conditions		Kindred Variables	Word Knowledge		Total
FRG	.176	.080	.163	.419	.054	.069	.123	.542
Finland	.190	.156	.052	.392	.073	.102	.175	.567
Ireland	.186	.070	.147	.403	.056	.109	.165	.568
Israel	.253	.019	.018	.290	.113	.132	.245	.535
Italy	.085	.106	.122	.313	.067	.144	.211	.524
Netherlands	.153	.226	.051	.430	.035	.054	.089	.519
New Zealand	.144	.204	.064	.412	.037	.134	.171	.583
United States	.204	.070	.028	.302	.099	.193	.292	.594
Mean	.174	.116	.080	.370	.067	.117	.184	.554

rows and columns used for the first four subjects has been transposed for the foreign language tables.

If we look first at Tables 4.3 through 4.6 we see that on the average the increment of R^2 for Block 3, the Recent conditions of learning, is least for Reading Comprehension and most for Civic Education. This holds whether we look at the means for all countries or the means for the common countries—that is, the four countries, namely Finland, Italy, New Zealand and the United States, that took all four subjects. The mean increments are:

	All countries	Common countries
Reading Comprehension	.026	.026
Science	.054	.038
Literature	.058	.062
Civic Education (Cognitive Score)	.081	.066

It was to be expected that the increment would be least for Reading Comprehension, since most of the teaching of reading occurs in lower grades, and its effects are wrapped up in Block 2. The teaching of Literature and Civic Education occurs later, while Science occupies an intermediate position.

Foreign Languages

If we turn now to the Foreign Languages we find on extracting the mean increments of R^2:

1. English	Blocks		
	3	4	3+4
(a) Reading: All Countries	.078	.070	.148
(b) Reading: Common Countries	.066	.073	.139
(c) Listening: All Countries	.048	.092	.140
2. French			
(a) Reading: All Countries	.103	.068	.171
(b) Reading: Common Countries	.094	.067	.161
(c) Listening: All Countries	.092	.118	.210

"Common Countries" in (b) means the same thing as "All Countries" in (c), but not in (a). For English (a) comprises French-speaking Belgium, FRG, Finland, Israel, Italy, the Netherlands and Sweden, of which FRG, Israel and the Netherlands are omitted from (b) and (c) because they did not take the Listening test. For French (a) comprises England, the Netherlands, New Zealand, Scotland and the United States. The Netherlands are omitted from (b) and (c) because they did not take the Listening test. Rumania is omitted altogether from the averaging because, as a Latin country taking French, it is *sui generis*.

It will be seen that for the Foreign Languages, and particularly for French, the combined effect of Blocks 3 and 4 is much greater than the effect of Block 3 in the four compulsory subjects. However, the most important time factor turns out to be Grade, which accounts for 0.087 out of the 0.103 for Block 3 in French Reading, and 0.038 out of 0.092 in French Listening. Years of studying French accounts for 0.016 and 0.050, and the contributions from Age and from Grade of beginning French are very small. Since Grade has been included in Block 2 for the compulsory subjects the contrast is not quite so sharp as it seems at first sight. The composition of the Block 3 account for French Listening is strikingly different in England and the United States, where it is made up mostly of Years of study, and New Zealand and Scotland, where it is mostly Grade.

The mean increments for Block 1 are Science 0.193, Reading Comprehension 0.192, Literature 0.171, Civic Education (Cognitive) 0.174, English (Reading) 0.145 and French (Reading) 0.075. This

Table 4.7. *Population II, English as a Foreign Language (Reading). Increment of R^2 by Blocks.*

Block	Belgium (Fr)	FRG	Finland	Israel	Italy	Netherlands	Sweden	Mean
1 Home	.142	.151	.257	.224	.012	.106	.124	.145
2 School Type	.210	.307	.404	.041	.075	.517	.000	.222
3 Time Factors	.065	.140	.058	.055	.054	.084	.087	.078
4 Learning Conditions	.098	.130	.021	.044	.132	.021	.042	.070
1+2+3+4	.515	.728	.740	.364	.273	.728	.253	.515
5 Kindreds	.055	.032	.033	.079	.028	.026	.215	.067
6 Word Knowledge	.000	.024	.009	.092	.060	.021	.076	.040
5+6	.055	.056	.042	.171	.088	.047	.291	.107
Total	.570	.784	.782	.535	.361	.775	.544	.622

shows the effect of selection for the foreign language courses, and particularly for French. Tables 4.9 and 4.12 show that when Listening replaces Reading as the criterion the contribution of Block 1 falls markedly. This fact, taken in conjunction with the much higher contribution from Block 3, shows that Listening to the foreign language, and particularly to French, depends more on school teaching, and less on Home background, than the other skills.

Table 4.8. *Population II, English as a Foreign Language (Listening). Increment of R^2 by Blocks.*

Block	Belgium (Fr)	Finland	Italy	Sweden	Mean
1 Home	.110	.273	.003	.116	.126
2 School Type	.104	.327	.110	.000	.135
3 Time Factors	.036	.056	.024	.075	.048
4 Learning Conditions	.181	.018	.127	.041	.092
1+2+3+4	.431	.674	.264	.232	.400
5 Kindreds	.037	.030	.015	.175	.064
6 Word Knowledge	.000	.008	.015	.063	.022
5+6	.037	.038	.030	.238	.086
Total	.468	.712	.294	.470	.486

Table 4.9. *Population II, English as a Foreign Language, Reading and Listening compared Increment of R^2 by Blocks.*

Block	Belgium (Fr) Listening	Belgium (Fr) Reading	Finland Listening	Finland Reading	Italy Listening	Italy Reading	Sweden Listening	Sweden Reading	Mean Listening	Mean Reading	Listening minus Reading
1 Home	.110	.142	.273	.257	.003	.012	.116	.124	.126	.134	−.008
2 School Type	.104	.210	.327	.404	.110	.075	.000	.000	.135	.172	−.037
3 Time Factors	.036	.065	.056	.058	.024	.054	.075	.087	.048	.066	−.018
4 Learning Conditions	.181	.098	.018	.021	.127	.132	.041	.042	.091	.073	.019
1+2+3+4	.431	.515	.674	.740	.264	.273	.232	.253	.401	.445	−.044
5 Kindreds	.037	.055	.030	.033	.015	.028	.175	.215	.064	.083	−.019
6 Word Knowledge	.000	.000	.008	.009	.015	.060	.063	.076	.022	.036	−.014
5+6	.037	.055	.038	.042	.030	.088	.238	.291	.086	.119	−.033
Total	.468	.570	.712	.782	.294	.361	.470	.544	.487	.564	−.077

"Unique" Contributions

Table 4.1 (M) sets out for Science the regression coefficients in Equation 3 of the variables in Block 3 that appeared consistently, and with consistent signs. Apart from Grade there were eight of them, of which only three appeared in a majority (seven or more) of the 12

Table 4.10. *Population II, French as a Foreign Language (Reading). Increment of R^2 by Blocks.*

Block	England	Netherlands	New Zealand	Rumania	Scotland	United States	Mean[a]
1 Home	.120	.037	.045	.106	.146	.025	.075
2 School Type		.123	.014	.028	.123	.009	.098
3 Time Factors	.107	.140	.092	.000	.137	.041	.103
4 Learning Conditions	.036	.074	.055	.148	.098	.079	.068
1+2+3+4	.485	.374	.206	.282	.504	.154	.344
5 Kindreds	.066	.038	.160	.048	.098	.068	.086
6 Word Knowledge	.034	.012	.072	–	.046	.056	.044
5+6	.100	.050	.232	.048	.144	.124	.130
Total	.585	.424	.438	.330	.648	.278	.474

[a] The Rumanian data have been excluded.

Table 4.11. *Population II, French as a Foreign Language (Listening). Increment of R^2 by Blocks.*

Block	England	New Zealand	Scotland	United States	Mean
1 Home	.087	.030	.116	.023	.064
2 School Type	.296	.001	.066	.007	.092
3 Time Factors	.142	.071	.089	.065	.092
4 Learning Conditions	.201	.084	.093	.094	.118
1+2+3+4	.726	.186	.364	.189	.366
5 Kindreds	.050	.074	.102	.082	.077
6 Word Knowledge	.015	.035	.036	.038	.031
5+6	.065	.109	.138	.120	.108
Total	.791	.295	.502	.309	.474

countries. The other subjects present similar pictures. Thus for Reading Comprehension only Grade and Homework appear in most countries with positive signs, and Grouping for reading with negative signs, indicating that this is an expedient adopted for weak readers. Having a mother tongue class appears frequently, the sign, with one exception, being positive.

Tables 4.13 through 4.18 set out the position for the six subjects in a slightly different form. In these tables the entry is not the regres-

Table 4.12. *Population II, French as a Foreign Language, Reading and Listening compared. Increment of R^2 by Blocks.*

Block	England Listening	England Reading	New Zealand Listening	New Zealand Reading	Scotland Listening	Scotland Reading	United States Listening	United States Reading	Mean Listening	Mean Reading	Listening minus Reading
Home	.087	.120	.030	.045	.116	.146	.023	.025	.064	.084	−.020
School Type	.296	.222	.001	.014	.066	.123	.007	.009	.092	.092	.000
Time Factors	.142	.107	.071	.092	.089	.137	.065	.041	.092	.094	−.002
Learning Conditions	.201	.036	.084	.055	.093	.098	.094	.079	.118	.067	.051
1+2+3+4	.726	.485	.186	.206	.364	.504	.189	.154	.366	.337	.029
Kindreds	.050	.066	.074	.160	.102	.098	.082	.068	.077	.098	−.021
Word Knowledge	.015	.034	.035	.072	.036	.046	.038	.056	.031	.052	−.021
Total	.791	.585	.295	.438	.502	.648	.309	.278	.474	.487	−.013

Table 4.13. Population II, Science. Between-Student b^2/c on Block 3.

	United States	Thailand	Sweden	Scotland	New Zealand	Netherlands	Japan	Italy	Iran	India	Hungary	Finland	FRG	England	Chile	Belgium (Fl)	Australia
Grade	2.1	4.0	6.3	0.9	5.3	3.0		0.8	1.4	2.4		3.9	3.0	0.2	0.1	1.1	4.5
Hours homework	0.9	0.7	0.2	1.1	0.8	0.2	1.4	0.3	0.7	0.3	2.1		0.4	1.0		1.6	2.0
Teacher preparation		2.1	0.4	0.1[a]	0.1[a]			0.1[a]	0.9[a]	0.1		0.5[a]	0.1		0.4	0.7[a]	0.5
Hours study science				0.8				0.1[a]	1.5[a]	0.3[a]		0.6		0.4		0.3[a]	0.2
Laboratory assistants	0.1[a]					0.2[a]				0.9				0.4		0.2	0.2
% Male teachers	0.3	0.5[a]	0.3[a]	0.3[a]	0.3	0.4[a]	0.9	0.5[a]		0.7	0.4[a]			0.2[a]			0.4[a]
Pupil/Teacher		0.2[a]			0.3	0.1		0.1	2.0	0.1[a]			0.2	0.2	1.1[a]		0.1
Taking science	1.1	0.8		0.7		0.1		1.7	0.4[a]	1.9	0.9			0.6	1.8	0.8	0.3
Time employed								0.5			0.3					1.1	0.2
Report to authorities	0.1	1.5[a]	0.1		0.1	0.2	0.1	0.2		0.1	0.1[a]	0.1[a]	1.1[a]	0.1		1.6	0.2
Specialist teacher science		0.5	0.2[a]			1.8		0.1					0.4	0.1[a]		1.8[a]	0.1[a]
Total science homework		0.2[a]	2.6[a]	0.1[a]							0.9[a]	0.5[a]				0.5[a]	0.1
Opportunity to learn				0.9	0.3						0.1	0.2					0.1
Subject association member	0.1[a]	0.8[a]		0.5		0.6			1.9	0.1[a]				0.3	0.4	0.5	0.1
% Teachers in science	0.1						0.3			0.1	0.1	0.2	1.9			1.2	0.1
Total enrollment		1.3			0.5												0.1
Total science study	0.2	0.9									0.2	1.1	0.8	0.6		0.5	
Teacher post-secondary education	0.2	0.1[a]				0.3	0.2	0.6	0.6	1.4[a]		0.1	0.6		0.7[a]	2.0	
Sex of teacher		0.3[a]	0.1[a]			0.4[a]	0.3[a]	0.6	0.2[a]		0.1		2.3[a]	0.3[a]	0.9[a]		
Practical work			0.2[a]				0.2						0.9	0.1			
Admission criteria, performance						0.9			2.3								
Type of community	0.1[a]	0.6[a]	0.1[a]			0.5[a]											
Highest grade	0.2[a]	1.5[a]															

Note: Missing data prevented the calculations being made for Belgium (Fr).

Table 4.14. Population II, Reading Comprehension Between-Student b^2/c on Block 3.

	United States	Sweden	Scotland	New Zealand	Netherlands	Italy	Israel	Iran	India	Hungary	Finland	England	Chile	Belgium (Fr)	Belgium(Fl)
Grade	3.1	1.2	0.4	5.4	2.6	0.6	1.7	1.7	4.6		3.2	0.1	5.1	3.5	2.2
Group for reading	0.1[a]		0.2[a]			0.2[a]		0.4[a]		0.2	0.1[a]			0.2[a]	2.1[a]
Hours homework per week	0.9		1.0	0.3	0.1	0.6	0.7	1.1	1.7	2.7		0.8	0.3	1.1	
Pupil/Teacher	0.1[a]	0.1[a]		0.6				2.4[a]		0.5[a]		0.1		1.9	0.8[a]
Mother tongue class	0.2	0.4	0.8	0.9	0.4	0.1		0.5		0.3	0.3[a]	0.7	0.8[a]	1.0	0.8
Sex of teacher	0.1[a]	0.2		0.2[a]	0.1	0.2[a]		0.6	1.3		0.3			0.5[a]	
Teacher post-secondary education			0.2[a]			0.2	0.2					0.2	0.5[a]	0.7	0.8
Report to authorities		0.1	0.5		0.8	0.1	0.9					0.2	0.1[a]	0.6	0.4[a]
Class grouping	0.2[a]	0.2[a]	0.2				1.6[a]	1.0[a]	0.3	0.2	0.1	0.1[a]	0.9[a]		
Specialist teacher mother tongue		0.1[a]	0.2	0.1		0.4				0.4	0.4[a]	0.1			2.6
Weeks per year/schooling						0.1[a]		0.7[a]	1.7						
Age of teacher	0.2		0.4[a]			0.3		0.6[a]		0.1[a]					
Type of community	0.3[a]	0.4[a]		0.2		0.1[a]	0.8[a]		0.7[a]						

[a] The sign of the regression coefficient is negative.

Table 4.15. *Population II, Literature. Between-Student b^2/c on Block 3.*

	Belgium (Fl)	Belgium (Fr)	Chile	England	Finland	Iran	Italy	New Zealand	Sweden	United States
Importance of exams	3.4		0.3ᵃ	0.3		1.5	0.3	0.1		
Impression of students	1.8	4.0	0.3		0.3				0.4ᵃ	
Methods–textbooks	1.1		0.9		0.1				0.5	0.3
Weeks per year school	0.7ᵃ	1.6ᵃ			0.3ᵃ		0.1ᵃ			
Teacher post-secondary education	0.7					2.8				
Hours homework/week	0.2		1.1	1.2	0.1	0.5	0.3	0.5		0.9
Admission criteria, performance	0.7				0.1	0.2		0.1		0.1
Grade	0.5	2.5	4.7	0.1	1.6	0.5	0.5	4.2	0.6	1.0
Teaching experience this school	0.3ᵃ				0.1		0.2			
Sex of teacher		2.2ᵃ				1.1ᵃ				0.2ᵃ
Age of teacher		0.5ᵃ		0.1	0.1	1.4ᵃ	0.2		0.1ᵃ	0.1
Write about literature		0.4		0.1		2.2	.	0.6	0.2ᵃ	0.4
Biographies of individual authors		0.3ᵃ			0.5ᵃ	3.4			0.4ᵃ	0.5
Class size literature			0.3	0.6	0.5	0.5ᵃ	0.1	0.9	0.6	0.2
Recite from memory				0.9ᵃ	0.5ᵃ	1.6ᵃ	0.3ᵃ	0.7ᵃ	2.3ᵃ	1.8ᵃ
% Teachers male				0.5ᵃ		3.3	0.6ᵃ		0.1ᵃ	0.1ᵃ
Proportion time literature				0.1						0.5
Decision–administration				0.1ᵃ	0.2	0.1		0.2ᵃ		
Hours homework literature				0.2ᵃ			0.1ᵃ		0.1	0.3ᵃ
Public library						2.8ᵃ			0.3	0.3
Pupil/Teacher						0.6				0.1ᵃ
Type of community							0.1	0.3		

ᵃ The sign of the regression coefficient is negative.

sion coefficient b; it is b^2/c, the so-called unique variance, or in other words the increment of R^2 when the relevant variable is the last to be entered in the regression. The diagonal element c is the reciprocal of the residual variance so that if P is the multiple correlation of the relevant variable with the other variables in the regression the quantity b^2/c may equally well be written as $b^2 (1-P^2)$.

If the sampling were simple random and all distributions normal we should have $c (1-R^2)/(d.f.)$ as the error variance for a regression coefficient, which gives t^2 or F, as $(b^2/c) (d.f.)/(1-R^2)$. For Australia

Table 4.16. *Population II, Civic Education Cognitive Total Corrected Score. Between-Students b^2/c on Block 3—Normal Order Regressions.*

	FRG	Fin-land	Ire-land	Italy	Nether-lands	New Zealand	United States
Grade beginning secondary school	0.4				0.3^a	0.9^a	0.1^a
Admission criteria examination	1.9						
Proportion minority group						0.6^a	
Sex of teacher	0.3^a	0.1^a	0.3	0.8		0.1^a	
Specialist teacher	0.0^b	0.2	0.8^a	0.8			
Post secondary education	0.9^a	0.1^a	0.3^a			0.1	
Hours preparation	0.2	0.2	0.2	1.0^a	0.2^a		0.2^a
Frequency use standardized tests	0.4^a			0.2^a		0.1^a	
Frequency use projects	0.1		0.7^a				
Frequency use printed drill	4.9^a	0.4^a	1.4^a				
Frequency use audio-visuals	0.7			1.4		0.1	0.4
Frequency use lectures	0.1^a			0.4^a	1.1		
Frequency use class grouping		0.2	0.3			0.1	0.1^a
Training civics, history, geography	0.1^a	0.6^a		0.2	1.5^a	0.1	
Sum of inservice training	1.2^a	0.7	1.3^a	1.7^a	0.2	0.9^a	
Subject association member			0.5^a	0.2^a	0.6^a	0.2	
Importance non-western cultures	0.4	0.8	0.3^a	0.6^a			
Importance own country po-litical history	1.1^a	0.1^a	0.7	1.5		0.4	
Tolerance of issue discussion	0.4^a	0.3^a		0.1			0.1
Teacher non-political-good citizenship	0.4	0.2	0.9^a	1.7^a			1.0
Grade	3.1	4.1	2.4		1.7	4.6	
Classroom independence	1.9	0.1	0.9	0.7	0.9	1.1	0.3
Classroom patriotism	1.4^a	2.4^a	4.6^a		1.1^a	2.6^a	0.8^a
Stress on facts in civics		0.1	1.1^a	0.3^a	0.1^a	0.1^a	

[a] The sign of the regression coefficient is negative.
[b] The variable entered the regression but has $b^2/c < 0.05$.

we have 5279 as the degrees of freedom in Equation 3 (Table 4.1 [A]) and 0.339 as R^2. These values lead to $t^2 = (b^2/c)/(1.25 \times 10^{-4})$, or $b^2/c = 0.000125 \, t^2$. The cut-off used was $F = 2$, which admits a variable to the regression if its $b^2/c = 0.00025$ or more. This is an extremely lenient cut-off value. If we were considering the Australian evidence in isolation it would be more reasonable to allow two standard errors for uncertainty and to take the jack-knife estimate of the standard error

Table 4.17. *Population II, English-Reading. Between-Student b^2/c on Block 4—Regression Order II.*

	Belgium (Fr)	FRG	Finland	Israel	Italy	Netherlands	Sweden	Thailand
Language auxiliaries, total	1.8^a		0.8				0.3^a	0.1
Classes conducted in English	2.7^a	1.6^a	0.1		0.3			0.4^a
Selection of English students	2.0	0.7	0.2		0.6	0.1^a		
Total time English beginning	2.7	0.1^a						
Total time English intermediate	2.4^a	3.4			0.1			
Sex of teacher	0.5^a		0.1		0.4^a			0.3
Hours marking papers	0.4	0.4^a	0.2					0.7
Other foreign language taught		0.2^a	0.1		0.5^a	0.1		0.7^a
Perceived listening skill, teacher		1.7			0.7		0.3^a	1.7
Perceived speaking skill, teacher			$0.0^{a,b}$			0.3		1.0
Perceived reading skill, teacher	4.0^a						0.4	
Perceived writing skill, teacher		4.0^a						0.2
Perceived pronunciation skill, teacher	1.5							2.2^a
Residence English-speaking country	0.5	0.6^a			0.3^a			
Years experience teaching foreign language		1.2	0.0^b	0.1	0.5	0.1	0.1	0.5
Teaching grammar		0.1		1.2	4.6^a	1.0	0.2^a	
Hours homework				2.0	2.0	$0.0^{a,b}$		1.8
Speaking English to teacher, sometimes	0.2	0.8	0.2	0.4		0.0^b	2.0	
Listening to teacher speaking mother tongue, sometimes					0.2^a	1.9^a		
Writing exercises in English		0.2	0.2	0.1	0.4	0.3	1.0	0.6
Reading for pleasure sometimes	0.8	0.1				0.2		0.5

^{a} The sign of the regression coefficient is negative.
^{b} The variable entered the regression but had $b^2/c < 0.05$.

(see Chapter 2). In the Australian case the average design effect for regression coefficients is 1.9, which gives $F = 7.6$, or 8, say, for an uncertainty of two standard errors, and a corresponding lower limit of 0.001 for b^2/c. This more severe standard would exclude the last seven variables shown in Equation 3 in Table 4.1 (A), of which six are

Table 4.18. *Population II, French Reading. Between Student b^2/c on Block 4.*

	Eng-land	Nether-lands	New Zealand	Rumania	Scot-land	United States
Coeducation		0.6	0.5ᵃ			0.2ᵃ
Number French teachers				3.8		1.5
Admission criteria—examination	0.9				0.5	0.5ᵃ
Class conducted in French: Grades 1–8			0.5ᵃ			
Total time beginning French		1.2ᵃ			0.8	0.1
Total time intermediate French	0.2	1.4ᵃ	0.2ᵃ			
Teacher sex			0.3	0.1	0.6	0.1
Hours marking papers	0.2	0.6ᵃ		0.7ᵃ		
Perceived listening skill, teacher		0.1		4.7	0.5ᵃ	
Perceived speaking skill, teacher	0.5				0.6ᵃ	0.2
Perceived reading skill, teacher				0.4ᵃ		
Perceived writing skill, teacher	0.2	0.5			0.5	0.3ᵃ
Perceived pronunciation skill, teacher				0.2ᵃ	0.8	
Residence in French country					0.6	0.1ᵃ
Years tertiary French				0.6ᵃ		0.1ᵃ
Years teaching foreign language						0.5
Method teaching grammar		0.1	0.1ᵃ			2.2
French in the classroom—speaking French	0.8		0.3	0.5	0.6	0.2
French in the classroom—writing exercises			0.6	0.2	0.8	0.1
French in the classroom—speaking in mother tongue	0.5ᵃ	0.2ᵃ	0.4ᵃ	1.5ᵃ	1.8ᵃ	0.1ᵃ
French in the classroom—translating		0.6	1.2			0.8
Teaching aids—variety and extent	0.1ᵃ	2.3ᵃ		0.2	1.8ᵃ	

ᵃ The sign of the regression coefficient is negative.

shown again in Table 4.13 because their b^2/c have been rounded *up* to 0.001 (and the last excluded because the four figure value is 0.0003). Excluding the last seven produces only a slight reduction in the estimate of R^2, which shrinks from 0.3388 to 0.3347, by 0.0041. The case for taking the extremely lenient $F=2$ as the cut-off rests on the fact that we have samples not from one country only but from many. Twelve developed countries are included in Table 4.1, with sample sizes ranging from 7 026 students in 210 schools in Hungary to 1 236 students in 50 schools in the Netherlands. All the samples are small, because of the limited resources of the project. From previous evidence, such as the Plowden studies, rough estimates of both the regression coefficients and the design effects could be made at the outset, and from these estimates it was clear that the probable result of taking anything but a lenient value for the cut-off would be to fill Tables 4.1 (M) and Tables 4.13 through 4.18 mainly with blanks. The result of taking the lenient cut-off $F=2$ would be to replace many of these blanks by small values which, though individually untrustworthy, might support each other by forming consistent patterns. In this way the evidence from different countries might be combined, and more variables might emerge as clearly deserving notice. As to the block increments, these would not be much affected by the choice of cut-off.

Cause and Effect

This, then, was how the position stood at the outset, and these were the considerations leading to the crucial decision to take $F=2$ as the cut-off. Bets must be placed before the race is run. How did things turn out? The forecasts of the size of the regression coefficients and the design effects proved to be quite accurate. But the forlorn hope that there would be an effective league of nations and that individually weak efforts would combine in united strength was largely disappointed. The tables were not left blank. They were filled, as may be seen, by numerous small, and individually untrustworthy, coefficients. But it was seldom that the same coefficient turned up frequently, and those that appeared for the majority of countries with the same sign were few indeed.

This was disappointing. That the results would have a more consistent pattern was from the outset a hope rather than an expectation, but it was not before the event a quite unreasonable hope, though a forlorn one. In each case the candidates, that is to say the variables in Block 3, were chosen with great care by the International Subject Committees, and it was reasonable to think that their choice would include any possible winners. But in fact the number of winners, with successes in several countries, turned out to be very small. Why?

Some reasons have been given earlier in this chapter, but they are perhaps worth recapitulation and expansion. In the first place all the variables in Block 3 were *recent* conditions of learning, operating only for a fairly brief interval before the survey. The longer term variables were included in Blocks 1 and 2, where they were very successful both in accounting for much of the criterion variation and in their capacity as a surrogate pre-test. This meant that on the average the coefficients for the Block 3 variables were bound to be small, but it did not preclude the possibility that some might be consistent from country to country. The low cut-off value was chosen to give this consistency the chance of showing itself, if it existed, at the expense of examining the distribution of sign among more coefficients than would have been admitted by a more severe cut-off. But even so comparatively little evidence of consistency appeared among the Block 3 variables. Taken together the Block 3 variables made contributions to the criterion variation ranging, in the compulsory subjects, from 2.6 % in Reading Comprehension to 8.1 % in Civic Education, and these amounts owed little to the low cut-off. But their composition varied from country to country. This suggests that apart from the few variables that appeared consistently there were others that have genuine but small effects, and which may or may not be picked up by the regression in samples of this size according to the luck of the draw.

However this may be, the total contribution of Block 3 remains small in comparison with the contribution of the long-term Blocks 1 and 2, as was to be expected. Taken together the first three blocks account for about a third of the variation in the students' criterion scores. What can account for the other two thirds? They can only be covered by the blanket phrase "Errors and omissions excepted," which in this context means that there are errors of measurement in the variables included (at both ends), and that other relevant variables have been perforce omitted. The omissions seem likely to cover more than the errors. For example, there is no measure of aptitude, scholastic talent, or IQ—different names for the same thing. Long standing and massive evidence has shown this to be a main determinant of school achievement in the subjects that are universally taught within a given system of compulsory education. That it is not entirely covered by our surrogates is shown by the fact that Blocks 5 and 6—the Word Knowledge and Reading Comprehension tests— add a quarter or more to the variation covered in Science, Literature and Civic Education, even though they were simultaneous and not prior tests.

If we regarded the equations in Table 4.1 as part of the network that would be needed to construct a path diagram with the last three blocks included as intervening variables (or the last two where there was no Reading Comprehension test) the final or direct paths would be the coefficients in the last equation. For all countries the most striking thing about the last equation is that the coefficient for Reading Comprehension (or for Word Knowledge if there is no Reading Comprehension test) is far larger than any other. In each table the coefficients in a row shrink as we go from left to right and move through equations bringing in more and more intervening variables. In the language of path analysis this is interpreted as meaning that part of the effect of earlier variables is transmitted through the later ones. Thus in the English case (Table 4.1 [B]) Equation 6 shows b for Reading Comprehension as 0.44, rounded from 0.437, so that $b^2 = 0.191$. The regression has reduced the residual variance of Reading Comprehension to 0.413, the reciprocal of the diagonal element, and $b^2 s^2 = 0.191 \times 0.413 = 0.0789$ the increment of R^2 shown as 0.079 in the second row of the table. It is because we have chosen a form of the path diagram in which this variable is taken last that its unique variance $b^2 s^2$ is identical with the increment of R^2. Every variable in the equation has its own b and s, and these are the same for any form of the path diagram provided that the same set of variables is finally in the regression, but $b^2 s^2$ is only identical with the increment of R^2 for which ever variable is taken last in the diagram as declared. There is nothing in the correlation matrix or the regressions derived from it to cause one path diagram rather than another to be declared. The declaration must depend on the taste and fancy of the analyst, that is to say on his view not of what is a conceivable but of what is a likely sequence of cause and effect, given both the immediate and the previous evidence, which includes all that he knows from his own experience and the reports of others about schools, teachers and parents. Analysts may, and frequently do, differ both as to their own experience and the set of reports with which they happen to be acquainted—for example, even within the English-speaking world people are more familiar with the professional literature of their own country as well as with its experience. This is only one of the many reasons that may lead to different interpretations of the same evidence. In the case before us there may well be differences of opinion on (1) what variables may reasonably be included in the path diagram and (2) in what order should they be taken? In particular is it reasonable to extend the path diagram by including the Reading tests as intervening variables, and, if so, where should they intervene? Excluding them means preferring Equation 3 in Table 4.1, or Equation 4 if Kindred variables are included. Including them means preferring Equation 5, or Equation 6 if both tests are included. For any of these choices the direct path coefficients are those shown in Table 4.1 for the relevant equation, but the earlier paths and the incremental account depend on the order in which the chosen variables are taken. The incremental account given at the head of each section of Table 4.1 takes the blocks in the order 1, 2, 3, 4, 5, 6. Altering the order would change the increments though not their total for any given choice of variables. Thus if in the English case Block 6, the Reading Comprehension test, were included and taken first it would at once account for $0.73^2=0.58$ of the criterion variation, as against the 0.08 that it accounts for above, when it is taken last after all the other variables in Equation 6. Thus if the Reading Comprehension test is included and taken first it is given a prime importance in the interpretation of the Science scores. If it is excluded it is given no importance. If it is included and taken last it is given some importance but not very much. Other examples of the effect of the choice of order are to be found in the chapter on the Newton and Spurrell analyses.

The main argument against including the Reading tests (i.e., the Word Knowledge and the Reading Comprehension tests) in the path diagram is that they were simultaneous and not previous tests. Against this it can be said that had they been pretests the correlations would not have been much changed; for example in Table 4.1 the first order criterion correlation for England is 0.73, and in the Plowden national sample for the same age group the correlation, covering an interval of four years, was 0.76, and many local studies in England and Scotland of selection for types of secondary school have given similar results. Compare also "Reading and Reasoning" (Thorndike, 1969). If one accepts this argument one will include the Reading tests in the path diagram, which will reduce the final paths for Block 3 to the values in Equation 6, and one will give the Reading tests an early place, which will make them bulk large in the incremental account and take the prime explanatory importance. The argument, like so many arguments in educational research, is not wholly free from circularity, and should not be pressed too far. What it amounts to is that if one believes in earlier evidence that something called reasoning ability is cardinal in much school achievement, and that a reading comprehension test is a good measure of this ability for students in the lower and middle grades of an established school system, then the IEA evidence lends support to this belief because it is compatible with it. The proviso is needed to indicate that it is not thought that reasoning ability would be assessed by the Reading Comprehension test in the absence of a school system, or given the same assessment in two quite different systems, such as those existing in a developed and a developing country. The cautious statement is needed because beliefs, if rational, can only rest on initial evidence with which new evidence is found compatible, and are always at risk of being falsified by the appearance of incompatible evidence. There can never be a guarantee that new incompatible evidence will not appear, but it can be said that if the weight of favorable evidence has increased over a long time it becomes increasingly unlikely that new evidence will call for more than minor modifications in the previously established range. Despite all the discoveries of modern physics, the Nautical Almanac is still calculated on Newtonian principles. In the social sciences, theory is in a much more primitive state and there are differences in kind that may make the analogy of physics inept, so that there is more ground for differences of opinion about the extent to which it is likely that new evidence may call for revisions of conclusions reasonably based on the old evidence. At present the evidence indicates that most of the causes of variation in school achievement lie outside the control of schools, but it is conceivable that this might be somewhat modified by new practices. On whether this is likely there is room for different opinions.

The immediate evidence has been set out in such a way that the reader can exercise his own preference. Equation 3 assesses the effect of the Recent learning conditions in Block 3 at about 5 % of the total variation in the case of Science. Equation 6 puts it at about half that amount. For Literature the amounts are about the same, and for Civic Education half as much again, with a further increase for the two Foreign Languages. On either reckoning the amounts are small. They are under-estimates of the total effect of teaching, because in the first place the variables include no direct assessment of how well teaching is done, and because the effects of earlier teaching, at home and in the primary school, are wrapped up in the first two blocks. On the other hand both general experience and longitudinal studies suggest that the degree of under-estimation cannot be very large. In all the developed countries several generations have passed through the schools, but the low level of literacy of some students is still a matter of complaint, which could hardly be the case if it were

Table 4.19. *Population I, Science. Increment of R^2 by Blocks.*

Block ... Country	1 Home Back- ground	2 Type of School	3 Learning Condi- tions	1+2+3	4 Kindred Vari- ables	5 Word Knowl- edge	4+5	Total
England	.212	.004	.030	.246	.070	.352	.422	.668
FRG	.077	.019	.096	.192	.043	.173	.216	.408
Finland	.144	.002	.043	.189	.068	.349	.417	.606
Hungary	.075	.001	.074	.150	.049	.277	.326	.476
Italy	.043	.000	.035	.078	.058	.385	.443	.521
Japan	.166	.002	.012	.180	.037	. −	−	−
Netherlands	.163	.012	.067	.242	.043	.301	.344	.586
Scotland	.220	.011	.054	.285	.075	.311	.386	.671
Sweden	.155	.001	.048	.204	.035	.354	.389	.593
United States	.176	.009	.088	.273	.071	.338	.409	.682
Mean (without Japan)	.140	.007	.060	.207	.057	.315	.372	.579
Mean (with Japan)	.143	.006	.055	.204	.054	. −	−	−

Note: Block 1 includes Sex and Age.

easily remediable by teaching. Some teachers can work miracles, but there is no reason to expect miracle workers to be more common among teachers than among the rest of us.

POPULATION I.
BETWEEN-STUDENT REGRESSION EQUATIONS

Science and Reading Comprehension

There were ten developed countries that took the Science tests for Population I, and nine that took the Reading Comprehension. Eight took both. Table 4.19 gives the incremental account for Science. Table 4.20 gives the incremental account for Reading Comprehension. Table 4.21 compares the mean increments in the two subjects for the countries that took both subjects. In these tables Block 2 plays a very small part, because there is not much differentiation of Type of school or Type of program before the age of 11. It will be seen from Table 4.21 that Home background plays a larger part for Reading Comprehension, and Recent conditions of learning for Science, as would be expected.

Table 4.20. *Population I, Reading Comprehension. Increment of R² by Blocks.*

Block ...	1 Home Back-ground	2 Type of School	3 Learning Condi-tions	1+2+3	4 Kindred Vari-ables	5 Word Knowl-edge	4+5	Total
Country								
England	.221	.004	.015	.240	.074	.374	.448	.688
Finland	.177	.000	.028	.205	.073	.330	.403	.608
Hungary	.187	.004	.038	.229	.056	.265	.321	.550
Israel	.254	.019	.037	.310	.057	.173	.230	.540
Italy	.096	.002	.045	.143	.038	.375	.413	.556
Netherlands	.111	.016	.040	.167	.097	.335	.432	.599
Scotland	.237	.003	.023	.263	.079	.323	.402	.665
Sweden	.114	.003	.029	.146	.037	.384	.421	.567
United States	.198	.010	.039	.247	.062	.373	.435	.682
Mean	.177	.007	.033	.217	.063	.326	.389	.606

Note: Block 1 includes Sex and Age.

More about Cause and Effect

The first four blocks are the same in these tables as for Population II, but the fifth block is not. In the tables for Population II Block 5 was the Word Knowledge score. Here it includes both the alien criteria— that is to say Word Knowledge and Reading Comprehension for Science, and Word Knowledge and Science for Reading Com-prehension. The computer printout does not give the complete

Table 4.21. *Population I, Science and Reading Comprehension. Mean Increment of R² by Blocks for the Eight Developed Countries that took both Subjects.*

Block ...	1 Home Back-ground	2 Type of School	3 Learning Condi-tions	1+2+3	4 Kindred Vari-ables	5 Word Knowl-edge	4+5	Total
(a) Science means	.148	.005	.056	.209	.059	.333	.392	.601
(b) Reading Com-prehension means	.167	.005	.033	.205	.064	.345	.409	.614
(c) Difference; (b)−(a)	.019	.000	−.023	−.004	.005	.012	.017	.013

Table 4.22. *Population I, Science and Reading Comprehension. Increment of R^2 by Selections of Blocks.*

Block ... Country		1 Home Background	2 Type of School	3 Learning Conditions	6 Reading Comprehension	Total	Reading Comprehension Coefficients		
							b	r	r^2
England	(a)	.212	.004	.030	–	.246			
	(b)	.212	.004	.030	.392	.638	.710	.768	.590
	(c)	.212	–	–	.443	.635	.718	.768	.590
Finland	(a)	.144	.002	.043		.189			
	(b)	.144	.002	.043	.384	.573	.689	.713	.508
	(c)	.144	–	–	.409	.553	.690	.713	.508
Hungary	(a)	.075	.001	.074		.150			
	(b)	.075	.001	.074	.295	.445	.609	.631	.398
	(c)	.075	–	–	.333	.408	.621	.631	.398
Italy	(a)	.043	.000	.035		.078			
	(b)	.043	.000	.035	.412	.490	.672	.684	.468
	(c)	.043	–	–	.436	.479	.679	.684	.468
Netherlands	(a)	.163	.012	.067		.242			
	(b)	.163	.012	.067	.321	.563	.626	.706	.498
	(c)	.163	–	–	.380	.543	.654	.706	.498
Scotland	(a)	.220	.011	.054		.285			
	(b)	.220	.011	.054	.346	.631	.674	.754	.569
	(c)	.220	–	–	.396	.616	.698	.754	.569
Sweden	(a)	.155	.001	.048		.204			
	(b)	.155	.001	.048	.364	.568	.669	.719	.517
	(c)	.155	–	–	.407	.562	.686	.719	.517
United States	(a)	.176	.009	.088		.273			
	(b)	.176	.009	.088	.369	.642	.696	.770	.593
	(c)	.176	–	–	.451	.627	.727	.770	.593
Mean	(a)	.148	.005	.055		.208			
	(b)	.148	.005	.055	.361	.569	.668	.718	.516
	(c)	.148	–	–	.395	.543	.675	.718	.516

Notes: Block 1 includes Sex and Age.

Blocks 1, 2 and 3 are in the (a) rows, 1, 2, 3 and 6 in the (b) rows and 1 and 6 in the (c) rows. The (b) and (c) rows also give the values of b, r and r^2 for Block 6 (Reading Comprehension) when it is included in the equation in the order indicated.

matrix after Block 4 is in the regression, so that it would be extremely laborious to separate the effects of the two variables by hand. But the print does give the complete matrix after the first block is in the regression, and again after the first three are in. This makes it

Table 4.23. *Population II, Science and Reading Comprehension. Increment of R^2 by Selections of Blocks.*

Block ...		1 Home Back- ground	2 Type of School	3 Learning Condi- tions	6 Reading Compre- hension	Total	Reading Comprehension Coefficients		
Country							b	r	r^2
England	(a)	.231	.168	.067	–	.466			
	(b)	.231	.168	.067	.164	.630	.544	.731	.534
	(c)	.231	–	–	.341	.574	.684	.731	.534
Finland	(a)	.220	.121	.034		.375			
	(b)	.220	.121	.034	.135	.500	.474	.597	.356
	(c)	.220	–	–	.240	.460	.547	.597	.356
Hungary	(a)	.139	.030	.051	–	.220			
	(b)	.139	.030	.051	.236	.456	.575	.630	.397
	(c)	.139	–	–	.302	.441	.611	.630	.397
Italy	(a)	.103	.046	.051	–	.200			
	(b)	.103	.046	.052	.157	.357	.459	.509	.259
	(c)	.103	–	–	.218	.321	.492	.509	.259
Netherlands	(a)	.193	.176	.074	–	.443			
	(b)	.193	.176	.074	.107	.550	.414	.595	.354
	(c)	.193	–	–	.273	.466	.558	.595	.354
Scotland	(a)	.289	.116	.081	–	.486			
	(b)	.289	.116	.081	.158	.644	.524	.734	.539
	(c)	.289	–	–	.297	.586	.634	.734	.539
Sweden	(a)	.175	.031	.036	–	.242			
	(b)	.175	.031	.036	.289	.531	.600	.651	.424
	(c)	.175	–	–	.341	.516	.621	.651	.424
United States	(a)	.217	.037	.048	–	.302			
	(b)	.217	.037	.048	.187	.489	.498	.611	.373
	(c)	.217	–	–	.242	.459	.536	.611	.373
Mean	(a)	.195	.092	.055	–	.342			
	(b)	.195	.092	.055	.179	.521	.511	.632	.399
	(c)	.195	–	–	.282	.477	.585	.632	.399

Notes: Block 1 includes Sex and Age.

Blocks 1, 2 and 3 are in (a) rows, 1, 2, 3 and 6 in (b) rows and 1 and 6 in (c) rows. The (b) and (c) rows also give the values of b, r and r^2 for Block 6 (Reading Comprehension) when it is included in the equation in the order indicated.

practicable to produce Table 4.22 by hand calculation without pro-hibitive labor. For each country in Table 4.22 there are three regression equations, (a), (b) and (c). The right hand side of (a) contains the first three blocks of variables, that of (b) contains the first three blocks and also the Reading Comprehension score, and that of (c) contains only the first block together with the Reading Comprehension score. The three rows (a), (b) and (c) for each country in the table show the corresponding increments of R^2, which are of course the same in all three rows for Block 1, and the same in rows (a) and (b) for Blocks 2 and 3. The three columns on the right of the table all relate to Block 6, the Reading Comprehension Score (RCS). The first gives the regression coefficient b in the relevant equation, the second the first order correlation r, and the third r^2, which is the increment of R^2 for the Reading Comprehension Score if taken first. The regression coefficients increase somewhat from row (b) to row (c), because Blocks 2 and 3 are omitted from Equation (c), but r and r^2 are the same in both rows.

Provided that the same set of variables is included in a regression equation the order in which they are put into the regression does not affect the final R^2, but it does affect the increments of which that total is composed. Thus in row (b) at the foot of the table we have a total of 0.569, made up of increments 0.148, 0.005, 0.055, 0.361 for Blocks 1, 2, 3, 6 in that order. If we changed the order to 6, 1, 2, 3 we should have 0.516 for 1, and the remainder 0.053 split between the other three blocks, instead of the 0.208 that they contain in (a) and (b) in the table. If we took the order 1, 6, 2, 3 we see from (c) that 1 and 6 would contain 0.148 and 0.395, leaving 0.569−0.543=0.026 to be split between 2 and 3, instead of the 0.060 that they contain in (b) and (c). These calculations apply also to the individual countries. They illustrate the fact that while different path diagrams for the same set of variables give the same final R^2, and the same final paths, the increments and the intermediate paths do depend on the order.

But which order is to be preferred? In particular, what is there to be said in favour of promoting the Reading Comprehension Score to an earlier place? In the Watergate inquiry the chairman was asked "How do you know that?" "Because" replied Senator Erwin "I understand the English language. It is my mother tongue." We begin to learn our mother tongue from our mothers, with some assistance from our fathers, and later from our companions and teachers, and some of us learn faster than others, first to speak and then to read. The world is full of a number of things, and as we grow older we are expected to understand more and more of them. We can only do this by first understanding something of what is said or written about them, and the advantage of the written or printed word is that one can go over it more than once. *Literia scripta manent.* What is said through the medium of the printed word remains to be looked at again, which is more than can be said for some other media, where what is not grasped at once is gone for ever. In this sense learning to read well is the most important of school achievements, and the foundation of the others. And for young children, at any rate, a reading comprehension test is a rather good measure of the ability to read well.

This argument and the effects of accepting it have already been discussed at the end of the previous section on Population II To make the parallelism clearer, Table 4.23 for Population II is in the same form as Table 4.22 for Population I. Here again we see, on looking at the mean rows at the foot of the table, that the first three blocks give $R^2=0.342$, that including the Reading Comprehension score raises R^2 to 0.521, and that Home background and Reading Comprehension score alone give $R^2=0.477$. Consequently $0.521-0.477=0.044$ is the increment of R^2 when Blocks 2 and 3 are added to the regression after Home background and Reading Comprehension score have been put into it. If Blocks 2 and 3 are put in after Home background but before the Reading Comprehension score we see from (a) or (b) that they add 0.147 to R^2, three times the previous assessment.

So far as the correlation matrices and the resulting regression equations go these are merely alternative ways of stating the same facts. It is only when we begin to think about interpreting the facts that the choice between the alternatives becomes important. All the variables that survive to the end of the regression runs do so because they have non-zero final regression coefficients, or final paths in the language of path analysis. But if we merely consider these final paths we interpret only the "unique" variance obtained by summing b^2/c, and leave the large remainder of R^2 out in the cold. This is a meagre interpretation, but to fill it out we have to go back behind the immediate evidence and try to use the whole background of what is known of schools and the history of education to exercise choice not only about what variables should be included but also about the order in the path diagram. Different choices lead to different results, of which some may appear more reasonable than others.

Tables 4.24 and 4.25, for Science and Reading Comprehension in Population I, follow the pattern of Tables 4.13 and 4.14 for Population II. The entries are b^2/c for the Block 3 variables when Blocks 1, 2 and 3 are in the regression in that order. As in the Population II case an (a) indicates a negative b, and only a few variables have consistent

Table 4.24. *Population I, Science. Between-Student b²/c on Block 3.*

	Belgium (Fl)	Belgium (Fr)	Chile	England	FRG	Finland	Hungary	India	Iran	Italy	Japan	Netherlands	Scotland	Sweden	United States
Design own experiments		0.3[a]	1.6[a]	1.1[a]	0.8[a]	0.6[a]	0.4[a]	0.8[a]	1.1[a]			1.9[a]	2.4[a]	1.8[a]	1.9[a]
Grade		12.7	2.4	0.3	0.8	1.1		1.6	1.6	0.5			1.2	1.5	2.6
Observations and experiments	2.4	1.1	0.3	0.5	0.4		0.7	0.2[a]	1.3	0.1		0.7[a]	0.2	0.4[a]	1.0
Science textbooks	0.8	1.3	1.5	0.3	1.7[a]	0.6	0.2	2.5	0.2	1.0		0.5		0.2	0.8
Pupil/Teacher		0.5			0.7[a]		0.4	3.9		0.4		0.7[a]	0.7[a]		0.2
Opportunity to learn				0.1	0.1	0.2		3.9					0.2		0.3
Coeducation Population I	0.8[a]	0.3[a]	0.4[a]	0.1	0.5[a]	0.3[a]	0.2[a]	0.7				0.2[a]	0.2		
Class size	0.7[a]			0.5	1.9		0.1[a]	0.2				0.2[a]	0.1		
Regular Science lessons	1.2	1.2	1.2	0.2[a]	0.5	0.2	1.3	1.2	0.3[a]		0.7	0.2			0.3
Sex of teacher							0.1	0.6	0.2[a]	0.6[a]					
% Teachers male		0.5[a]				0.3[a]	0.2[a]	0.1[a]	0.1	1.3[a]		1.3	0.3[a]		0.2
Hours homework							0.5		0.1		0.5				
Total enrollment	0.3		1.2[a]	0.2[a]	0.3		1.4[a]	4.3[a]							0.4[a]

[a] The sign of the regression coefficient is negative.

Table 4.25. Population I, Reading Comprehension. Between-Student b^2/c on Block 3.

	Belgium (Fl)	Belgium (Fr)	Chile	England	Finland	Hungary	India	Iran	Israel	Italy	Netherlands	Scotland	Sweden	United States
Grade	1.4	13.2	1.9	0.4	1.0	0.7	0.3	1.5	0.9	0.8		0.9	1.7	3.4
Class size				0.2	0.3[a]		0.6[a]	0.6	0.8	0.2				
Library in class	5.7	1.9	0.2[a]	0.2	0.6[a]	0.5	0.4				2.7		0.1	
PTA raises money	1.3[a]		0.2[a]	0.1		0.2[a]	0.1							0.1[a]
Grouping for reading	2.9[a]		0.8	0.1[a]		0.4[a]	0.7	0.7[a]	0.3[a]					
Assessment homework		1.2	0.1	0.1	0.2	0.1[a]	1.1[a]	1.2	0.2[a]			0.3[a]		
Advocate reading for discussion	0.3[a]	1.0	0.8	0.1[a]	0.5	0.8	1.2	0.2[a]	0.1		0.2		0.2[a]	
Subject association members			0.7	0.1[a]		0.1[a]	0.1[a]		0.9		0.3	0.4[a]	0.1	
Audio-Visual materials used	1.6[a]		3.1[a]			0.5								
Hours homework		0.5				0.3	0.9[a]		0.2			0.3[a]		
Hours mark papers		0.2	0.6[a]			0.2	0.3	2.5	0.2[a]		0.5			
Importance of textbooks		0.3				0.2[a]			0.6[a]					
Years principal	0.9	1.3[a]	0.1[a]			0.1	7.3	0.7[a]		0.1				
PTA activities—Parent Education	1.3				0.4		1.4[a]			1.1	0.1[a]	0.2	0.3	
Teacher aids			0.3[a]				0.6			1.9	0.5[a]		0.1[a]	0.4[a]

[a] The sign of the regression coefficient is negative.

signs across countries. Grade is positive everywhere. In Science, Observation and experiment, Having a science text-book, Having regular science lessons, and Opportunity to learn are consistently positive, and Designing one's own experiments quite consistently negative. In Reading Comprehension there is little consistency apart from Grade, and this supports the view of reading as the fundamental skill continually exercised and depending more on home background and the earliest school stages than on later sources of variation.

POPULATION IV.
BETWEEN-STUDENT REGRESSION EQUATIONS

In the developed countries education is compulsory at least up to the age of Population II. But at the age of Population IV attendance is voluntary; only part of the age group is still in school, and the part varies from 9 % in the Federal Republic of Germany to 75 % in the United States. The range of Home background is no longer fully representative, and those from the lower end of the range who are still in school are likely to be untypical. In addition, the instructional variables have operated over a longer period. For these reasons Home background may be expected to account for less of the variation of achievement among the volunteers of Population IV than among the conscripts of Populations I and II.

Another difference is that, in some countries at least, there is some specialization by subject among the older students, which does not arise at the earlier ages.

Science, Reading Comprehension, Literature
and Civic Education

Tables 4.26 through 4.29 give the block increments for Population IV for Science, Reading Comprehension, Literature and Civic Education. In Table 4.30 the block averages over countries are given for the four subjects; the figure in brackets indicates in each case the number of countries in the average. There is a marked contrast between the row for Science and the next three rows for the other subjects; to bring out this contrast these three rows are themselves averaged in the fifth and lowest row of the table. Thus for the first block the top row contains 0.162, and the fifth row 0.088. For the third block we have 0.237 and 0.042. The explanation is not far to seek. The first block contains not only Home background but also Age and Sex. As may be seen in Comber and Keeves (1973) boys do

Table 4.26. *Population IV, Science. Increment of R^2 by Blocks.*

Country	Home Background (1)	Type of School (2)	Learning Conditions (3)	1+2+3	Kindred Variables (4)	Word Knowledge (5)	Reading Comprehension (6)	4+5+6 Total
Australia	.134	.033	.204	.371	.066	.081		
England	.129	.016	.412	.557	.052	.035	.050	.137	.694
FRG	.132	.115	.075	.322	.065	.030		
Finland	.249	.193	.072	.514	.042	.041	.045	.128	.642
Hungary	.114	.134	.097	.345	.066	.037	.070	.173	.518
Italy	.096	.022	.157	.275	.028	.032	.057	.117	.392
Netherlands	.211	.053	.307	.571	.054	.016	.031	.101	.672
New Zealand	.129	.013	.307	.449	.093	.045	.048	.186	.635
Scotland	.190	.013	.340	.543	.084	.045	.024	.153	.696
Sweden	.181	.082	.204	.467	.053	.066	.054	.173	.640
United States	.184	.088	.081	.353	.039	.108		
Mean (11 countries)	.159	.069	.205	.433	.058	.049		
Mean (8 countries)	.162	.066	.237	.465	.059	.040	.047	.146	.611
France[a]	.159	.259	.045	.463	.026	.032		

[a] The French details are given separately because the primary sampling unit was the complete class.

better than girls in the Science tests, and increasingly so as the age increases. Sex differences exist in the other subjects, but they are comparatively slight. It is this that accounts for the much larger part played by the first block in Science. Home background by itself plays a small part, relatively to the part it plays in Populations I and II, in Science as in the other subjects. The reason for the relatively large part played in Science by the third block is specialization by subject. The two variables Science study and homework, and Years of science study, if taken by themselves after Blocks 1 and 2, can account for most of the Block 3 increment—for example, 0.185 out of 0.204 in Australia, 0.275 out of 0.307 in New Zealand, and 0.304 out of 0.340 in Scotland. In the United States, where the block increment is only 0.081, these two variables account for 0.062, and they are in fact the only variables that appear consistently, in all the countries. In other words the students who give more time to the study of Science and have more teaching in the subject learn more about Science, and less

Table 4.27. *Population IV, Reading Comprehension. Increment of R^2 by Blocks.*

Block ... Country	1 Home Background	2 Type of School	3 Learning Conditions	1+2+3	4 Kindred Variables	5 Word Knowledge	4+5	Total
England	.024	.018	.046	.088	.075	.159	.234	.322
Finland	.115	.023	.023	.161	.059	.079	.138	.299
Hungary	.069	.085	.049	.203	.069	.063	.132	.335
Israel	.086	.194	.151	.431	.038	.061	.099	.530
Italy	.096	.079	.050	.225	.028	.075	.104	.329
Netherlands	.010	.084	.038	.132	.031	.047	.078	.210
New Zealand	.090	.016	.019	.125	.067	.151	.218	.343
Scotland	.040	.014	.035	.089	.113	.205	.318	.407
Sweden	.042	.140	.017	.199	.050	.169	.219	.418
United States	.175	.080	.029	.284	.052	.201	.253	.537
Mean	.075	.073	.046	.194	.058	.121	.179	.373

about other things, than other students, and there is much more variation among students of this age in the amount of attention given to Science than in the amount of attention given to the other three subjects in Table 4.30. This is a rather convincing explanation of the fact that in Block 3 the increment for Science is six times the average increment for the other subjects, which is only 4 %.

Table 4.28. *Population IV, Literature. Increment of R^2 by Blocks.*

Block ... Country	1 Home Background	2 Type of School	3 Learning Conditions	1+2+3	4 Kindred Variables	5 Word Knowledge	6 Reading Comprehension	4+5+6	Total
England	.073	.008	.007	.088	.048	.056	.145	.249	.337
Finland	.057	.003	.027	.087	.051	.050	.101	.202	.289
Italy	.107	.033	.054	.194	.029	.053	.124	.206	.400
New Zealand	.087	.017	.020	.124	.041	.089	.097	.227	.351
Sweden	.051	.044	.018	.113	.032	.099	.133	.264	.377
United States	.163	.034	.050	.247	.060	.085	.138	.283	.530
Mean	.090	.023	.029	.142	.043	.072	.123	.238	.380

Table 4.29. *Population IV, Civic Education (Cognitive Score). Increment of R^2 by Blocks.*

Block ...	1 Home Back-ground	2 Type of School	3 Learning Condi-tions	1+2+3	4 Kindred Vari-ables	5 Word Knowl-edge	4+5	Total
Country								
FRG	.047	.006	.068	.121	.050	.095	.145	.266
Finland	.138	.029	.009	.176	.099	.075	.174	.350
Ireland	.090	.008	.090	.188	.040	.197	.237	.425
Netherlands	.082	.080	.051	.213	.051	.034	.085	.298
New Zealand	.081	.002	.033	.116	.077	.141	.218	.334
Sweden	.075	.150	.060	.285	.041	.103	.144	.429
United States	.183	.090	.041	.314	.068	.160	.228	.542
Mean	.100	.052	.050	.202	.061	.115	.176	.378

Foreign Languages

Tables 4.31 and 4.32 give the block increments for English and French as Foreign Languages with Reading as the criterion. In the English table the blocks have the usual meaning. In the French table the Time factors have been made into a separate block. There is a striking contrast between the first rows in the two tables, showing that the students who take French as a Foreign Language are more highly selected than those who take English, and perhaps supporting the view that today English is regarded as the more utilitarian and

Table 4.30. *Population IV, Science, Reading Comprehension, Literature and Civic Education (Cognitive Score). Increment of R^2 averaged over countries.*

Block ...	1 Home Back-ground	2 Type of School	3 Learning Condi-tions	1+2+3	4 Kindred Vari-ables	5 Word Knowl-edge	6 Reading Compre-hension	Total
Subject								
1 Science (8)	.162	.066	.237	.465	.059	.040	.047	.611
2 Reading Com-prehension (10)	.075	.073	.046	.194	.058	.121		.373
3 Literature (6)	.090	.023	.029	.142	.043	.072	.123	.380
4 Civics (7)	.100	.052	.050	.202	.061	.115		.378
5 (1+2+3)/3	.088	.049	.042	.179	.054	.103	–	–

Note: The figures in brackets after the name of each subject indicate the number of countries in the averages.

Table 4.31. *Population IV, English as a Foreign Language. Increment of R^2 by Blocks.*

Block	FRG	Fin-land	Hun-gary	Is-rael	Italy	Swe-den	Mean
1 Home Background	.036	.091	.029	.153	.190	.031	.088
	.011						
2 Type of School	.047	.000	.127	.097	.292	.195	.120
3 Recent Conditions of Learning	.118	.147	.187	.098	.240	.051	.140
4 Kindred	.077	.133	.063	.047	.046	.117	.081
5 Word Knowledge	.104	.058	.009	.042	.008	.087	.051
Total	.346	.429	.415	.437	.776	.481	.480

French as the more cultural of the two languages. As in Population II, the teacher's self-ratings of skill in reading, pronouncing and listening to the foreign language were among the variables contributing to the increment, and in general the pattern of contributions was rather more consistent than in other subjects. This suggests that the school plays a somewhat larger part relatively to the home among students of foreign languages. For Population II Tables 4.9 and 4.12 showed that this effect was even stronger for Listening than for Reading, and this holds also for Population IV.

Table 4.32. *Population IV, French as a Foreign Language. Increment of R^2 by Blocks.*

Block	Eng-land	Nether-lands	New Zealand	Scot-land	Swe-den	United States	Mean
1 Home Background	.026	.008	.020	.027	.025	.033	.023
2 Type of School	.049	.004	.000	.004	.000	.024	.014
3 Time Factors	.071	.048	.024	.051	.290	.071	.092
4 Recent Conditions of Learning	.060	.050	.144	.106	.225	.136	.120
5 Kindred	.184	.126	.127	.234	.000	.126	.133
6 Word Knowledge	.050	.032	.061	.106	.070	.081	.067
Total	.440	.268	.376	.528	.610	.471	.449

Variations in Retentivity in Population IV

In the IEA study the word "retentivity" was used to denote the proportion of the age group still in school. For Population IV this varied in the developed countries from 9 % in the Federal Republic of Germany to 75 % in the United States. One would expect high retentivity to maximize success, and low retentivity to minimize failure, since with high retentivity most children with talent will stay on, as well as many children who lack talent, while with low retentivity few children who lack talent will stay on, but not all the children with talent will stay on. The top of the milk contains the highest proportion of cream, but it does not contain all the cream.

The expectation that high retentivity will maximize success can be checked from the IEA evidence by extracting from the Population IV sample for each country a subsample containing the np highest scorers, where n is the number of children in the sample and p is chosen so that the subsample contains the same proportion of the age group in each country. In other words $p=k/R_C$ where R_C is the retentivity of the country. The largest admissible value of the constant k is R_G, the retentivity in the Federal Republic of Germany. If we chose p as R_G/R_C the subsample will comprise the whole sample in Germany and the best 12 % (i.e. 0.09/0.75) in the United States. If we now take the variables:

X_1 The country mean score for Population II
X_2 The retentivity function $R^*=R^{\frac{1}{2}}$
X_3 The country mean score for the whole sample of Population IV
X_4 The country mean score for the subsample of Population IV

and regress the scores on the first two variables we obtain the standardized equations:

(*a*) Science

$$x_3=0.396x_1- 0.695x_2+x_{3.12}, R^2=0.702$$
$$x_5=0.538x_1+ 0.218x_2+x_{4.12}, R^2=0.311$$

(*b*) Reading

$$x_3=0.128x_1- 0.667x_2+x_{3.12}, R^2=0.500$$
$$x_4=0.186x_1+ 0.447x_2+x_{4.12}, R^2=0.197$$

(*c*) Literature

$$x_3=0.396x_1- 0.695x_2+x_{3.12}, R^2=0.516$$
$$x_4=0.772x_1+ 0.218x_2+x_{4.12}, R^2=0.522$$

These equations bear out the expectations, since the coefficient of the retentivity function, x_2, is always positive for the subsample and negative for the whole sample. The coefficient of x_1 is always positive, because the scores of Population IV depend partly on the scores at the previous stage. The reason for taking the retentivity function R^* as $R^{\frac{1}{2}}$ is that it is plain that a small increase in R from a low value will produce a greater effect than the same increase from a high value, so that what we need for R^* is a function whose rate of increase with R declines as R increases. $R^{\frac{1}{2}}$ is the simplest function that meets this need, and in fact gives a better fit than either R or $R^{\frac{1}{4}}$.

SUMMARY

In this chapter we have considered the range of variation in student achievement at the ages of 10, 14 and 18 in the developed countries and have used the other information in the survey to attempt to account for some of the variation. Our starting point is that the student's achievement at 14 say, is built on his achievement at 13, which in turn is built on achievement at 12, and so on back to the age at which his schooling began. At this point there was already a wide variation, which must represent variation in heredity and early environment. For exemple, some children, already able to read by the time they begin school, read better than some who are at the end of grade 3. Such children have an early lead, which usually, though not invariably, increases as they grow older, because the learning process is cumulative, with each step depending on its predessor so that those who begin as fast learners tend to continue as fast learners. There is an analogy with physical growth. Tall 5-year-olds tend to become tall 10-year-olds, and children who are tall at 10 tend to be tall at 14, and so on, with the range at 18 much greater than the range at 5. The growth does not progress evenly; there are well recognized spurts at certain ages, which are not the same for boys as for girls, and growth that would otherwise occur may be prevented by malnutrition. In the same way mental malnutrition—lack of good teaching—may inhibit mental growth that would otherwise occur.

Suppose that we wished to estimate the effect on growth of supplying milk in schools to children during their tenth year. The likelihood of getting a useful estimate would be much greater if (1) some children drank their milk and others did not, and (2) we had the children's measurements at the beginning as well as at the end of the year. If all children drank all their milk, no estimate would be possible; if all drank some but the amounts varied, an estimate would be possible but less accurate. If we did not know the measurements at the beginning of the interval, we should not know how much to attribute to milk and how much to growth before the interval began. And even if we did know we should still be at risk of attributing to milk gains that were really brought about by other causes.

The analogy with physical growth is helpful in several ways. In the first place it draws our attention to the fact that, subject to adequate nutrition, children grow, and grow at very different rates. "Subject to adequate nutrition" does not mean that the children must have a special diet. It means that they must have enough food. Provided the food contains the necessary nutrients, including vitamins, there is little to choose between a wide range of possible diets. Starvation and scurvy are both inimical to growth, but there is plenty of scope for individual preference in the choice of diet, provided that enough is available to make choice possible. In the same ways children grow mentally, and grow at very different rates, subject to adequate mental nutrition. If they are mentally starved, or if their mental food is unsuitable, growth is inhibited, but if the diet is then improved growth will begin again. The mental stature at any time is the sum of all preceding growth, through good intervals and bad. The variation in stature at any time is attributable partly to nutrition in the most recent interval, partly to nutrition in all the preceding intervals, and partly to a "natural" tendency to be tall or short. To speak of a "natural" tendency does not explain that tendency. It means that we recognize it as an important fact that is not to be ignored when we are trying to assess the effects of variation in nutrition.

In our analyses the block of variables described as Recent conditions of learning contains our evidence about recent nutrition. As evidence it is far from complete, since it contains little about the quality of teaching, and the meaning of "recent" is rather vague. Our evidence about what happened before these conditions became operative is also rather vague; it is contained in the other blocks of variables. There is a strong case for putting the first two blocks— Home background with Sex and Age, and Type of program and Type of school, into the regression before the Recent conditions of learning in the third block. The first two blocks are certainly correlated with the growth that has taken place before the recent conditions begin to operate, and can therefore stand in as surrogates for that growth, but are they the best combination available? In particular, is there anything to be said for including the two Reading tests in the surrogate? At first sight the fact that the tests were simultaneous appears to be conclusive. If we were concerned with physical growth one would not include a simultaneous measure of arm-span in an equation intended to explain growth in stature. But all the information that generates the variables is in fact collected at the same time, and we do not accept the simultaneity argument against the first two blocks. This is because we believe that the simultaneous information in them can also stand for an earlier state of affairs. Boys will be boys, and girls, girls; age increases uniformly with time, and family circumstances are usually fairly stable. The child usually remains in the type of program or school to which he is first transferred. These are the grounds for giving priority to the first two blocks, despite the fact that the information that they contain was collected at the same time that the tests were held. Can anything analogous be said to apply to the Reading tests? There is evidence not only that skill in reading is the foundation on which much other school achievement rests but that it is relatively stable from its first beginning; the precocious reader becomes the assiduous reader. If so, there is a case for putting the Reading tests into the regression for the other five subjects, and particularly for the foreign languages which begin late and are taught to selected students.

The consequences of putting the Reading tests into the regression are clearer than the case for doing so. The effect is twofold, as may be seen by comparing equations 4, 5 and 6 with equation 3 in Table 4.1, and again in Tables 4.22 and 4.23, and later in the section on the Newton and Spurrell analyses (Chapter 6). In the first place more of the variance is explained. Secondly the amount attributed to the Recent conditions of learning in the third block is reduced. If we refrain from putting the Reading tests into the regression we have a larger residual variance which is unexplained. Unexplained, that is to say, by any of the measured variables, though we may have a strong conviction that much of it is to be explained in another sense by the general activity or lethargy of the mental processes. If so we could represent in by a hypothetical variable called IQ, for want of a better name, and bring this hypothetical variable into the equations, where it would play much the same part as the reading tests. In particular it would reduce the amount attributable to the third block, besides increasing the total of the explained variance.

These questions are difficult, but they are also unavoidable if we are to make much sense of the results of the study. The immediate evidence, from the study itself, is embodied in the regression equations. But these equations can be interpreted in many ways. The way which makes most sense is that which is most compatible with all the previous evidence. Some of the previous evidence is embodied in formal studies, but far more of it is uncodified and even unrecorded. Let the reader think of any child he actually knows very well—that is to say better than he knows other children. In such a case he will be familiar with certain regularities of behavior, and this will enable him to make predictions about future behavior which are more often right than wrong, at any rate in broad outline. This is easier with one's own children and grandchildren, owing to the persistence of hereditary traits, recognized in the phrase "a strong family resemblance," but even in this case he will have many surprises, and be driven to recognize that much of human nature will escape any set of variables. Every case is unique, which is the reason why there are no universal rules of good teaching. The most that can be said is that some rules succeed more often than not, and that the best teachers, like the best doctors, may recognize some cases where the rules do not apply and need to be replaced by a quite different treatment. If the reader is old enough to be a grandfather he will also perceive that his behavior, and that of his contemporaries, is easier to predict successfully than that of children, and particularly young children, because habits tend to become fixed with age. This applies alike to good and bad habits, and shows the importance of forming good habits early; the prime purpose of school education is to increase the prospect of this happening, within the limits imposed by heredity and family background.

Schools are concerned with a wide spectrum of habits but since this chapter is about school achievement the habit to which it directs our attention is the habit of study, that is, of becoming interested in the matter in hand and applying one's mind to it. This habit, like others, depends partly on heredity and early family life, so that there is already a wide range by the time children begin school. Because each step depends on its predecessor, this range becomes wider with the years if each child receives a fair deal in school. If those with an initial lead receive a better deal the increased width will be somewhat greater; if they receive a worse deal the increase will be somewhat less. This is the conclusion to which common observation of children at home and in school points. It is consonant with the results of more formal longitudinal studies. It is also consonant with the IEA evidence, on the interpretation suggested above, which indicates that variations in the conditions of learning operating through a fairly short interval of school life do have an effect, but an effect that is rather small in comparison with the effect of what has gone before.

What is maintained here is not that no other interpretation is possible, but that an interpretation which is compatible with the previous evidence is more likely, and that it increases the total weight of evidence in favor of that view.

To avoid the risk of being misunderstood two points should be added. The first is that to say that most of the variation in achievement within a country's educational system is caused by factors outside the control of the school is by no means to say that schools and teachers matter little. The success of a lesson, or of a course of study, is to be judged by the amount of learning that has taken place, and not by the change, if any, that has occurred in the relative standing of the students. The total amount of learning that now takes place in the schools in a developed country is much greater today than formerly, because the educational system has now existed over several generations. This point is so plain that it would not be worth mention were it not that experience shows that misunderstanding can occur.

The second point is that there is no suggestion that special educational efforts in deprived areas should not be undertaken, or that if undertaken such enterprises are doomed to futility. Whether they should be undertaken is an ethical question. The evidence suggests that the difficulties are likely to be formidable, but not that success is impossible. The evidence also suggests that the enterprise should begin when the children are very young, and that success is likely to depend mainly upon the extent to which their parents can be persuaded to participate.

Table 4.1. *Population II, Science. The Regression Equations (Between-Students).*

	(A) *Australia*					
Equation	0	1	2	3	4	5
R^2		.160	.232	.339	.392	.504
Increment R^2		.160	.072	.107	.053	.112
Increment R^2 with Grade in Block 2			.115	.064		

Block	Variable	r	b	b	b	b	b
I	SHS	.33	.35	.27	.18	.12	.07
	Sex	−.20	−.22	−.23	−.27	−.23	−.23
II	Type of program	.32		.26	.19	.13	.10
	Type of school	.17		.08	.01	.00	−.02
III	Grade	.26			.24	.24	.15
	Homework	.33			.17	.10	.07
	Teacher preparation	.09			.08	.08	.07
	Hours study science	.19			.05	.06	.04
	Laboratory assistants	.10			.06	.06	.05
	% Teachers male	.03			−.07	−.07	−.05
	Pupil/Teacher	.11			.04	.04	.02
	Taking science	.20			.06	.04	.02
	Time employed	.00			.04	.05	.04
	Report to authorities	.03			.04	.05	.03
	Specialist teacher science	.05			−.03	−.05	−.04
	Science homework	.20			.03	.02	.03
	Opportunity to learn	.10			.03	.03	.02
	Subject association member	.07			.03	.03	.02
	% Teachers in science	.02			.03	.03	.02
	Total enrollment	.04			.03	.02	.00
	Total science study	.12			−.02	−.02	.00
IV	Expected education	.38				.16	.10
	Science interests	.36				.14	.13
	Reading for pleasure	.23				.07	.02
	Like school	.21				−.03	−.02
	School motivation	.16				.02	.00
V	Word Knowledge	.58					.40

Note: Throughout the table the column headed 0 gives the first order correlations with criterion variable, and the columns headed 1, 2, 3 etc. give the regression coefficients for first, second, third etc. equation.

Table 4.1 (continued).

		(B) *England*						
Equation		0	1	2	3	4	5	6
R^2			.231	.399	.466	.519	.595	.674
Increment R^2			.231	.168	.067	.053	.076	.079
Block	Variable	r	b	b	b	b	b	b
I	SHS	.45	.47	.26	.20	.15	.08	.01
	Sex	−.09	−.14	−.23	−.19	−.11	−.10	−.11
	Age	.09	.11	.09	.05	.06	.04	.02
II	Type of school	.51		.39	.31	.29	.21	.15
	Type of program	.37		.15	.11	.08	.05	.02
III	Science study	.43			.10	.08	.04	.03
	Homework	.46			.13	.08	.05	.03
	Taking science	.22			.08	.07	.04	.01
	Laboratory assistants	.34			.07	.07	.06	.05
	Hours study science	.38			.08	.04	.06	.06
	Sex of teacher	.04			−.09	−.07	−.07	−.06
	% Teachers male	−.01			−.07	−.04	−.02	−.01
	Subject association member	.23			.06	.05	.05	.03
	Pupil/Teacher	−.24			.05	.05	.05	.02
	Grade	.10			.05	.07	.04	.04
	Specialist teacher science	.33			−.05	−.05	−.03	−.03
	Report to authorities	.04			.03	.03	.03	.00
	Practical work	.05			.03	.02	.00	.00
	Opportunity to learn	.28			−.02	−.02	−.01	−.01
IV	Science reading	.37				.15	.13	.12
	Science interests	.39				.12	.12	.10
	Expected education	.45				.11	.08	.05
	Like school	.19				−.05	−.05	−.05
V	Word Knowledge	.63					.35	.15
VI	Reading Comprehension	.73						.44

Table 4.1 (continued).

(C) *Federal Republic of Germany*

Equation		0	1	2	3	4	5
R^2			.181	.204	.345	.378	.463
Increment R^2			.181	.023	.141	.033	.085
Increment R^2 with Grade in Block 2				.069	.095		
Block	Variable	r	b	b	b	b	b
I	SHS	.31	.30	.23	.15	.09	.03
	Sex	−.30	−.29	−.28	−.28	−.24	−.25
II	Type of school	.28		.17	.12	.09	.01
III	Grade	.20			.19	.20	.12
	Teacher post-secondary education	.29			.13	.12	.06
	Sex of teacher	−.25			−.18	−.17	−.12
	% Teachers in science	−.04			.17	.18	.16
	Practical work	.08			.11	.12	.11
	Report to authorities	−.13			−.12	−.12	−.10
	Total science study	−.01			.10	.11	.09
	Specialist teacher science	.30			.10	.11	.10
	Homework	.15			.07	.03	.01
	Pupil/Teacher	−.12			.07	.08	.07
	Teacher preparation	.21			.06	.04	.01
IV	Science interests	.27				.11	.10
	Expected education	.31				.14	.09
	Like school	.13				.04	.04
	Reading for pleasure	.11				.03	.01
	School motivation	.12				.03	.04
V	Word Knowledge	.53					.38

Table 4.1 (continued).

		(D) Finland						
Equation		0	1	2	3	4	5	6
R^2			.220	.276	.375	.436	.488	.548
Increment R^2			.220	.056	.099	.061	.052	.060
Increment R^2 with Grade in Block 2				.121	.034			
Block	Variable	r	b	b	b	b	b	b
I	SHS	.34	.35	.21	.13	.05	.03	.01
	Sex	−.30	−.31	−.33	−.37	−.28	−.28	−.25
	Age	.09	.08	.08	−.05	−.03	−.02	−.02
II	Type of program	.34		.27	.40	.32	.18	.06
III	Grade	.18			.25	.23	.16	.12
	Total science study	.17			.11	.10	.07	.05
	Hours study science	.40			.12	.14	.16	.17
	Science homework	.18			−.08	−.11	−.09	−.06
	Teacher preparation	.18			−.10	−.09	−.10	−.08
	Opportunity to learn	.01			.05	.06	.04	.03
	% Teachers in science	.09			.05	.04	.93	.01
	Report to authorities	−.05			−.04	−.05	−.03	−.02
	Teacher post-secondary education	.13			.03	.03	.03	.02
IV	Science reading	.40				.20	.18	.16
	Expected education	.31				.12	.10	.06
	Reading for pleasure	.09				.07	.04	.01
	Science interests	.32				.07	.06	.05
	Like school	.04				−.04	−.03	−.04
V	Word Knowledge	.48					.28	.13
VI	Reading Comprehension	.60						.36

Table 4.1 (continued).

(E) *Hungary*

Block	Variable	0	1	2	3	4	5	6
	Equation	0	1	2	3	4	5	6
	R^2		.139	.169	.220	.308	.370	.489
	Increment R^2		.139	.030	.051	.088	.064	.117
		r	*b*	*b*	*b*	*b*	*b*	*b*
I	SHS	.31	.32	.27	.23	.07	.04	−.02
	Sex	−.19	−.20	−.24	−.25	−.19	−.20	−.18
	Age	−.02	−.06	−.08	−.05	−.03	−.02	−.03
II	Type of program	.22		.12	.08	.06	.04	.02
	Type of school	.20		.07	.04	.04	.05	.02
III	Homework	.21			.16	.09	.06	.02
	Taking science	.17			.10	.09	.07	.04
	Science homework	−.03			−.10	−.12	−.11	−.07
	Pupil/Teacher	−.16			−.08	−.06	−.06	−.04
	Science study	.08			.05	.04	.03	.01
	Time employed	.06			.05	.04	.05	.05
	Report to authorities	−.05			−.04	−.05	−.05	−.04
	% Teachers in science	.04			.04	.04	.04	.03
	Sex of teacher	.10			.04	.02	.01	.00
	Opportunity to learn	.03			.02	.02	.02	.01
	% Teachers male	−.08			.03	.04	.01	.02
	Specialist science teachers	.13			.02	.00	.00	−.02
IV	Science interests	.36				.17	.15	.11
	Expected education	.38				.19	.13	.06
	Science reading	.30				.11	.10	.07
	Reading for pleasure	.19				.03	.00	−.03
V	Word Knowledge	.43					.28	.12
VI	Reading Comprehension	.63						.46

Table 4.1 (continued).

		(F) *Italy*						
Equation		0	1	2	3	4	5	6
R^2			.103	.143	.200	.243	.321	.391
Increment R^2			.103	.040	.057	.043	.078	.070
Increment R^2 with Grade in Block 2				.046	.051			
Block	Variable	r	b	b	b	b	b	b
I	Sex	−.22	−.22	−.23	−.23	−.18	−.20	−.19
	SHS	.16	.18	.11	.09	.02	−.02	−.03
	Age	.16	.16	.12	.06	.07	.07	.06
II	Type of school	.17		.16	.13	.14	.07	.02
	Type of program	.19		.14	.14	.10	.05	.01
III	Taking science	.09			.16	.16	.13	.10
	Grade	.21			.16	.18	.13	.09
	Sex of teacher	.10			.08	.08	.06	.05
	Teacher post-secondary education	.10			.08	.09	.07	.06
	% Teachers male	.04			−.08	−.08	−.05	−.05
	Time employed	.04			.08	.08	.08	.07
	Homework	.07			.05	.02	.01	−.01
	Report to authorities	.03			.04	.05	.04	.03
	Teacher preparation	−.03			−.04	−.04	−.05	−.04
	Laboratory assistants	.19			.04	.02	.02	.02
	Science homework	.12			.05	.03	.04	.04
	Hours study science	.10			−.04	−.04	−.02	+.01
	Specialist teacher science	.05			−.02	−.02	−.02	−.02
	Practical work	−.07			−.02	−.02	−.02	−.03
IV	Science reading	.24				.12	.11	.08
	Expected education	.20				.11	.06	.03
	Science interests	.23				.09	.09	.08
	Reading for pleasure	.06				.03	.01	.00
V	Word Knowledge	.39					.32	.17
VI	Reading Comprehension	.51						.35

Table 4.1 (continued).

	(G) *Japan*					
Equation		0	1	2	3	4
R^2			.234	.235	.272	.297
Increment R^2			.234	.001	.037	.125
Block	Variable	r	b	b	b	b
I	SHS	.38	.38	.37	.33	.11
	Sex	−.28	−.27	−.27	−.29	−.16
	Age	.11	.11	.11	.09	.07
II	Type of school	.12		.03	.03	.00
III	Homework	.17			.12	.06
	Laboratory assistants	.15			.10	.07
	Time employed	.8			.04	.02
	Sex of teacher	−.08			−.05	−.05
	Practical work	.11			.04	.03
	% Teachers in science	.00			.06	.05
	Teacher post-secondary education	.09			.05	.04
IV	Science interests	.49				.27
	Expected education	.47				.25
	Reading for pleasure	.23				.07

Table 4.1 (continued).

(H) The Netherlands

Equation	0	1	2	3	4	5	6
R^2		.193	.339	.443	.491	.540	.588
Increment R^2		.193	.146	.104	.048	.049	.048
Increment R^2 with Grade in Block 2			.176	.074			

Block	Variable	r	b	b	b	b	b	b
I	Sex	−.32	−.33	−.29	−.39	−.28	−.28	−.29
	SHS	.27	.28	.05	.01	−.04	−.05	−.05
	Age	.11	.09	.10	.02	.02	.02	.01
II	Type of program	.49		.45	.23	.23	.13	.05
III	Grade	.26			.19	.22	.17	.13
	Specialist Teacher science	.38			.31	.33	.30	.29
	% Teachers in science	.04			.09	.07	.07	.04
	Homework	.32			.05	.02	.05	.01
	Admission criteria, performance	.16			.11	.11	.12	.11
	Laboratory assistants	.38			−.10	−.17	−.16	−.15
	Type of community	−.02			−.08	−.10	−.10	−.10
	Teacher post-secondary education	.11			.07	.08	.08	.07
	Sex of teacher	−.28			−.09	−.10	−.10	−.10
	% Teachers male	.18			−.11	−.10	−.09	−.10
	Report to authorities	.26			.05	.04	.04	.01
	Taking science	.13			.04	.03	.02	.01
	Time employed	−.08			.05	.04	.03	.01
IV	Science reading	.31				.13	.12	.11
	Expected education	.40				.15	.13	.10
	Science interests	.26				.10	.09	.08
	Like school	.03				−.04	−.04	−.05
V	Word Knowledge	.49					.27	.14
VI	Reading Comprehension	.60						.32

113

Table 4.1 (continued).

		(I) New Zealand						
Equation		0	1	2	3	4	5	6
R^2			.169	.291	.375	.446	.530	.630
Increment R^2			.169	.122	.084	.071	.084	.100
Increment R^2 with Grade in Block 2				.185	.021			
Block	Variable	r	b	b	b	b	b	b
I	SHS	.33	.34	.20	.14	.09	.05	.04
	Sex	−.21	−.22	−.26	−.28	−.20	−.19	−.18
	Age	.11	.11	.12	−.01	.00	.00	.00
II	Type of program	.42		.38	.30	.24	.13	.04
III	Grade	.35			.27	.29	.20	.12
	Homework	.29			.10	.04	.03	.01
	Laboratory assistants	.10			.05	.05	.04	.03
	Taking science	.15			.06	.05	.03	.00
	Total enrollment	.04			.07	.07	.06	.02
	Opportunity to learn	.09			.06	.06	.04	.01
	Report to authorities	−.03			.03	.04	.04	.04
	Teacher preparation	.05			−.03	−.03	−.03	−.02
IV	Science interests	.38				.14	.13	.13
	Science reading	.32				.15	.14	.13
	Expected education	.34				.10	.07	.05
	Like school	.20				−.06	−.03	−.03
	Reading for pleasure	.20				.04	.00	−.03
	School motivation	.18				.03	.02	.01
V	Word Knowledge	.59					.36	.14
VI	Reading Comprehension	.70						.47

114

Table 4.1 (continued).

(J) *Scotland*

Equation		0	1	2	3	4	5	6
R^2			.289	.397	.486	.550	.625	.688
Increment R^2			.289	.108	.089	.064	.075	.063
Increment R^2 with Grade in Block 2				.116	.081			
Block	Variable	r	b	b	b	b	b	b
I	SHS	.48	.48	.32	.23	.17	.10	.06
	Sex	−.21	−.21	−.21	−.19	−.13	−.12	−.11
	Age	.12	.10	.10	.04	.07	.05	.03
II	Type of program	.48		.26	.20	.15	.08	.03
	Type of school	.42		.15	.12	.12	.09	.07
III	Hours study science	.39			.13	.08	.09	.08
	Opportunity to learn	.33			.11	.12	.12	.10
	Homework	.38			.13	.05	.02	.01
	Grade	.13			.12	.15	.11	.09
	Taking science	.24			.12	.09	.07	.05
	Subject association member	.22			.07	.06	.03	.02
	Laboratory assistants	.10			−.06	−.05	−.04	−.04
	Science homework	.13			−.04	−.04	−.02	−.01
	Teacher preparation	.09			−.03	−.04	−.03	.02
IV	Science reading	.40				.15	.14	.14
	Science interests	.42				.14	.11	.08
	Expected education	.46				.13	.07	.05
V	Word Knowledge	.63					.35	.15
VI	Reading Comprehension	.73						.40

Table 4.1 (continued).

		(K) Sweden						
Equation		0	1	2	3	4	5	6
R^2			.175	.175	.242	.358	.460	.577
Increment R^2			.175	.000	.067	.116	.102	.117
Increment R^2 with Grade in Block 2				.031	.036			
Block	Variable	r	b	b	b	b	b	b
I	SHS	.28	.28	.28	.27	.16	.10	.05
	Sex	−.22	−.24	−.24	−.28	−.18	−.19	−.19
	Age	.21	.21	.21	.00	.00	.00	.00
III	Grade	.27			.25	.27	.21	.17
	Science homework	−.15			−.17	−.16	−.11	−.04
	Total homework	.02			.04	−.03	−.01	.00
	Teacher preparation	.06			.07	.05	.05	.01
	Specialist teacher science	−.02			−.04	−.04	−.03	−.03
	% Teachers male	−.05			−.06	−.04	−.03	−.03
	Type of community	−.01			−.04	−.05	−.05	−.02
	Practical work	−.03			−.04	−.02	−.02	.00
	Report to authorities	.05			.04	.04	.03	.01
	Sex of teacher	.02			−.03	−.04	−.03	−.02
IV	Science reading	.37				.26	.22	.18
	Expected education	.31				.20	.14	.06
	Like school	.20				.04	.03	.02
	Reading for pleasure	.05				.04	.01	−.04
V	Word Knowledge	.50					.36	.15
VI	Reading Comprehension	.65						.47

Table 4.1 (continued).

			(L) *United States*				
Equation		0	1	2	3	4	5
R^2			.217	.236	.302	.363	.521
Increment R^2			.217	.019	.066	.061	.158
Increment R^2 with Grade in Block 2				.037	.048		
Block	Variable	r	b	b	b	b	b
I	SHS	.40	.40	.36	.30	.24	.13
	Sex	−.22	−.21	−.21	−.23	−.18	−.18
	Age	.09	.10	.09	.00	.00	.02
II	Type of program	.24		.13	.10	.08	.03
	Type of school	.12		.05	.08	.08	.03
III	Grade	.19			.17	.19	.09
	Taking science	.14			.11	.09	.08
	Homework	.19			.10	.04	.00
	% Teachers male	.11			.06	.07	.04
	Teacher post-secondary education	.08			.05	.05	.05
	Total science study	.15			.05	.03	.01
	Type of community	−.06			−.05	−.07	−.05
	% Science teachers	.04			.03	.03	.02
	Admission criteria, performance	.08			.04	.04	.05
	Report to authorities	.02			.03	.02	.02
	Practical work	.03			.04	.03	.03
	Laboratory assistants	−.04			−.03	−.04	−.02
	Subject association member	.01			−.03	−.02	−.02
IV	Science interests	.35				.20	.17
	Reading for pleasure	.20				.09	.03
	Expected education	.28				.10	.06
V	Word Knowledge	.61					.47

117

Table 4.1 (continued). *(M) The Regression Coefficients in Equation 3 of the Variables Block 3 that appear consistently.*

Variable	Australia	England	FRG	Finland	Hungary	Italy	Japan	Netherlands	New Zealand	Scotland	Sweden	United States	Mean	+	I	
Grade	.26	.05	.19	.25	–	.16	–	.19	.27	.12	.25	.17	.16	10	0	
Homework	.17	.13	.07	–	.16	.05	.12	.05	.10	.13	.04	.10	.09	11	0	
Taking science	.06	.08	–	–	.10	.16	–	.04	.06	.12	–	.11	.06	8	0	
Subject association member	.03	.06	–	–	–	–	–	–	–	.07	–	–.03	.02	3	1	
% Teachers male	.03	–	.17	.05	.04	–	.06	.09	–	–	–	.03	.04	7	0	
Total science study	−.02	.10	.10	.11	.05	–	–	–	–	–	–	.05	.03	5	1	
Teacher post-secondary education	–	–	.13	.03	–	.08	.05	.07	–	–	–	.05	.03	6	0	
Sex of teacher[a]		.09	.18	–	–.04	.08	.08	.09	–	–	.03	–	.04	6	1	
Opportunity to learn	.03	–	–	.05	.02	–	–	–	.06	.11	–	–	.04	5	0	

[a] Sex of Teacher—The signs have been reversed in this row, so that a positive sign means that men do better.

118

Chapter 5

The Regression Analyses Between Schools in Developed Countries

HOW MUCH VARIATION LIES BETWEEN SCHOOLS

In the previous chapter we were concerned with analyses where the unit of analysis was the individual student. In this chapter the unit is the school, represented by those students in it who appeared in the sample. The average numbers per school in the samples are shown by Population in Table 5.1, where it will be seen that for Population I the averages ranged from 32 in Hungary to ten in Japan, with a mean of 22. In Population II the range was from 33 in Hungary to ten in Japan, with a mean of 24. In Population IV the range was from 73 in Hungary to 19 in Scotland, with a mean of 32.

With these numbers of students per school in the samples we should expect the variances of school means to be about four percent of the student variance if each school contained a random sample of the whole population. This is plainly not the case, and Table 5.2 shows the extent to which it is not. This table shows the percentage ratio of the variance between schools to the variance between students for the test scores in the three Stage 2 subjects (i.e., Science, Reading Comprehension and Literature) for each population. Time ran out before the corresponding analyses for the subjects in stage 3 could be made. It will be seen that the general average ratio is 25 %, with population averages of 24 %, 28 % and 23 %. In all three populations the highest ratios are in Israel and Italy, and the lowest in Sweden.

The variation among these ratios, or in other words the varying extent to which they depart from the random sample value of 4 %, must be the effect of many causes. A minor cause is the variation between countries and populations in the average size of the samples, which replaces the general expectation of 4 % by an expectation of $100/n$ percent for a country and population for which the average size of the School sample is n. Thus in Population I the expectation for Sweden is $100/21 = 5 \%$, and for Japan $100/10 = 10 \%$, the actual values being 13 % and 19 %, so that the excesses are almost equal. In

Table 5.1. *Average number of Students per School in the IEA Samples for Science, Reading Comprehension and Literature.*

Country	Population I	II	IV
Australia	–	24	22
England	22	22	32
FRG	26	27	25
Finland	13	30	23
Hungary	32	33	73
Israel	17	16	22
Italy	15	22	65
Japan	10	10	–
Netherlands	27	25	31
New Zealand	–	27	25
Scotland	21	28	19
Sweden	21	26	21
United States	21	24	23
Mean	22	24	32

Table 5.2. *Percentage Ratios of the Variance Between-Schools to the Variance Between-Students by Population and Subject.*

Country	Population I Science	Reading	Mean	Population II Science	Reading	Literature	Mean	Population IV Science	Reading	Literature	Mean
Australia	–	–	–	16	–	–	16	16	–	–	16
England	20	20	20	37	37	37	37	14	14	17	15
FRG	25	–	25	38	–	–	38	20	–	–	20
Finland	16	14	15	20	38	29	29	09	16	12	12
Hungary	41	31	36	28	26	–	27	27	21	–	24
Israel	–	37	37	–	55	–	55	–	57	–	57
Italy	55	36	45	42	42	35	40	65	44	38	49
Japan	19	–	19	20	–	–	20	–	–	–	–
Netherlands	21	21	21	41	40	–	40	29	18	–	24
New Zealand	–	–	–	12	13	17	14	13	08	09	10
Scotland	23	16	20	32	28	–	30	17	17	–	17
Sweden	13	13	13	08	09	15	11	50	35	24	36
United States	32	26	29	23	27	24	25	17	16	13	15
Mean	26	24	25	26	31	26	28	25	25	19	23

Population II the expectations for England and the United States are the same, but the actual values are 37 % and 25 %, the English values being higher owing to the selective system for types of secondary schools. This applies also to the higher values for Scotland, the Federal Republic of Germany, Italy and the Netherlands. In Population IV, on the other hand, the ratios for England, Scotland and the United States are much the same, and quite low, though the reasons are not the same. In all three countries the schools are relatively homogeneous, but in England and Scotland only about a fifth of the age group is still at school at this level; in the United States about three quarters. Sweden, which has the lowest ratio for Populations I and II, has the third highest for Population IV.

The variance ratios can be used to put the standardized incremental accounts between schools on the same scale as the standardized accounts between students. For example, in Tables 5.11, 5.12 and 5.13 row (a) in each section contains the standardized account for schools, row (b) the standardized account for students, and row (c) is row (a) multiplied by the mean variance ratio to put the items on the same scale as in row (b). It is tempting to guess that the differences between rows (b) and (c) will give the account for students within schools, but this is not the case. It is true that the variances and covariances for students can be partitioned into the amount between schools and the amount within schools, so that we can write $V = V_b + V_w$, and $C = C_b + C_w$, but we then find that

$$C_b^2 / V_b + C_w^2 / V_w - C^2/V = (C_w V_b - C_b V_w)^2 / V V_b V_w$$

and the right hand side is essentially positive. Short of a fantastically improbable coincidence to make the right hand side zero, the regression sums of squares between schools and between students within schools must add to more than the regression sum of squares for students overall. An example may be seen in the Reading Comprehension section of Table 5.13, where for Block 1 we find 0.075 in row (b) and 0.078 in row (c), which would imply a negative variance for students within schools if the additive rule held. Similar instances are quite common in the analogous tables for individual countries. For example, there are three cases out of eight in Table 5.14.

BLOCK INCREMENTS BETWEEN SCHOOLS

Tables 5.3 through 5.10 give the block increments between-schools for the three Stage 2 subjects in Populations I, II and IV. There was

Table 5.3. *Increments of R^2 by Blocks for Science—Population I.*

Block ...	1	2	3	1+2+3	4	5	6	4+5+6	
Country	Home Background[b]	Type of School	Learning Conditions		Kindred Variables	Word Knowledge	Reading Comprehension		Total
England	.665	.000	.021	.686	.016	.117	.037	.170	.856
FRG	.297	.031	.338	.666	.015	.071	–	–	–
Finland	.176	.035	.108	.319	.087	.207	.055	.349	.668
Hungary	.154	.000	.199	.353	.019	.070	.159	.248	.601
Italy	.080	.000	.123	.203	.123	.269	.126	.518	.721
Japan	.375	.000	.015	.390	.032	–	–	–	–
Netherlands	.534	.020	.076	.630	.047	.082	.126	.255	.885
Scotland	.665	.011	.048	.724	.000	.055	.053	.108	.832
Sweden	.301	.019	.107	.427	.058	.171	.141	.370	.797
United States	.668	.000	.079	.747	.039	.086	.021	.146	.893
Mean[a]	.392	.011	.111	.514	.044	.125	.091	.260	.774

[a] The column means are based on the number of items in the column, except for the last two entries, which are obtained by adding along the mean row. The column means for these two entries are 0.270 and 0.782.

[b] Includes Sex and Age.

Table 5.4. *Increments of R^2 by Blocks for Reading Comprehension—Population I.*

Block ...	1 Home Background[a]	2 Type of School	3 Learning Conditions	1+2+3	4 Kindred Variables	5 Word Knowledge	4+5	Total
England	.593	.000	.000	.593	.043	.166	.209	.802
Finland	.255	.000	.240	.495	.134	.076	.210	.705
Hungary	.467	.000	.070	.537	.020	.111	.131	.668
Israel	.661	.000	.008	.669	.054	.086	.140	.809
Italy	.167	.000	.105	.272	.104	.290	.394	.666
Netherlands	.400	.000	.100	.500	.187	.123	.310	.810
Scotland	.701	.009	.000	.710	.032	.062	.094	.804
Sweden	.218	.028	.132	.378	.027	.230	.257	.635
United States	.629	.013	.062	.704	.030	.130	.160	.864
Mean	.454	.005	.079	.538	.070	.142	.212	.750

[a] Includes Sex and Age.

Table 5.5. *Increment of R^2 by Blocks for Science—Population II.*

Block ...	1	2	3	1+2+3	4	5	6	4+5+6	
Country	Home Background	Type of School	Learning Conditions		Kindred Variables	Word Knowledge	Reading Comprehension		Total
Australia	.487	.023	.152	.662	.021	.141	–	–	–
England	.664	.153	.041	.858	.013	.022	.021	.056	.914
FRG	.529	.033	.264	.826	.027	.013	–	–	–
Finland	.708	.055	.119	.882	.004	.031	.008	.043	.925
Hungary	.199	.039	.065	.303	.135	.042	.063	.240	.543
Italy	.332	.035	.050	.417	.022	.162	.014	.198	.615
Japan	.495	.000	.097	.593	.072	–	–	–	–
Netherlands	.523	.247	.163	.933	.004	.000	.008	.012	.945
New Zealand	.549	.102	.113	.764	.000	.031	.011	.042	.806
Scotland	.812	.034	.025	.871	.022	.029	.025	.076	.947
Sweden	.131	.149	.286	.566	.064	.107	.056	.227	.796
United States	.672	.000	.105	.777	.016	.046	–	–	–
Mean[b]	.508	.072	.124	.704	.033	.057	.026	.116	.820

[a] Includes Sex and Age.

[b] The column means are based on the number of items in the column, except for the last two entries, which are obtained by adding along the mean row. The column means for these two entries are 0.112 and 0.811.

In New Zealand 0.084 for Grade, and in Sweden 0.149 for Grade, have been transferred from Block 3 to Block 2. These are the only countries where Grade appears in the analyses.

no time for the corresponding analyses for the Stage 3 subjects. In Table 5.11, for Population I, the mean increments over countries are shown for Science and Reading Comprehension; in both sections of the table the first row gives the increments between-schools, the second the increments between-students, as in Chapter 4, and the third the increments between-schools rescaled, by multiplying by the mean variance ratio, to put them on the same basis as the increments between-students. Tables 5.12 and 5.13 repeat this for Science, Reading Comprehension and Literature in Populations II and IV. In every case it will be seen, from the Total column, where the three entries are always in descending order of size, that the explained variance between-schools is a large fraction of the total variance between-schools (first row) but a small fraction of the total variance

Table-5.6. *Increment of R^2 by Blocks for Reading Comprehension—Population II.*

Block ... Country	1 Home Back-ground[a]	2 Type of School	3 Learning Condi-tions	1+2+3	4 Kindred Vari-ables	5 Word Knowl-edge	4+5	Total
England	.687	.126	.021	.834	.047	.038	.085	.919
Finland	.763	.086	.015	.864	.033	.020	.053	.917
Hungary	.594	.049	.059	.702	.047	.054	.101	.803
Israel	.641	.049	.069	.759	.068	.027	.095	.854
Italy	.512	.101	.023	.636	.060	.087	.147	.783
Netherlands	.511	.357	.027	.895	.009	.014	.023	.918
New Zealand	.646	.068	.137	.851	.006	.042	.048	.899
Scotland	.748	.078	.009	.835	.043	.052	.095	.930
Sweden	.109	.000	.224	.333	.215	.098	.313	.646
United States	.686	.000	.055	.741	.117	.055	.172	.913
Mean	.590	.091	.064	.745	.064	.049	.113	.858

[a] Includes Sex and Age.

Table 5.7. *Increment of R^2 by Blocks for Literature—Population II.*

Block ... Country	1 Home Bakcground[a]	2 Type of School	3 Learning Conditions	1+2+3	4 Kindred Variables	5 Word Knowledge	6 Reading Comprehension	4+5+6	Total
England	.683	.107	.015	.805	.026	.000	.000	.026	.831
Finland	.791	.055	.000	.846	.005	.036	.041	.082	.928
Italy	.483	.087	.017	.587	.021	.051	.104	.176	.763
New Zealand	.598	.032	.082	.712	.105	.036	.000	.141	.853
Sweden	.052	.000	.398	.450	.076	.048	.000	.124	.574
United States	.549	.000	.082	.631	.198	.000	.000	.198	.829
Mean	.526	.047	.099	.672	.072	.029	.024	.125	.797

[a] Includes Sex and Age.

Table 5.8. Increment of R^2 by Blocks for Science—Population IV.

Block ...	1 Home Background[b]	2 Type of School	3 Learning Conditions	1+2+3	4 Kindred Variables	5 Word Knowledge	6 Reading Comprehension	4+5+6	Total
Australia	.423	.046	.123	.592	.067	.058	–	–	–
England	.664	.048	.173	.885	.000	.011	.010	.021	.906
FRG	.482	.124	.099	.705	.031	.042	–	–	–
Finland	.383	.055	.171	.609	.035	.081	.022	.138	.747
Hungary	.587	.114	.135	.836	.041	.017	.021	.079	.915
Italy	.279	.000	.224	.503	.078	.055	.021	.154	.657
Netherlands	.627	.084	.188	.899	.040	.019	.008	.067	.966
New Zealand	.456	.037	.253	.746	.087	.000	.012	.099	.845
Scotland	.505	.041	.213	.759	.060	.051	.027	.138	.897
Sweden	.473	.111	.302	.886	.020	.015	.018	.053	.939
United States	.435	.060	.131	.626	.061	.060	–	–	–
Mean[a]	.483	.065	.183	.731	.047	.037	.017	.101	.832

[a] The column means are based on the number of items in the column, except for the two last entries, which are obtained by adding along the mean row. The column means for these two entries are 0.094 and 0.859.

[b] Includes Sex and Age.

(third row), and that it is always less than half the explained variance between-students.

Deprived Areas

Table 5.14 gives the same three sets of increments country by country for Science in Population II. The eight countries included are those that took the Reading Comprehension test as well as the Word Knowledge test, so that they have an entry for Block 6. If we look at the last two rows at the foot of the table and divide row (c) by row (b) we can obtain:

Block	1	2	3	1+2+3	4	5	6	4+5+6	Total
$t\,\dfrac{\text{Row }(c)}{\text{Row }(b)}$	0.75	0.28	0.42	0.55	0.12	0.21	0.07	0.13	0.39

This shows that the effect of aggregating by schools is to increase the proportion of variance explained by the early variables, and diminish

125

Table 5.9. *Increment of R^2 by Blocks for Reading Comprehension—Population IV.*

Block ... Country	1 Home Background[b]	2 Type of School	3 Learning Conditions	1+2+3	4 Kindred Variables	5 Word Knowledge	4+5	Total
England	.101	.096	.177	.374	.158	.037	.195	.569
Finland	.230	.000	.109	.339	.023	.032	.055	.394
Hungary	.589	.088	.101	.778	.028	.022	.050	.828
Israel	.218	.293	.016	.527	.019	.072	.091	.618
Italy	.294	.078	.073	.445	.112	.097	.209	.654
Netherlands	.498	.000	.048	.546	.094	–	–	–
New Zealand	.151	.113	.116	.380	.080	–	–	–
Scotland	.334	.044	.136	.514	.082	.107	.189	.703
Sweden	.180	.337	.051	.568	.050	.144	.194	.762
United States	.526	.000	.000	.526	.014	.133	.147	.673
Mean[a]	.312	.105	.083	.500	.066	.081	.147	.647

[a] The column means are based on the number of items in the column, except for the last two entries, which are obtained by adding along the mean row. The column means for these two entries are 0.148 and 0.650.

[b] Includes Sex and Age.

Table 5.10. *Increment of R^2 by Blocks for Literature—Population IV.*

Block ... Country	1 Home Background[a]	2 Type of School	3 Learning Conditions	1+2+3	4 Kindred Variables	5 Word Knowledge	6 Reading Comprehension	4+5+6	Total
England	.397	.048	.180	.625	.033	.000	.115	.148	.773
Finland	.197	.000	.137	.334	.128	.088	.074	.290	.624
Italy	.344	.028	.126	.498	.128	.066	.091	.285	.783
New Zealand	.345	.040	.193	.578	.191	.011	.024	.226	.804
Sweden	.141	.172	.138	.451	.056	.095	.108	.259	.710
United States	.316	.000	.223	.539	.065	.019	.102	.186	.725
Mean	.290	.048	.166	.504	.100	.047	.085	.232	.736

[a] Includes Sex and Age.

Table 5.11. *Mean Increments in R^2 by Blocks and Level of Analysis for Science and Reading Comprehension—Population I.*

Block[a]...	1	2	3	1+2+3	4	5+6	4+5+6	
Subject and Level of Analysis	Home Background[c]	Type of School	Learning Conditions		Kindred Variables	Word Knowledge and Reading Comprehension		Total
Science								
(a) Between-Schools	.392	.011	.111	.514	.044	.216	.260	.774
(b) Between-Students	.143	.006	.055	.204	.054	.315	.369	.573
(c) Between-Schools Rescaled[b]	.098	.003	.028	.129	.011	.054	.065	.194
Reading Comprehension								
(a) Between-Schools	.454	.005	.079	.538	.070	.142	.212	.750
(b) Between-Students	.177	.007	.033	.217	.063	.326	.389	.606
(c) Between-Schools Rescaled[b]	.105	.001	.018	.124	.016	.033	.049	.473

[a] In the Science analysis Blocks 5 and 6 were merged. In the Reading Comprehension analysis Block 6 does not appear, since it is the criterion. Thus the last three entries in each row for Reading Comprehension are for Blocks 5, 4+5, and 1+2+3+4+5.

[b] Rescaled by multiplying the original Between-School figure by the mean variance ratio, which is 0.25 for Science and 0.23 for Reading Comprehension.

[c] Includes Age and Sex.

the proportion explained by the late comers. The same point can be seen in Tables 5.11 through 5.13. It suggests that the between-school variance increments may be well approximated by a weighted mean of the variance ratio and the between-student increments.

If we explore this suggestion for the increments in the first column of Table 5.14 we obtain:

Column 1   Standard Form   Metric Form
$$x_3 = 0.73x_1 + 0.65x_2 \quad R^2 = 0.96 \quad X_3 = 5X_1 + X_2 - 186$$

where X_1, X_2 and X_3 stand for the variance ratio and the first column entries in row (b) (Between-Students) and row (c) (Between-Schools rescaled). Similarly, for the Total column we find:

Total Column   Standard Form   Metric Form
$$x_3 = 0.96x_1 + 0.38x_2 \quad R^2 = 0.95 \quad X_3 = 9X_1 + 0.5X_2 - 311$$

127

Table 5.12. *Mean Increments in R^2 by Blocks and Level of Analysis for Science, Reading Comprehension and Literature—Population II.*

Block[a]...	1	2	3	1+2+3	4	5	6	4+5+6	
Subject and Level of Analysis	Home Background[b]	Type of School	Learning Conditions		Kindred Variables	Word Knowledge	Reading Comprehension		Total
Science									
(a) Between-Schools	.508	.072	.124	.704	.033	.057	.026	.116	.820
(b) Between-Students	.193	.091	.054	.338	.068	.085	.082	.235	.573
(c) Between-Schools Rescaled	.133	.019	.032	.183	.009	.015	.007	.031	.214
Reading Comprehension									
(a) Between-Schools	.590	.091	.062	.745	.064	.049		.113	.858
(b) Between-Students	.192	.129	.026	.347	.089	.117		.206	.553
(c) Between-Schools Rescaled	.183	.028	.019	.230	.020	.015		.035	.265
Literature									
(a) Between-Schools	.526	.047	.099	.672	.072	.285	.024	.1245	.796
(b) Between-Students	.171	.078	.058	.307	.066	.078	.129	.273	.580
(c) Between-Schools Rescaled	.137	.012	.026	.175	.019	.007	.006	.032	.207

[a] The mean variance ratio is 0.26 for Science, 0.31 for Reading Comprehension and 0.26 for Literature. See Table 5.2 for the variance ratios by countries.
[b] Includes Sex and Age.

The high values of R^2 show that in both cases the approximation is remarkably good, as the reader can easily check by using the two metric forms on the evidence in Table 5.14. The metric forms have been slightly rounded to make this easier, but the reader will find that they give the right values of R^2 to two decimal places. The equations show that in Column 1 the variance ratio and the between-student increment are of roughly equal importance, whereas in the Total column the variance ratio predominates.

The Row (c)/Row (b) ratios also suggest that there will be a high negative correlation between the Block 1 increments and the final subtotal, and on exploring this we obtain:

Table 5.13. *Mean Increments in R^2 by Blocks and Level of Analysis for Science, Reading Comprehension and Literature—Population IV.*

Block[a]...	1	2	3	1+2+3	4	5	6	4+5+6	
Subject and Level of Analysis	Home Background[b]	Type of School	Learning Conditions		Kindred Variables	Word Knowledge	Reading Comprehension		Total
Science									
(a) Between-Schools	.483	.065	.183	.731	.047	.037	.017	.101	.834
(b) Between-Students	.159	.069	.205	.433	.058	.049	.047	.154	.587
(c) Between-Schools Rescaled	.121	.016	.046	.183	.012	.009	.004	.025	.208
Reading Comprehension									
(a) Between-Schools	.312	.105	.083	.500	.066	.081	–	.147	.647
(b) Between-Students	.075	.073	.046	.194	.058	.121	–	.179	.373
(c) Between-Schools Rescaled	.078	.026	.021	.125	.017	.020	–	.037	.162
Literature									
(a) Between-Schools	.290	.048	.166	.504	.100	.047	.085	.232	.736
(b) Between-Students	.090	.023	.029	.142	.043	.072	.123	.238	.380
(c) Between-Schools Rescaled	.055	.009	.032	.096	.019	.009	.016	.044	.140

[a] The mean variance ratio is 0.25 for Science, 0.25 for Reading Comprehension, and 0.19 for Literature. See Table 5.2 for the variance ratios by countries.
[b] Includes Age and Sex.

	Science	Reading	Literature	Mean
Population I	−0.84	−0.78	–	−0.81
Population II	−0.84	−0.73	−0.61	−0.73
Population IV	−0.72	−0.38	−0.65	−0.58
Mean	−0.80	−0.63	−0.62	−0.69

Since the subtotal comprises the residuals of the Kindreds and the Reading Comprehension tests this suggests in turn that there is likely to be a negative correlation between the variance ratio and the Reading Comprehension score, carrying with it negative correlations between the variance ratio and the other subjects since these depend on Reading. On checking this conjecture we find the following correlations over countries between the variance ratio and the test score:

Table 5.14. *Increments of R^2 by Block, Country and Level of Analysis for Science—Population II.*

Block ...		1	2	3	1+2+3	4	5	6	4+5+6	
Country		Home Background[a]	Type of Program	Learning Conditions		Kindred Variables	Word Knowledge	Reading Comprehension		Total
England	(a)	.664	.153	.041	.858	.013	.022	.021	.056	.914
	(b)	.231	.168	.067	.466	.053	.076	.079	.208	.674
.37	(c)	.246[b]	.057	.015	.318	.005	.008	.008	.021	.338
Finland	(a)	.708	.055	.119	.882	.004	.031	.008	.043	.925
	(b)	.220	.121	.034	.375	.061	.052	.060	.173	.548
.20	(c)	.142	.011	.024	.177	.001	.006	.002	.009	.185
Hungary	(a)	.199	.039	.065	.303	.135	.042	.063	.240	.543
	(b)	.139	.030	.051	.220	.088	.064	.117	.269	.489
.28	(c)	.056	.011	.018	.085	.038	.012	.018	.067	.152
Italy	(a)	.332	.035	.050	.417	.022	.162	.014	.198	.615
	(b)	.103	.046	.051	.200	.043	.078	.070	.191	.391
.42	(c)	.139[b]	.015	.021	.175	.009	.068	.006	.083	.258
Netherlands	(a)	.523	.247	.163	.933	.004	.000	.008	.012	.945
	(b)	.193	.176	.074	.443	.048	.049	.048	.145	.588
.41	(c)	.214[b]	.101	.067	.382	.002	.000	.003	.005	.387
New Zealand	(a)	.549	.098	.099	.764	.000	.031	.011	.042	.806
	(b)	.169	.185	.021	.375	.071	.084	.100	.255	.630
.12	(c)	.066	.012	.012	.102	.000	.004	.001	.005	.108
Scotland	(a)	.812	.034	.025	.871	.022	.029	.025	.076	.947
	(b)	.289	.116	.081	.486	.064	.075	.063	.202	.688
.32	(c)	.260	.011	.008	.279	.007	.009	.008	.024	.303
Sweden	(a)	.131	.148	.290	.569	.064	.107	.056	.227	.796
	(b)	.175	.031	.036	.242	.116	.102	.117	.335	.577
.08	(c)	.010	.012	.023	.045	.005	.009	.004	.018	.063
Mean	(a)	.490	.101	.107	.698	.033	.053	.026	.112	.810
	(b)	.190	.109	.052	.351	.068	.072	.082	.222	.573
.26	(c)	.142	.029	.023	.194	.008	.015	.006	.029	.223

Note: (a) Between-Schools, (b) Between-Students, (c) Between-Schools Rescaled (Rescaled by multiplying the original Between-School figure by the mean variance ratio listed under the country name for each country).
[a] Includes Sex and Age.
[b] Instances where (c) exceeds (b).

Population ...	I	II	IV	Mean
Science	−0.25	−0.37	−0.42	−0.35
Reading Comprehension	−0.44	−0.56	−0.65	−0.55
Literature	−	−0.55	−0.67	−0.61
Mean	−0.35	−0.49	−0.58	−0.49

This makes sense. A large variance ratio implies that there must be some schools fed mainly by deprived areas which find it hard to get off the ground in Reading Comprehension and hence in other subjects, and this drags down the average performance by more than the amount by which it is raised by the schools at the other end of the scale.

ALTERNATIVE FORMS OF THE REGRESSION

One effect of the preponderance of the Home background variable where the variance ratio is large is to reduce the number of Block 3 variables that appear in the regression equations. There is only one such variable in the equations for Science in Population I for England. This makes it possible to use this case to illustrate, without an inordinate amount of hand calculation, the alternative form of the regression equations, on which the use of R^2 as the indicator of the size of an effect depends. In other cases the fact that the computer print gives the complete matrix at only two points would make the amount of hand calculation rebarbative. Table 5.15 covers this case.

In Table 5.15 (a) the equations are given in the form extensively illustrated in Table 4.1. The regressors are the correlated variables x_1, x_2, x_3, x_4, x_5 and x_6. Because these variables are correlated bringing another variable into the equation changes the coefficients of the variables that have already become regressors. In the top row, for example, there is a dramatic change from 0.811 to 0.326, which occurs mainly at the fifth step, when Word Knowledge is brought in. In Table 5.15 (b) the regressors are the uncorrelated residuals $x_1, x_{2.1}$, $x_{3.12}, x_{4.123}, x_{5.1234}$ and $x_{6.12345}$. Because these variables are uncorrelated, their coefficients remain unchanged along the rows. It will be seen that these coefficients are the same as those in the final diagonal of the preceding table. The original variables were standardized, with unit variance. The variances of $x_{2.1}, x_{3.12}, x_{4.123}$, etc. are given on the right of the table. Multiplying each of these variances by the square of the corresponding coefficient gives the increment of R^2 for the

Table 5.15. *Alternative Forms of Between-School Regression Equations. Science Achievement, England—Population I.*

Equations	0	1	2	3	4	5	6
		(X_1)	(X_1+X_2)	$(X_1...X_3)$	$(X_1...X_4)$	$(X_1...X_5)$	$(X_1...X_6)$
R^2		.657	.664	.685	.689	.701	.818
Increment R^2		.657	.007	.021	.004	.012	.117

		Beta	Partial betas				
(a) Regressors							
Home X_1	.811	.811	.811	.801	.806	.753	.326
Sex X_2	−.078		−.083	−.111	−.105	−.094	−.056
Experiments X_3	.184			.147	.158	.171	.139
Like Science X_4	.020				−.065	−.140	−.032
Science Motivation X_5	.380					.145	−.030
Word Knowledge X_6	.872						.615
(b) Regressors							
X_1	.811	.811	.811	.811	.811	.811	.811 $(1.00)^a$
$X_{2.1}$	−.083		−.083	−.083	−.083	−.083	−.083 $(1.00)^a$
$X_{3.12}$	.147			.147	.147	.147	.147 $(0.958)^c$
$X_{4.123}$	−.065				−.065	−.065	−.065 $(0.949)^c$
$X_{5.1234}$	.145					.145	.145 $(0.584)^c$
$X_{6.12345}$	.615						.615 $(0.310)^c$

[a] The variances in the last column are the variances of the regressors. Thus $S^2_{5.1234}=0.584$.

step. Thus the variance of $x_{5.1234}$ is 0.584, as shown in the right hand column, and $0.145^2 \times 0.584 = 0.012$, the corresponding increment.

The two sections of the table *look* very different, but the equations in each pair are in fact identical. Thus for the fourth pair we have:

(a) $x_0 = 0.806x_1 - 0.105x_2 + 0.158x_3 - 0.065x_4 + x_{0.1234}$

and

(b) $X_0 = 0.811x_1 - 0.083x_{2.1} + 0.147x_{3.12} - 0.065x_{4.123} + x_{0.1234}$

If in (b) we replace $x_{2.1}, x_{3.12}$, and $x_{4.123}$ by their values in terms of x_1, x_2, x_3 and x_4, which are

$x_{2.1} = x_2 + 0.007x_1$

$x_{3.12} = x_3 - 0.072x_1 - 0.191x_2$

and

$x_{4.123} = x_4 - 0.073x_1 - 0.101x_2 - 0.166x_3$

we obtain (*a*). Similar relations can be written down for any other pair; they all emerge in the process of solving the normal equations by pivotal condensation of the correlation matrix.

There is nothing to choose, then, between the two members of any pair of equations in Table 5.15 if they are thought of as predictors of x_0. Each member says exactly the same thing as the other, in different but convertible language. It is only when we move on from prediction and try to think in causal terms that a distinction emerges. One way of thinking in causal terms is to use the language of path analysis. If we are using this language, and if we have chosen to take the variables in the order 1, 2, 3, 4, 5, 6, we say that the coefficients in (*a*) are the direct paths, and those in (*b*) the total paths. Thus in the sixth pair the total path for variable 1 (Home background) is 0.811, but the direct path is only 0.326, the rest of the total effect being thought of as transmitted through the intervening variables. The proviso about order is cardinal. The same variables in a different order would give the same equation 6 (*a*), but a quite different 6 (*b*). Thus if Word Knowledge (x_6) were taken first instead of last its coefficient in 6 (*a*) would still be 0.615, but its coefficient in **6** (*b*) would now be 0.872. That is, its total path would be 0.872, and its direct path 0.615, with the rest of its effect transmitted through what would now be the intervening variables. In short, path analysis demands a prior judgment about what is transmitted through what, and some such act of judgment is always needed to cover the move from prediction to causation. Without it all that can be said is that association may or may not be evidence of cause. In our case, as was said in the preceding chapter, there is strong evidence—both from common observation in schools and from longitudinal inquiries— that is consonant with the judgment adopted, both about the order of the variables and about the use of the increment of R^2 as the indicator of the relative importance of the blocks. The object here has been to illustrate the need for judgment in a slightly different way, and to show that the use of R^2 as the indicator of relative importance is tantamount to putting the stress on the second form of the regression equation—to use 6 (*b*) rather than 6 (*a*).

Should the Reading Tests be included as Independent Variables for Science?

As in the preceding chapter there is a question about the part to be played by the last three blocks. Should they be included in the causal sequence, or should that sequence end with the third block? The argument for including the two Reading tests (Word Knowledge and Reading Comprehension) in the sequence has been set out in the preceding chapter. The author finds it rather convincing, but it is for the reader to say. Its main importance is that it strengthens the case for saying that if special educational efforts are undertaken in deprived areas these enterprises should begin when the children are very young and should involve the parents. In the more immediate context it can be said that the effect (of accepting or rejecting the argument) on the assessment of the variables in Block 3 is not very great. For example the preceding equations contain only one variable from Block 3 (x_3, Experiments). In Set (a) from Table 5.15 the regression coefficients are 0.147, 0.171 and 0.139 when the regression is stopped after Blocks 3, 4 and 5. (N.B., Block 4 includes variables 4 and 5). If we call these b_3, b_4, b_5 we find the following for the five countries in which the variable appears:

	b_3	b_4	b_5	b_6
England	147	171	139	
Scotland	090	090	080	
Finland	241	246	219	200
Hungary	250	225	185	116
United States	090	061	038	
Mean (5)	164	158	132	
Mean (2)	246	235	202	158

Note: The first mean is for all five countries, and the second for the two that include the Reading Comprehension test as well as b_6 the Word Knowledge.

The mean effect of including the kindred variables and the two Reading tests in the regression is to reduce the regression coefficient for the variable in the third block by about 40%, which is neither negligible nor catastrophic. The effect on the corresponding coefficient in the (b) set of equations would depend on the order. If the Kindreds and the Reading tests were included after the third block there would be no change. But if they were regarded as intervening variables and put before the third block the effect would be the same as in set (a). If the coefficient is reduced to 60% of its former value the increment will be reduced to about 36%, since it is b^2/c, and c will not change much.

How would this affect our earlier estimates? In Tables 5.11 through 5.13 we obtained, for the Block 3 estimates in the third rows:

134

Table . . .	5.11	5.12	5.13	
Population . . .	I	II	IV	Mean
Science	0.028	0.032	0.046	0.035
Reading Comprehension	0.018	0.019	0.021	0.019
Literature	–	0.026	0.032	0.029
Mean	0.023	0.026	0.033	0.028

That is, between-schools the Block 3 variables accounted for about
3 % of the total variance in Science and Literature, and about 2 % in
Reading. If we now take the view that Reading should be included as
an intervening variable for Science and Literature the effect would
be to reduce the 3.4 % for Science to 3.4 % × 36 % = 1.2 %, and the
3.1 % for Literature to 1.1 %, on the assumption that the reduction in
the English case is fairly typical.

THE "UNIQUE" CONTRIBUTIONS OF THE SHORT-TERM VARIABLES

Table 5.16, for Science in Population I, gives the "unique" contributions of those short term variables that survive most consistently in
the analyses after the variables in the first two blocks have been
partialled out. The tabulated quantity b^2/c is the increment of R^2
corresponding to the variable when it is the last comer of the variables so far included in the regression. "Unique" is in quotation
marks to remind us that these quantities would usually be reduced if
more variables (e.g., the scores in the Reading tests) intervened in the
regression. The contributions are summed at the foot of the table,
and compared with the increment of R^2 for the whole block when it is
taken after the first two blocks. The difference is accounted for in
two ways. In the first place, a variable has to appear in at least two
columns (countries) to be regarded as a "consistent" survivor. Were it
not for this rule there would be more entries in each column. Secondly, the variables that do appear are usually positively correlated
in each country, and this fact alone would make the sum less than the
increment.

Tables 5.17, 5.18 and 5.19 are in the same form for Science in
Population II, Reading Comprehension in Population II, and Science in Population IV. For Reading Comprehension in Populations I
and IV, and for Literature in Populations II and IV, there are not
enough consistent variables to make tabulation worthwhile. Grade
appears for Reading Comprehension in Population I, but it really

Table 5.16. *"Unique" Variances for Science, Population I: Values of b^2/c for the Most Consistent Variables in Block 3 after the First Two Blocks have been Partialled Out.*

Variable	England	FRG	Finland	Hungary	Italy	Japan	Netherlands	Scotland	Sweden	United States
Experiments	2.1		3.5	5.8				0.6		0.6
Audio-Visual aids				3.2	1.8			1.4		0.8
Science text books		9.0	1.9		3.5		1.8		2.6	
Regular science lessons		3.3								0.7
% Male teachers							4.3		1.9	
Design own experiments								1.1[a]		2.8[a]
Grade			2.5							1.9
Sum of b^2/c	2.1	12.3	7.9	9.0	5.3	0.0	6.1	3.1	4.5	6.8
Block increment in R^2	2.1	33.8	10.8	19.9	12.3	1.5	7.6	4.8	10.7	7.9
Between-schools % (Variance Ratio)	20	25	16	41	55	19	21	23	13	32

[a] Negative b.

Table 5.17. *"Unique" Variances for Science, Population II: Values of b^2/c for the Most Consistent Variables in Block 3, after the First Two Blocks have been Partialled Out.*

Variable	Australia	England	FRG	Finland	Hungary	Italy	Japan	Netherlands	New Zealand	Scotland	Sweden	United States
Science homework	3.6				1.0	1.7	2.1	12.0	1.4		5.0	1.9
Science study		1.0		0.6	1.8			0.6[a]		0.9		0.6
Opportunity to learn				1.3		1.3				0.5		2.1
School behavior		0.5	0.9	1.6	1.4		1.5	2.2	3.8			1.2
Ancillary staff		0.6					3.1		3.9			
Sum of b^2/c	3.6	2.1	0.9	3.5	4.2	3.0	6.7	14.8	9.1	1.4	5.0	5.8
Block increment in R^2	15.2	4.1	26.4	11.9	6.5	5.0	9.7	16.3	11.3	2.5	28.6	10.5
Between-schools % (Variance Ratio)	16	37	38	20	28	42	20	41	12	32	8	23

[a] Negative b.

Table 5.18. *"Unique" Variances for Reading Comprehension, Population II: Values of b^2/c for the Most Consistent Variables in Block 3, after the First Two Blocks have been Partialled Out.*

Variable	England	Finland	Hungary	Israel	Italy	Netherlands	New Zealand	Scotland	Sweden	United States
Total homework			2.5	3.0	1.4		2.2			1.3
School behavior	0.7	1.0	0.7	1.8		1.5	2.7	0.9		0.8
Sex of teacher		0.4[a]			0.8[a]	1.1[a]			3.6	0.5[a]
Sum of b^2/c	0.7	1.4	3.2	4.8	2.2	2.6	4.9	0.9	3.6	2.6
Block increment R^2	2.1	1.5	5.9	6.9	2.3	2.7	13.7	0.9	22.4	5.5
Between-schools % (Variance Ratio)	37	38	26	55	42	40	13	28	9	27

[a] Negative b (i.e. Women do better).

Table 5.19. *"Unique" Variances for Science, Population IV: Values of b^2/c for the Most Consistent Variables in Block 3, after the First Two Blocks have been Partialled Out.*

Variables	Australia	England	FRG	Finland	Hungary	Italy	Netherlands	New Zealand	Scotland	Sweden	United States
Science study		6.7	1.1	1.6			2.9	12.9	14.7	0.9	8.1
Science homework	1.9					13.2			3.6[a]	2.0	0.7
Total homework					5.0	1.5[a]	0.7				
Ancillary staff						4.6				0.6	
Opportunity to learn	1.6	0.8		2.1				1.6[a]			
Teacher education	1.4			3.2			1.5		1.3		1.9
Teacher experience		0.5							2.7		
Total enrollment								3.1			1.6
Sum of b^2/c	4.9	8.0	1.1	6.9	5.0	19.3	5.1	17.6	22.5	3.5	12.3
Block increment in R^2	12.3	17.3	9.9	17.1	13.5	22.4	18.8	25.3	21.3	30.2	13.1
Between-schools % (Variance Ratio)	16	14	20	9	27	65	29	13	17	50	17

[a] Negative b.

belongs to the second block. For Reading Comprehension in Population IV the nearest approach to consistency is made by Homework and the Study of the mother tongue, with *b* negative in each case, which seems likely to reflect the fact that at this age it is only in the weaker schools that much attention is given to reading as such. In Table 5.18, for Reading in Population II Homework and School behaviour appear consistently. These two variables "express the common theme of a serious, industrious approach to learning," to quote from the report on Reading Comprehension. For Literature there are no variables that appear commonly with consistent signs.

As in the previous chapter it is in Science that the short term variables show the most consistent pattern, at all three ages. In Table 5.19 the most notable variable is the Amount of science study, which shows up strongly in countries where it has a long range because at this age specialization has begun. The same effect is visible in the analyses between-students in the previous chapter, not only for Science but also for the modern languages (which were not analyzed between schools). This after all is what would be expected. Like the Opportunity to learn variable it illustrates the importance of teaching; children learn what they are taught, and don't learn what they are not taught. Where, as in Reading, all children are taught, the effects of teaching in school do not show up much. It is only where, as in the foreign languages, the amount of teaching varies markedly according to the option exercised that the importance of teaching stands out in the analyses. To stand out in an analysis of variation a variable must vary; practices that are relatively uniform will not stand out, but this does not mean that they are ineffective, any more than that the relative uniformity of the human diet means that there is no difference between food and poison, or between an adequate and an inadequate diet. Without food we should starve, and without teaching we should remain ignorant. The point is plain enough, and only worth reiterating because the relative uniformity of schools in comparison with homes has misled some commentators into thinking that schools and teachers don't matter.

SUMMARY

In this chapter we have seen that the proportion of the test variance that lies between-schools ranges from 8 % in Sweden for Science in Population II to 65 %, also for Science, in Italy in Population IV. The general average is 25 %. Our chosen variables can account for a larger part of this proportion, mainly because the Home background plays an even more predominant role when the evidence is aggregated by schools. When the variance between-schools is put on the same scale as the variance between-students, by multiplying it by the variance ratio, we can compare the block increments between-schools with the corresponding block increments between-students, and note that the between-school proportion is relatively large for the early variables, and relatively small for the late comers. This suggests that between-countries the test scores will be negatively correlated with the variance ratio, and in fact the correlations turn out to be uniformly negative and quite substantial, with a mean value of 0.49. In Population I the values are -0.44 for Reading and -0.25 for Science. Since a large variance ratio implies that there must be some schools in the system that are fed mainly by deprived areas, and therefore find it hard to get off the ground in Reading, and hence in other subjects, it may be inferred that these schools drag down the average achievement by more than it is raised by the schools at the other end of the scale.

A consequence of the predominance of Home background is that comparatively few variables appear in the equations. In particular there is only one variable in the third block for Science in Population I in England. This makes it possible, without an inordinate amount of hand calculation, to use this case to illustrate the alternative form of the regression equations in which the correlated pristine variables are replaced by their uncorrelated residuals. Algebraically there is nothing to choose between the two forms, which are identically equivalent, but using the second form, like using the increment of R^2, which is essentially the same thing, brings out the importance, for interpretation, of the order as well as of the choice of variables.

The arguments for and against including the two Reading tests in the equations for other subjects have been discussed in the preceding chapter. In this chapter it is shown that the effect of so including them is not only to increase substantially the total amount of variation that can be accounted for but also, if they are included as intervening variables, to diminish the amount of variation attributable to the variables in the third block—the Recent conditions of learning. Between-schools this is in any case small—about 3 % of the student variance—and including the Reading tests as intervening variables reduces it to 1 %. This reduction may be somewhat overstated because it includes the effect of including the Kindred variables as interveners, as well as the Reading tests. Owing to the form of the computer print an inordinate amount of hand calculation would be needed to exclude this supplement, but it is not likely to be large.

There is a general conformity between the assessments in this chapter and in Chapter 4 of the individual effects of the variables comprised in the third block, of Recent conditions of learning. The assessments show most consistency in Science, and particularly in Population IV, where Science study has entries almost everywhere, and very large entries for England, Scotland and New Zealand. In England and Scotland certainly, and perhaps in New Zealand, this reflects the degree of specialization at this level. Several other variables are modestly consistent across countries.

In Reading Comprehension there is no consistent variable for Population I, but School Environment and Homework are consistent for Population II, with positive signs. But in Population IV Homework and Study in the mother tongue are modestly consistent with negative signs, perhaps because at this level it is only in the weaker schools that much attention is given to reading as such. In Literature there are no variables that appear commonly with consistent signs.

In short, on the evidence considered in this chapter few of the short-term variables seem to have any effect consistent across countries on the variation of achievement between-schools, and even when the effect is consistent it is a very small part of the total variation between students. The predominant variables are those relating to Home background and early schooling.

The reason is not far to seek. It is that parents and children vary far more than school practices. In order to stand out in an analysis of variation a variable must vary. If it is relatively uniform it will have little effect on the variation in the system in comparison with variables that vary more widely. Where, as in the optional subjects and particularly at their later stages, the short-term variables *do* vary widely their effects do stand out; where they are relatively uniform this is not the case. But although the differential effects of relatively uniform practices will not stand out it would be a mistake to conclude that the practices are therefore unimportant, in the same way that it would be a mistake to conclude that food was unimportant because the human diet is relatively uniform. Because it is relatively uniform differential effects are small, but this does not alter the fact that without food we should starve. Without schools and teachers we should remain ignorant.

Chapter 6

Some Effects of Varying the Order in the Regression

THE NEWTON AND SPURRELL SHORT CUT

In the two previous chapters reasons have been given for preferring the order used there for the entry of blocks of variables in the regression. In this chapter we explore some of the effects of varying that order. For n blocks there are $n!$ possible orders, and the corresponding increments of R^2 could be obtained by making $n!$ regression runs. But Newton and Spurrell (Applied Statistics, 1967) showed that this work could be greatly shortened by obtaining their $2^n - 1$ "elements" instead. Once these elements have been obtained all possible increments can be obtained from them by suitable additions. The elements can be tabulated in a display that makes the rules of selection for these additions very easy to follow.

For Stage 2 of the IEA study a program was made to give the elements for the first four blocks of variables. To avoid confusion between names and numerical values the names of the blocks were changed from 1, 2, 3, 4 to A, B, C, D. The 15 (i.e., 2^4-1) elements can then be named A, B, C, D; AB, AC, AD, BC, BD, CD; ABC, ABD, ACD, BCD; ABCD. There are 8 elements whose names contain the letter A, namely A; AB, AC, AD; ABC, ABD, ACD; ABCD, and similarly for any other letter. The sum of any such set of 8 elements is R^2 for the corresponding block, taken by itself. The element A is the unique variance associated with the Block A; the element AB is associated with Blocks A and B, the element ABC with Blocks A, B and C, and the element ABCD with Blocks A, B, C and D, and so on. The elements with names containing more than one letter exist because the blocks are intercorrelated among themselves; but for this only A, B, C and D would exist, and interpretation would be less perplexing.

Newton and Spurrell analyses were made for the three subjects in the second stage of the IEA study, namely Civic Education, and English and French as Foreign Languages. To illustrate the analyses

141

Table 6.1.- *The Newton and Spurrell Elements for the Civics Cognitive Score by Block by Country—Population II.*

	Home Background (A)	Type of Program (B)	Conditions of Learning (C)	Kindred Variables (D)
1. *Federal Republic of Germany*				
A	.0198			
B		.0007		
C			.1280	
D				.0541
AB	.0135	.0135		
AC	.0103		.0103	
AD	.0049			.0049
BC		.0410	.0410	
BD		.0038		.0038
CD			.0492	.0492
ABC	.0433	.0433	.0433	
ABD	.0016	.0016		.0016
ACD	.0193		.0193	.0193
BCD		.0198	.0198	.0198
ABCD	.0638	.0638	.0638	.0638
Proportion Variance Explained If Alone	.1764	.1874	.3746	.2165
2. *Finland*				
A	.0161			
B		.0229		
C			.0652	
D				.0733
AB	.0008	.0008		
AC	.0134		.0134	
AD	.0070			.0070
BC		.0228	.0228	
BD		.0197		.0197
CD			.0258	.0258
ABC	.0207	.0207	.0207	
ABD	.0073	.0073		.0073
ACD	.0096		.0096	.0096
BCD		.0463	.0463	.0463
ABCD	.1155	.1155	.1155	.1155
Proportion Variance Explained If Alone	.1904	.2560	.3193	.3045

Table 6.1 (continued).

	Home Background (A)	Type of Program (B)	Conditions of Learning (C)	Kindred Variables (D)
3. Ireland				
A	.0270			
B		.0118		
C			.1291	
D				.0562
AB	.0090	.0090		
AC	.0267		.0267	
AD	.0121			.0121
BC		.0172	.0172	
BD		.0090		.0090
CD			.0407	.0407
ABC	.0217	.0217	.0217	
ABD	.0135	.0135		.0135
ACD	.0270		.0270	.0270
BCD		.0093	.0093	.0093
ABCD	.0489	.0489	.0489	.0489
Proportion Variance Explained If Alone	.1859	.1405	.3206	.2167
4. Italy				
A	.0221			
B		.0562		
C			.0965	
D				.0676
AB	.0105	.0105		
AC	.0013		.0013	
AD	.0073			.0073
BC		−.0021	−.0021	
BD		.0367		.0367
CD			.0257	.0257
ABC	.0057	.0057	.0057	
ABD	.0213	.0213		.0213
ACD	.0002		.0002	.0002
BCD		.0145	.0145	.0145
ABCD	.0169	.0169	.0169	.0169
Proportion Variance Explained If Alone	.0852	.1597	.1587	.1902

Table 6.1 (continued).

	Home Background (A)	Type of Program (B)	Conditions of Learning (C)	Kindred Variables (D)
5. *Netherlands*				
A	.0078			
B		.0882		
C			.0682	
D				.0354
AB	.0169	.0169		
AC	.0045		.0045	
AD	.0082			.0082
BC		.0309	.0309	
BD		.0422		.0422
CD			.0063	.0063
ABC	.0176	.0176	.0176	
ABD	.0531	.0531		.0531
ACD	.0001		.0001	.0001
BCD		.0406	.0406	.0406
ABCD	.0447	.0447	.0447	.0447
Proportion Variance Explained If Alone	.1530	.3343	.2129	.2308
6. *New Zealand*				
A	.0091			
B		.0506		
C			.1070	
D				.0378
AB	.0101	.0101		
AC	.0300		.0300	
AD	.0096			.0096
BC		.0533	.0533	
BD		.0271		.0271
CD			.0135	.0135
ABC	.0251	.0251	.0251	
ABD	.0239	.0239		.0239
ACD	.0059		.0059	.0059
BCD		.0162	.0162	.0162
ABCD	.0301	.0301	.0301	.0301
Proportion Variance Explained If Alone	.1439	.2364	.2811	.1640

Table 6.1 (continued).

	Home Background (A)	Type of Program (B)	Conditions of Learning (C)	Kindred Variables (D)
7. *United States*				
A	.0452			
B		.0418		
C			.0244	
D				.0993
AB	.0262	.0262		
AC	.0052		.0052	
AD	.0491			.0491
BC		−.0016	−.0016	
BD		.0266		.0266
CD			.0040	.0040
ABC	.0019	.0019	.0019	
ABD	.0596	.0596		.0596
ACD	.0045		.0045	.0045
BCD		.0029	.0029	.0029
ABCD	.0121	.0121	.0121	.0121
Proportion Variance Explained If Alone	.2038	.1694	.0534	.2582

the first of these has been chosen. Table 6.1 displays the elements for seven countries, and Table 6.2 shows the effect on the third block of partialling out one or more of the other blocks.

In each of the seven parts of Table 6.1 the elements are printed for convenience in the following form:

	A	B	C	D
A	A			
B		B		
C			C	
D				D
AB	AB	AB		
AC	AC		AC	
AD	AD			AD
BC		BC	BC	
BD		BD		BD
CD			CD	CD

Total T	TA	TB	TC	TD
ABC	ABC	ABC	ABC	
ABD	ABD	ABD		ABD
ACD	ACD		ACD	ACD
BCD		BCD	BCD	BCD
ABCD	ABCD	ABCD	ABCD	ABCD
Total T	TA	TB	TC	TD

There are 15 elements altogether, all shown once in the column on the left. The column headed A contains all the elements that have the letter A in their names, the column headed B all those with B, and so on. There are eight elements in each of these columns, elements with two letters appearing twice, those with three three times, and ABCD four times. The total TA is the value of R^2 when Block A is in the regression by itself, and similarly for TB, TC and TD. If we let TB.A stand for the increment of R^2 for Block B when it follows Block A in the regression, TC.AB for the increment for Block C when it comes after A and B, and TD, ABC for Block D after A, B and C the values are

1. TB.A=B+BC+BD+BCD
2. TC.AB=C+CD
3. TD.ABC=D

Thus TB.A comprises the elements in the B column that do not appear in the A column, TC.AB the elements in the C column that do not appear in either the A or the B columns, and TC.ABD the single element D that does not appear in the columns A, B or C. Thus TA+TB.A+TC.AB+TD.ABC=T, the sum of all the elements —in other words the sum of the increments is equal to R^2, as it should be. The increments for any other of the 24 possible orders of the four blocks can be obtained in the same way, by adding all the elements in one column, then all those in the next column that have not already appeared, and so on. If there were n blocks there would be 2^n-1 elements in the same binomial pattern, or 2^n if the final residual is counted.

In the upper part of Table 6.2 the values of TA, TB.A, TC.AB and TD.ABC are given. This part of Table 6.2 merely reproduces Table 4.6, except that Grade is now included in the third block instead of the second, because it was so included at the time when the Newton and Spurrell program was run, and could not now be transferred without a re-run. The main interest however lies in the effects on the third block of partialling out one or more of the other blocks,

Table 6.2. *Increments of R^2 by Blocks when the First Four Blocks are taken in Various Orders. Civics, Cognitive Score—Population II.*

	FRG	Fin-land	Ire-land	Italy	Nether-lands	New Zealand	United States	Mean
TA	0.176	0.190	0.186	0.085	0.153	0.144	0.204	0.163
TB.A	0.065	0.112	0.047	0.105	0.202	0.147	0.070	0.107
TC.AB	0.177	0.091	0.170	0.122	0.075	0.120	0.028	0.112
TD.ABC	0.054	0.073	0.056	0.068	0.035	0.038	0.099	0.060
Total	0.473	0.466	0.459	0.380	0.465	0.449	0.401	0.442
TC	0.375	0.319	0.321	0.159	0.213	0.281	0.053	0.246
TC.A	0.238	0.160	0.196	0.135	0.146	0.190	0.030	0.156
TC.B	0.207	0.114	0.223	0.124	0.079	0.156	0.038	0.134
TC.D	0.223	0.122	0.195	0.101	0.121	0.216	0.030	0.144
TC.AB	0.177	0.091	0.170	0.122	0.075	0.121	0.028	0.112
TC.AD	0.169	0.088	0.146	0.094	0.099	0.160	0.023	0.111
TC.BD	0.138	0.079	0.156	0.098	0.073	0.137	0.030	0.102
TC.ABD	0.128	0.065	0.129	0.096	0.068	0.107	0.024	0.088
Total[a]	1.655	1.038	1.536	0.929	0.874	1.368	0.256	1.093

Note: The table is interpreted as follows: A is the Home block, B the Type of program, C the Recent conditions of learning, D the Kindred variables. TA is the value of R^2 when Block A stands alone in the regression. TB.A is the increment for Block B when it follows A in the regression. The entries are obtained by adding in the columns of Table 6.1 and rounding to three decimal places.

[a] The total serves as a check since it is equal to $8C+4(AC+BC+CD)+2(ABC+ACD+BCD)+ABCD$.

that is in TC, TC.A, TC.B, TC.D, TC.AB, TC.AD, TC.BD and TC.ABD. These values are set out in the lower part of Table 6.2. Their relation to the elements in Table 6.1 is:

1. TC $=C+AC+BC+CD+ABC+ACD+BCD+ABCD$
2. TC.A $=C+BC+CD+BCD$
3. TC.B $=C+AC+CD+ACD$
4. TC.D $=C+AC+BC+ABC$
5. TC.AB $=C+CD$
6. TC.AD $=C+BC$
7. TC.BD $=C+AC$
8. TC.ABD $=C$

It will be seen that these equations are merely rules for selecting elements from the C column. TC contains all the elements in the C column. The elements containing the letter A are omitted from TC.A, the elements containing the letters A or B are omitted from TC.AB, and the elements containing A, B or D from TC.ABD. It is plain that the total (1) through (8) is

$$8C+4(CA+CB+CD)+2(ABC+ACD+BCD)+ABCD$$

and this serves as a check on the calculations.

The equations in the preceding paragraph, and the resulting section (2) of Table 6.2, concentrate on Block C. Analogous equations concentrating on Blocks A, B or D can easily be written down, to produce corresponding tables for these blocks. Thus in a section concentrating on the Home background Block A the top row, TA, would contain the totals for column A in Table 6.1, and the lowest row would contain only the values of the element A given at the head of the A columns in Table 6.1—the so-called unique variances. Similarly analogous tables for the upper section of Table 6.2 can be obtained by suitable additions in the columns of Table 6.1. In short, from the Newton and Spurrell elements the increments for any chosen selection and order of the blocks can at once be obtained. But the question remains—which choice is to be preferred? The literature shows that this is a greatly controverted question. It has been argued that no choice is to be preferred, and that at most the unique variance—the single letter element—can be assigned to each block, with all the rest of the explained variance assigned to the blocks jointly. At first sight this agnostic position appears safe, if unenterprising, but the safety is only apparent, since the "unique" variances are unique only for a particular choice of variables. There is nothing absolute about their uniqueness.

In Chapters 4 and 5 reasons have been given for choosing Blocks A, B, C and D, in that order; in other words, Home background followed by Type of program and/or Type of school followed by Recent conditions of learning followed by Kindred (or Concomitant) variables. The IEA computer program mainly followed this order, with the Reading tests as supplementary blocks. It would however be a mistake to regard it as the Athanasian creed of IEA, as may be seen from the subject volumes, and indeed, in advocating it the present author sometimes felt himself in the position of Athanasius *contra mundum*. For example, the argument for including the B block—Type of school and/or program—is that it is the best surrogate available in the IEA evidence for past achievement. But is it no more? Is it not that the student in an advanced program or school

148

receives a different treatment, and because of this makes more rapid progress than he would in a less advanced program or school? And since this different treatment is reflected to some extent in Block C, the Recent conditions of learning, does not partialling out Block B, which diminishes the increment for Block C, produce more distortion than it avoids? Or, to put the matter another way, do the students in more advanced programs do better because they have different treatment, or do they have different treatment because they can do better? It is plain that to some extent the different treatment is merely a matter of adapting the teaching to the capacity of the student, in the same way that first grade and twelfth grade students receive different treatment, but is this the predominant element?

A COMPARISON WITH A LONGITUDINAL STUDY

Some earlier work by the present author, reported in *The Plowden Children Four Years Later* (Peaker, 1971), throws some light on this. The Plowden study surveyed an English national sample in 1964 and again in 1968. Of the six cohorts in the sample, two cohorts, of boys and girls respectively, belonged to Population I, as defined by IEA, in 1964 and consequently to Population II in 1968. When tested in 1964 these two cohorts were in primary schools, but immediately afterwards they made the move to the various types of secondary school in which they continued at least to 1968. Consequently we have a longitudinal study in which the chronological order is free from any doubt, and in which the 1964 tests can be regarded as pretests from the standpoint of 1968. In Table 6.3 we have Newton and Spurrell analyses in the same form as in Tables 6.1 and 6.2 for the three Blocks A (Home background), P (the pretests: i.e., the 1964 tests) and B, the Type of school from 1965 to 1968 or later. From sections (ii) and (iii) of the table we see that Home background accounts for 24 % of the 1968 test variance, and that Type of school, if taken after Home background and without regard to the 1964 tests accounts for another 20 % (TB.A). On the other hand the 1964 tests taken after Home background and without regard to Type of school account for 36 % (TP.A), and then Type of school accounts for only 3 % more (TB.AP). This suggests that while Type of school (and/or program) can serve as a useful surrogate for a pretest, it is not a very efficient surrogate although, as in the IEA case, it may be the best available. To pursue this question further the author extracted

149

Table 6.3. *The Newton and Spurrell Elements for the 1968 Cognitive Tests. England—Population II.*

	Boys			Girls			Mean		
	Home Back-ground[a] 1964 (A)	Pre-Tests 1964 (P)	School Type[b] (B)	Home Back-ground[a] 1964 (A)	Pre-Tests 1964 (P)	School Type[b] (B)	Home Back-ground[a] 1964 (A)	Pre-Tests 1964 (P)	School Type[b] (B)
(i)									
A	.010			.009			.010		
P		.193			.186			.190	
B			.025			.039			.032
AP	.063	.063		.061	.061		.062	.062	
AB	.005		.005	.009		.009	.007		.007
PB		.184	.184		.158	.158		.171	.171
APB	.142	.142	.142	.170	.170	.170	.156	.156	.156
Total	.220	.582	.356	.249	.575	.376	.235	.579	.366
(ii)									
TA		.220			.249			.235	
TP.A		.377			.344			.361	
TB.AP		.025			.039			.032	
Total		.622			.632			.628	
(iii)									
TA		.220			.249			.235	
TB.A		.209			.197			.203	
Total		.429			.446			.438	

Note: Source of data—*The Plowden Children Four Years Later* (Peaker, 1971).

[a] For 1964.

[b] For 1965–68.

Tables 6.4, 6.5 and 6.6 from the evidence published in *The Plowden Children Four Years Later,* by some supplementary calculation. If the reader would like to check the work he should begin with Table 6.6, from which Table 6.4 can be obtained. Table 6.5 can then be obtained from Table 6.4. But for the immediate exposition it is more convenient to take the tables in the order in which they are printed.

Table 6.4 gives the Newton and Spurrell elements for Home background 1964, the 1964 tests, the Type of school from 1965 to 1968, and Homework in 1968. In the full analysis there are ten

Table 6.4. *The Newton and Spurrell Elements for the 1968 Cognitive Tests, Boys. England—Population II.*

	Home Background[a] (A)	Pre-Tests 1964 (P)	Type of School[b] (B)	Homework 1968 (H)
A	.006			
P		.141		
B			.014	
H				.030
AP	.033	.033		
AB	.002		.002	
AH	.004			.004
PB		.078	.078	
PH		.052		.052
BH			.011	.011
APB	.040	.040	.040	
APH	.029	.029		.029
ABH	.002		.002	.002
PBH		.105	.105	.105
APBH	.104	.104	.104	.104
Total	.220	.582	.356	.337

Note: Source of data—*The Plowden Children Four Years Later* (Peaker, 1971).

[a] For 1964.

[b] For 1965–68.

variables in the third block (Recent conditions of learning) but Homework proves to be the most potent, with Maturity of staff in second place. Homework will therefore serve for our present purpose, which is to see the effect on the third block of having a real pretest besides the surrogate supplied by Type of school. As a check on Table 6.4 we may note that omitting H should make it condense to Table 6.3 (i). And so it does; thus A in Table 6.3 (i) is 0.010, as is A+AH in Table 6.4. In moving from Table 6.4 to Table 6.3 (i) we merge H in the residual, and merge each of the other terms with H in their name with the appropriate term in Table 6.3 (i).

We can now use the elements to write down Table 6.5, which gives the increments of R^2 for each of the possible 24 orders of APBH. This task is easy, because for each order the first and last entries are already given at the foot and head of the appropriate columns in Table 6.4. Thus for order (1) we find 0.220 at the foot of the A column in Table 6.4, and 0.030 at the head of the H column. The

Table 6.5. *The Increments of R^2 for the Four Blocks in the 24 Possible Orders.*

	1		2		3		4		5		6	
	A	.220	A	.220	A	.220	A	.220	A	.220	A	.220
	P	.376	P	.376	B	.208	B	.208	H	.198	H	.198
	B	.025	H	.041	P	.193	H	.082	P	.219	B	.092
	H	.030	B	.014	H	.030	P	.141	B	.014	P	.141
Total		.651		.651		.651		.651		.651		.651

	7		8		9		10		11		12	
	P	.582	P	.582	P	.582	P	.582	P	.582	P	.582
	A	.014	A	.014	B	.029	B	.029	H	.047	H	.047
	B	.025	H	.041	A	.010	H	.034	A	.008	B	.016
	H	.030	B	.014	H	.030	A	.006	B	.014	A	.006
Total		.651		.651		.651		.651		.651		.651

	13		14		15		16		17		18	
	B	.356	B	.356	B	.356	B	.356	B	.356	B	.356
	A	.072	A	.072	P	.255	P	.255	H	.115	H	.115
	P	.193	H	.082	A	.010	H	.034	P	.174	A	.039
	H	.030	P	.141	H	.030	A	.006	A	.006	P	.141
Total		.651		.651		.651		.651		.651		.651

	19		20		21		22		23		24	
	H	.337	H	.337	H	.337	H	.337	H	.337	H	.337
	A	.081	A	.081	P	.292	P	.292	B	.134	B	.134
	P	.219	B	.092	A	.008	B	.016	A	.039	P	.174
	B	.014	P	.141	B	.014	A	.006	P	.141	A	.006
Total		.651		.651		.651		.651		.651		.651

Note: R^2 for pairs of blocks:

PH	.629	BH	.471
PB	.611	AB	.428
PA	.596	AH	.418

third entry is obtained by adding two items—e.g., 0.014 and 0.011 in the B column for B taken third in order (1)—and the second entry is then given by subtracting the entries already obtained from the total R^2, which is 0.651 the sum of all the elements. A check is supplied by the fact that the second entries in orders (1) and (2), (3) and (4), and so on must be the same, though they are obtained in different ways. From the main table we can at once obtain R^2 for the six possible pairs of blocks, and these are given at the foot of the table. It will be seen that all the pairs involving P are much more powerful than any pair without P. This is to be expected, since, as may be seen from Table 6.6, P has much the highest correlation with the criterion T.

Each of the 24 orders can be thought of as corresponding to a causal flow, and it is plain that if they are so thought of they attach very different degrees of importance to the four blocks. Perhaps the most striking contrast is between the first order and the last. The first order reckons forward, with the blocks in chronological order, APBH. The last reckons backward, with the reversed chronological order, HBPA. In the first R^2 is 0.220 for A; in the last Inc. R^2 for A is only 0.006. In the last R^2 is 0.337 for H; in the first Inc. R^2 for H is only 0.030.

Which of the 24 orders is to be preferred? Plainly there is much to be said in favor of reckoning forwards rather than backwards, and if this is agreed there are only two serious candidates, namely (1) and (2). These differ only in the order of B and H in the two last places, with a slight balance in favor of (1), since B is type of school from 1965 to 1968 and H is Homework 1968. So let us adopt (1) as the most favored candidate.

Now let us compare the assessment of H in (1) with its assessment without the benefit of the pretest P. For this we turn to order (4), where H immediately follows A and B. In (4) Inc. R^2 for H is 0.082; in (1) it is only 0.030. So the presence of the pretest reduces the assessment of H by more than half, and this will hold for other Block 3 variables as well. In other words the IEA estimates for the Recent conditions of learning are almost certainly exaggerated owing to the absence of a pretest, for which Type of school and/or program provides only a poor substitute, particularly in cases where Type of school and/or program is not sharply differentiated. This may be seen by omitting B from the reckoning. In order (2) H follows A and P, and Inc. R^2 for H is 0.041. In order (5) H follows A alone, and Inc. R^2 for H is 0.198—five times as much as when it follows A *and* P, and more than six times as much as when it follows A, P and B. On the other hand when, as in order (11), it follows P alone, the Inc. R^2 for H is only 0.047, very little more than when it follows both A and P in order (2). The point here is that it is unlikely that the absence of a pretest from a survey can affect the real importance of any Recent condition of learning. What the absence of a pretest can do is to exaggerate the estimate of that importance. Where there is a difference in Type of school, or Type of program, there is a surrogate for a pretest, which, though not a very good surrogate, is better than nothing. In the English case Type of school was a less effective surrogate in the IEA than in the Plowden survey, owing to the increase in the proportion of comprehensive schools between the surveys, but even for Plowden it was a relatively ineffective variable compared with the pretest four years earlier.

Altogether the Plowden survey followed three age groups from 1964 to 1965. The youngest group were aged seven in 1964, and the oldest were aged 14 in 1968, so that seven years of school life were covered. The correlations between the 1964 and the 1968 tests were 0.72, 0.76, and 0.76 for the youngest, the middle, and the oldest groups. This illustrates the cumulative nature of learning and its corollary that the individual pace of learning does not vary much in ordinary conditions; those who begin as fast or slow learners usually continue as such. The increment of R^2 for Recent conditions of learning averaged 4 % for the three groups, against 34 % for the pretest four years earlier, 24 % for Home background and, for the two older groups, 3 % for Type of school. All this evidence strongly suggests that the main source of variation is to be found in the student himself and his family, and that school variations, within a well established system, have a comparatively slight effect on the variation among students.

This is also suggested by the fact that in the Plowden survey the average achievement of the boys and girls who went from their primary schools to the comprehensive part of the secondary system differed little from that of those who went to the multitype part. The multitype part held a slight lead, of 9 % of a standard deviation, reduced from 10 % by the adjustment for creaming which it was possible to make because the 1964 tests and other variables were available for all children. When the two systems are working side by side there may be a tendency for the multitype system to receive more and the comprehensive side less than its share of able children. This is what is meant by creaming. Its extent could be assessed in the Plowden survey by the 1964 evidence relating to the children in both systems before the transfer took place. This evidence showed that creaming was mainly a London phenomenon, and was sometimes negative in other parts of the country; over the country as a whole the adjustment on the pretest and family background variables turned out to be only 1 % of a standard deviation. This again suggests that in the IEA survey, Type of school is mainly important as a surrogate for a pretest. It is not, however, so cogent on the interpretation of Type of program, since advanced programs exist in both systems.

154

Table 6.6. *The Correlation Matrix for Boys, and its Reduction by Pivotal Condensation.*
England—Population II.

(i) and (ii)

	Home A	Pre-Tests 1964 P	School Type B	Home Work H	Tests 1968 T	Home A	Pre-Tests P	School Type B	Home Work H	Tests 1968 T
A	1.000					1.000	0.475	0.367	0.352	0.469
P	0.475	1.000				−0.475	0.774			
B	0.367	0.602	1.000			−0.367	0.428	0.865		
H	0.352	0.517	0.473	1.000		−0.352	0.350	0.344	0.876	
T	0.469	0.763	0.597	0.581	1.000	−0.469	0.540	0.425	0.416	0.780

(iii) and (iv)

	Home A	Pre-Tests 1964 P	School Type B	Home Work H	Tests 1968 T	Home A	Pre-Tests P	School Type B	Home Work H	Tests 1968 T
A	1.292	−0.614	0.104	0.137	0.137	1.309			0.112	0.116
P	−0.614	1.292	0.553	0.454	0.698	−0.522	1.779		0.319	0.587
B	−0.104	−0.553	0.628			−0.166	−0.881	1.592	0.240	0.201
H	−0.137	−0.454	0.151	0.718		−0.112	−0.319	−0.240	0.682	0.142
T	−0.137	−0.698	0.126	0.172	0.403	−0.116	−0.587	−0.201	0.142	0.378

(v)

	Home A	Pre-Tests 1964 P	School Type B	Home Work H	Tests 1968 T
A	1.327				0.093
P	−0.470	1.928			0.521
B	−0.127	−0.769	1.676		0.151
H	−0.162	−0.468	−0.352	1.466	0.208
T	0.903	0.521	0.151	0.208	0.348

Note: At each step the matrix is of the form:

$$\frac{R_{pp}^{-1} \quad \mid \quad R_{pp}^{-1}R_{pq}}{-R_{qp}R_{pp}^{-1} \mid R_{qq}-R_{qp}R_{pp}^{-1}R_{pq}}.$$

where p denotes the variables that are, and q those that are not yet, in the regression. The top left contains the inverse matrix of regressors, the top right the regression coefficients, the bottom left the regression coefficients transposed with reversed signs, and the bottom right contains the residual variance–covariance matrix. Source of data—*The Plowden Children Four Years Later* (Peaker, 1971).

SOME PATH DIAGRAMS

Each of the 24 orders displayed in Table 6.5 has a path diagram to correspond. To obtain all of them by hand calculation would be too formidable a task, but we can at least examine the case of the first order. For this Table 6.6 displays the detail of the reduction of the

155

Table 6.7. *Path Coefficients for Various Orders. England—Population II.*

All paths				Total paths			
Path	b	Residual		Path	b	Variances²	Increment R²
(i) *Order APBHT (Home, Pretests, Schooltype, Homework, Tests)*							
AP	.475	P	.774	AT	.469	1.000	.220
AB	.104						
PB	.553	B	.628	(P.A)T	.698	0.774	.376
AH	.112						
PH	.319						
BH	.240	H	.682	(B.AP)T	.201	0.628	.025
AT	.093						
PT	.521						
BT	.151						
HT	.208	T	.348	(H.APB) T	.208	0.682	.030
(ii) *Order ABHT (Home, Schooltype, Homework, Tests)*							
AB	.367	B	.865	AT	.469	1.000	.220
AH	.206						
BH	.398	H	.739	(B.A)T	.491	0.865	.208
AT	.220						
BT	.358						
HT	.334	T	.489	(H.AB)T	.334	0.739	.082
(iii) *Order APHT (Home, Pretests, Homework, Tests)*							
AP	.475	P	.774	AT	.469	1.000	.220
AH	.137						
PH	.452	H	.718	(P.A)T	.698	0.774	.376
AT	.104						
PT	.590						
HT	.240	T	.363	(H.AP)T	.240	0.718	.041

The letters have the same meaning as in Table 6.6 from which order one was extracted. Orders two and three are extracted from similar tables not printed.

Source of data—*The Plowden Children Four Years Later* (Peaker, 1971).

correlation matrix when the variables are taken in the order APBH—the chronological order. The decision to take this order means that we need paths from A to P, B, H and T, from P to B, H and T, from B to H and T, and finally from H to T. The path values are the regression coefficients displayed in Table 6.6, and repeated, in the order AP; PA, PB; AH, PH, BH; AT, PT, BT, HT, on the left of section (i) of Table 6.7. After each step we have the residual of the variable that was the destination of the step. These are also shown in Table 6.6, and they are repeated (0.774 for P, 0.628 for B, etc.) in order in Table 6.7. In the path diagram their square roots are the external paths. On the right of section (i) we have the total paths, running to T from the uncorrelated variables A, (P.A), (B.AP), (H.ABP), with their coefficients and the variances of their starting points, which are the residuals shown as such on the left. For each total path b^2s^2 is the corresponding increment of R^2, as shown on the right.

In the second section of Table 6.7 we have the analogous details for the order ABH, with P omitted, and the third section covers the order APH, with B omitted. The reductions from which these paths are obtained are not shown, but the work follows the pattern of the first section.

Let us now look at the assessments of the effect of Homework (H), in either Table 6.7 or the corresponding diagrams in Figure 6.1. We find:

	Path HT	Inc. R^2
(i) H after A, P and B	0.208	0.030
(ii) H after A and B	0.334	0.082
(iii) H after A and P	0.240	0.041

Whether we look at the path coefficient or the increment we have the largest assessment when only B is present, and the least when both B and P are present, but the assessment for P alone is not much greater than that for both B and P.

For the effect of Type of school (B) we have:

	Path BT	Inc. R^2
(i) P included	0.151	0.025
(ii) P excluded	0.358	0.208

The large apparent effect of B in (ii) is seen to be brought about by the exclusion of P from the reckoning. In other words there is strong support for the view that students in advanced programs have different treatment because they can do better, rather than the view that they do better because they have different treatment. To take an analogy from league football—players are chosen for first division sides because they are the best players; they do not become the best players because they are chosen for first division sides. But because first division football is a more advanced game the players do improve somewhat from their experience in it. The path and the

157

Figure 6.1. *The Path Diagrams corresponding to Table 6.7.*

(i) Order (APBHT)

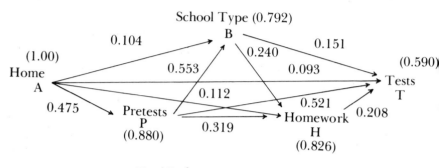

All Paths

School Type (0.792)

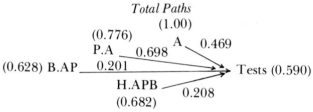

Total Paths

(ii) Order (ABHT)

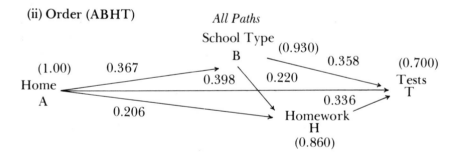

All Paths

School Type

Total Paths

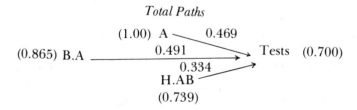

Figure 6.1 (continued).

ii) Order (APHT)

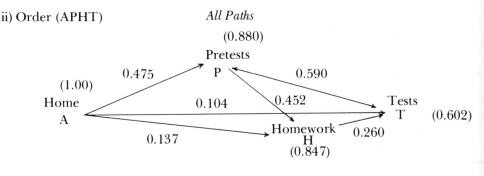

All Paths

(0.880)

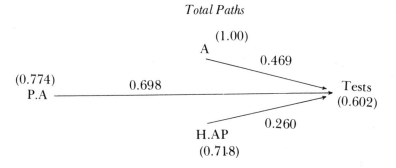

Total Paths

increment in (i) are much smaller than those in (ii), but they are not entirely negligible.

It might be said that what applies to BT and HT should apply equally to AT, which is also much smaller in (i) than in (ii) or (iii). But the cases are different, AT is the direct path for A, and represents only the residual that has not been transmitted by other routes. The total effect of A is shown by the increment on the right, as nine times the effect of B.

It has been possible to illustrate these points from the English case because the existence of a national longitudinal study provided a pretest. This is the essential point, not the existence of different types of school. What can be said about differences between types of school can equally be said about differences between types of program in the same school, or about differences in grade. In each case we have groups of students doing more advanced work because they have shown themselves capable of it. So we have three blocks of variables—the analogues of A, B and H in Tables 6.3 through 6.7. There are six possible orders for these blocks, and the interpretation

159

depends on the choice of order. If we accept the argument about the causal flow being forward through time we prefer the order ABH, and this gives estimates of the effects of H, the Recent conditions of learning. But if we also had a pretest, as in the English longitudinal study, we should again find that the estimates of H made without taking the pretest into account were too large, although they are the best that we have without the pretest. As in Table 6.7 we should also find that the estimates for the path BT and for Inc. R^2 for B made in the absence of the pretest were too large. They were too large because they did not take enough account of events that had already taken place.

Let us now step back from the details of the analyses and consider them in the light of the ordinary practice of schools. When a teacher receives a new class she will also receive a record of the past performance of each student as a guide. This will warn her against attempting too much with the children whose past performance has been poor. But, if she is a good teacher, it will also warn her against attempting too little, because she will have learnt from experience that some children with poor past records can be brought to do rather better in future, and that some children with good past records can be brought to do even better. The good teacher's purpose in two-fold—to confirm past judgments when they are favorable, and to confute them when they are not. She will not expect miracles, but she will not on that account desist from the attempt to bring all the children in the class on as far as possible, and she will find a modicum of success rewarding.

Anyone who is familiar with many schools knows that they contain good teachers who are following this line, but that they also contain students who remain backward despite the teachers' utmost endeavors. Against this massive experience it is not to be expected that experiments in compensatory education will be conspicuously successful, and abundant evidence testifies that they are not. The fact that all such experiments have disappointed the more sanguine hopes entertained of them is no reason for desisting from the attempt; here, as with the individual teacher, there is a moral imperative, and a modicum of success is rewarding.

It seems probable that in both cases the reason for the relative lack of success is that while the past record may sometimes be misleading, it does not mislead very often; more commonly the backward child remains backward because he lacks talent. At the other end of the scale this is plain enough; most of us recognise that no amount of education would have made us into a Newton, a Mozart, or an Olympic champion. Enough is known about genetics for it to be clear that the accidents of conception play a part in all our lives.

It also seems probable that they play a large though concealed part in the IEA analyses. To be sure, they do not appear directly; they are wrapped up in the long term and middle term variables, to begin with. Just as intrafamilial variation provides evidence of the genetic origin of differences in IQ, so social mobility suggests evidence of the genetic part in socioeconomic status. In both cases the facts accord with the probability model of genetics, and not with the principle that like begets like. Socioeconomic status can account for some of the variation in achievement because it is mildly correlated with talent owing to the variation between siblings. The middle-term variables pick up some of the intersibling variation which escapes the first group. One argument for putting both groups in the regression before the short-term group is that doing so helps to prevent the apparent effect of the latter group being inflated by the genetic variation. A similar argument can be urged in favor of giving priority to the Reading tests. When both steps are taken the effects of the short-term variables are reduced to a level consonant with the results of daily experience and deliberate experiment, and this is what all the arguments rest on finally.

SUMMARY

In this chapter we revert to the question of the order in which our variables should be considered, and see again that the order makes a great difference to the interpretation. We also see that if we had more information about the previous history of the student the interpretation of our variables would again be affected. This leads to the consideration, in the second half of the chapter, of a national survey where such earlier information was secured.

We begin with the Newton and Spurrell analyses (sometimes called commonality analyses) for Population II in seven developed countries in the IEA survey. These analyses are between-students and are concerned with the Cognitive Test in Civic Education. The details are set out in Tables 6.1 and 6.2. Because our blocks of variables are heavily correlated with each other the main weight of the elements lies in the lower part of each of the national sections into which Table 6.1 is divided. These are the elements common (hence "commonality") to two, three or all of the four blocks, so that the block that is taken first absorbs the lion's share of the explained variance and the block that is taken last the least share. As to which is the right order it is argued that the chronological order is to be preferred, and that this order is Home background followed by Type of program and/or Type of school and Grade, followed by Recent conditions of learning followed by Kindred (or Concomitant) variables, if indeed these last should be included at all.

In Table 6.2 it is shown that the assessment of the third block, the Recent conditions of learning, in which the initial interest of the IEA survey lay, is highly sensitive to the choice and order of the preceding blocks. In the IEA survey the choice of preceding variables was limited by the fact that all the evidence had to be gathered at the same time, so we turn to another national survey to which this limitation did not apply. This survey was reported by the present author in *The Plowden Children Four Years Later*, and as the name implies, it extended from 1964 to 1968. Consequently the 1964 tests could be used as pretests for the 1968 evidence. Moreover there were three cohorts (or six if boys and girls are reckoned separately, as they were). The youngest cohort was aged seven in 1964, and the oldest 14 in 1968, so that altogether seven years of school life were covered. In Table 6.3 the commonality analysis for the boys and the girls in the oldest cohort are given for Home background 1964, Pretest (i.e. the 1964 tests) and Type of school from 1965 to 1968. In the lower sections of the table it is shown that the assessment of the effect of Type of school is reduced, by a factor of seven by the inclusion of the pretest.

The Plowden evidence included altogether ten variables in the Recent conditions of learning block, but one of them—Homework—accounted for more than a third of the explained variance. Consequently this variable is brought into another commonality analysis in Table 6.4, where it is called H, along with Home background (A), Pretest (B) and Type of School (B). Table 6.4 is then used to obtain Table 6.5, in which the increments of R^2 are given for each of the possible 24 orders of the four blocks, and also for the six possible pairs of blocks. The dominance of P is clearly visible in this table. When taken first it accounts for 90 %, and when taken last for more than 20 %, of the explained variance. Taken, as it should be on the chronological argument, after A but before B and H, it adds 38 % *to* the explained variance (or nearly 60 % *of* the 65 % explained). The presence of P also reduces the assessment of B by a factor of nine, and the assessment of H by a factor of three. (The factor of nine is greater than the seven in Table 6.3 because the latter did not include H.)

To put these points in another way, and also to examine the side effect of B, we proceed to Table 6.6, which gives the correlation matrix and its reduction, and to Table 6.7, which gives the resulting path diagrams in both forms. In Table 6.7 we see that the direct path from B (i.e., BT) is reduced by P from 0.36 to 0.15. The large path without P indicates that in the absence of P the Type of school variable acts mainly as a surrogate for the pretest. The small path when P is present indicates some inequity in the distribution of resources. That this inequity is probably small is indicated not only by the small path but also by the comparison between the average achievement of the comprehensive and the multitype systems. The 1964 variables were used to make the necessary adjustment for creaming, and after this had been done it was found that the multitype system held a slight lead, of 9 % of a standard deviation. Had the inequity been very serious the sign of this difference would have been reversed.

Chapter 7

Country Means

RELATIONS BETWEEN COUNTRY MEAN SCORES FOR POPULATIONS I AND II

In this chapter we explore some relations between the mean scores for those countries where the Reading Comprehension and/or the Science tests were taken by Populations I and II. These populations were aged 10 and 14, and there is a prior expectation that their scores will be in the ratio of their ages, provided that the two sets of tests are on the same scale. At first sight the proviso seems to make the proposition a mere tautology, and so of course it would be if we looked merely at the ratio of the means aggregated over all countries and re-scaled one set of tests until we obtained the expected result. The interest lies in seeing how far the ratios for the individual countries depart from the general average.

In Table 7.1 columns A and B give RCI and RCII—the Reading Comprehension means for Populations I and II. The column means are 15.5 and 22.3, and their ratio is 1.44, which is close enough to 1.4 to need no adjustment. The country ratios are set out in column C, where it will be seen that 11 out of the 14 ratios lie within the range from 1.2 to 1.6. The three outliers are Hungary (1.8), Iran (2.1) and India (0.6).

Columns D and E give ScI and ScII—the Science means for Populations I and II. The column means are 14.5 and 19.0, in the ratio 1.31. If we multiply this ratio by 1.1 we obtain 1.44, the ratio of the column means for Reading Comprehension, so we now multiply the scores in column E by 1.1 and enter the results in column F. The ratios F/D are given in column G, where it will be seen that of the 16 ratios 11 lie in the range from 1.2 to 1.6. The five outliers are Federal Republic of Germany (1.75), Hungary (1.9), Scotland (1.7), Iran (2.05) and India (1.0). Altogether we have 30 ratios in columns C and G, of which 22 lie in the range from 1.2 to 1.6.

In column H the ratios in columns C and G are averaged for the cases where both exist. There are 13 such cases; 10 lie in the range from 1.2 to 1.6, the three outliers being Hungary (1.9), Iran (2.1) and India (0.8).

Finally, in column I we have G/C, the growth ratio for Science

Table 7.1. *Country Mean Scores in Reading Comprehension and Science—Populations I and II.*

Country	A RCI	B RCII	C B/A	D ScI	E ScII	F ScII×1.1	G F/D	H ½(C+G)	I G/C
Belgium (Fl)	17.5	24.6	1.41	17.9	21.2	23.3	1.30	1.36	0.92
Belgium (Fr)	17.9	27.2	1.52	13.9	15.4	16.9	1.22	1.37	0.80
England	18.5	25.3	1.37	15.7	21.3	23.4	1.49	1.43	1.09
FRG				14.9	23.7	26.1	1.75		
Finland	19.4	27.1	1.40	17.5	20.5	22.5	1.29	1.34	0.92
Hungary	14.0	25.5	1.82	16.7	29.1	32.0	1.92	1.87	1.05
Israel	13.8	22.6	1.64						
Italy	19.9	27.9	1.40	16.5	18.5	20.4	1.24	1.32	0.89
Japan				21.7	31.2	36.3	1.58		
Netherlands	17.7	25.2	1.42	15.3	17.8	19.6	1.28	1.35	0.90
Scotland	18.4	27.0	1.47	14.0	21.4	23.5	1.68	1.58	1.14
Sweden	21.5	25.6	1.19	18.3	21.7	23.9	1.31	1.25	1.10
United States	16.8	27.3	1.62	17.7	21.6	23.8	1.34	1.48	0.83
Chile	09.1	14.1	1.55	09.1	09.2	10.1	1.11	1.33	0.72
India	08.5	05.2	0.61	08.5	07.6	08.4	0.99	0.80	1.62
Iran	03.7	07.8	2.11	04.1	07.8	08.6	2.05	2.08	0.97
Thailand				09.9	15.6	17.1	1.74		
Mean	15.5	22.3	1.47	14.5	19.0	20.9	1.46	1.43	1.00

Note: RCI=Reading Comprehension—Population I; RCII=Reading Comprehension—Population II; ScI=Science—Population I; ScII=Science—Population II.

divided by the growth ratio for Reading Comprehension. Again there are 13 of these ratios, but this time they are centred on unity, with nine lying in the range from 0.9 to 1.1, the four outliers being Belgium (Fr.) (0.8), United States (0.8), Chile (0.7) and India (1.5).

The tendency of all these ratios to converge within a narrow range supports the view that between-countries, as between-schools and between-students, the pace of learning has a tendency to stay constant, with initially fast learners continuing fast, and slow, slow.

HOW WELL DO COUNTRY MEANS FOR POPULATIONS PREDICT?

Table 7.2 (1) sets out the correlation matrix for the 13 countries for which all the scores shown in Table 7.1 exist. To the variables RCI, ScI, RCII, ScII a fifth variable G has been added. G is a dummy or grouping variable that separates the ten developed and the three

Table 7.2. *The Correlation Matrix, and its Reduction, for Thirteen Countries.*

	G	RCI	ScI	RCII	ScII
(1)					
Grouping Variable	1.000	0.917	0.915	0.963	0.872
Reading Comprehension Population I	0.917	1.000	0.912	0.911	0.722
Science Population I	0.915	0.912	1.000	0.892	0.866
Reading Comprehension Population II	0.963	0.911	0.892	1.000	0.832
Science Population II	0.872	0.722	0.866	0.832	1.000
(2)					
Grouping Variable	1.000	0.917	0.915	0.963	0.872
Reading Comprehension Population I	−0.917	0.159	0.073	0.028	−0.078
Science Population I	−0.915	0.073	0.163	0.011	0.068
Reading Comprehension Population II	−0.963	0.028	0.011	0.073	−0.008
Science Population II	−0.872	−0.078	0.068	−0.008	0.240
(3)					
Grouping Variable	6.289	−5.767	0.494	0.802	1.322
Reading Comprehension Population I	−5.767	6.289	0.459	0.176	−0.491
Science Population I	−0.494	−0.459	0.129	−0.002	0.104
Reading Comprehension Population II	−0.802	−0.176	−0.002	0.068	0.006
Science Population II	−1.322	0.491	0.104	0.006	0.202
(4)					
Grouping Variable	8.180	−4.009	−3.829	0.810	0.924
Reading Comprehension Population I	−4.009	7.922	−3.558	0.183	−0.861
Science Population I	−3.829	−3.558	7.752	−0.015	0.806
Reading Comprehension Population II	−0.810	−0.183	0.015	0.068	0.008
Science Population II	−0.924	0.861	−0.806	0.008	0.118

(5) (Omitting G)

	(1)				(2)			(3)
	ScI	RCII	ScII		RCII	ScII		ScII
RCI	0.912	0.911	0.722	RCI	0.580	−0.407	RCI	−0.791
ScI	0.168	0.061	0.208	ScI	0.363	1.238	ScI	0.998
RCII	0.061	0.170	0.174	RCII	0.148	0.098	RCII	0.662
ScII	0.208	0.174	0.479	ScII	0.098	0.222	ScII	0.157

developing countries. In sections (2), (3) and (4) of Table 7.2 the variables are entered successively in the regression, in the order G, RCI, ScI. In section (5) G is omitted and the others entered in the same order as before, with a final step in which RCII becomes a regressor for ScII.

Table 7.3. *Newton and Spurrell (Commonality) Analyses Between Countries, Derived from Table 7.2.*

	Criterion RCII					Criterion ScII			
	G	RCI	ScI	Total		G	RCI	ScI	Total
(i) Including G									
Grouping	.080			.080	Grouping	.104			.104
Reading					Reading				
Comprehension		.004		.004	Comprehension		.028		.028
Science			.000	.000	Science			.084	.084
G×RCI	.052	.052		.052	G×RCI	.000	.000		.000
G×ScI	.022		.022	.022	G×ScI	.173		.173	.173
RCI×ScI		.001	.001	.001	RCI×ScI		.010	.010	.010
G×RCI×ScI	.773	.773	.773	.773	G×RCI×ScI	.483	.483	.483	.483
Total	.927	.830	.796	.932	Total	.760	.521	.750	.882

	Criterion RCII				Criterion ScII		
(ii) Omitting G	RCI	ScI	Total		RCI	ScI	Total
RCI	.056		.056	RCI	.028		.028
ScI		.022	.022	ScI		.257	.257
RCI×ScI	.774	.774	.774	RCI×ScI	.493	.493	.493
Total	.830	.796	.852	Total	.521	.750	.778

In Table 7.3 we have the Newton and Spurrell, or commonality, analyses. In section (i) G is included; it will be seen that its unique variance is 0.080 for RCII, and 0.104 for ScII. The two tables in (i) are then condensed to the two in (ii) by the omission of G. The unique variances of G in (i) disappear, with consequent reductions in the final values of R^2; the elements G×RCI in (i) are merged with RCI in (ii), and those of G×ScI with ScI, and the elements G×RCI×ScI are merged with RCI×ScI.

The regression equations and path diagrams in Table 7.4 are either copied directly from the lower slabs of Table 7.2 or calculated from the first slab. The first equation shows that RCII is quite closely predicted by RCI and ScI. In the second we see that the prediction can be improved by replacing ScI by G, with the coefficient of RCI reduced by two thirds. In (iii) ScI is brought back, but it now has a negligible coefficient and the prediction is unchanged from (ii). In (iv) ScII is predicted by ScI and RCI; R^2 is 0.78, which is only slightly

167

more than the 0.75 given by ScI alone (see Table 7.3), and the coefficient of RCI is negative. In (v) RCI is replaced by G; the prediction is slightly improved and the coefficient of ScI reduced by about two thirds. In (vi) RCI is brought back; R^2 is increased from 0.79 to 0.88, all the coefficients are large, and that of RCI is negative.

PATH DIAGRAMS AND HIDDEN VARIABLES

The values of R^2 shown in Figure 7.1 can also be obtained from Table 7.3, and a comparison of the two tables is illuminating. The small unique and the large interaction terms in Table 7.3 show why, in Figure 7.1, bringing in new variables does not add very much to the prediction but makes great changes in the regression coefficients. The large interaction terms arise because the variables are highly correlated and therefore interchangeable to a large extent. Each can act as a partial surrogate for the others. The case provides a good illustration of the problem of the hidden variable. Without G the variables RCI and ScI appear important in their own right, since they have large coefficients; bringing in G adds to the variance accounted for, but also makes RCI and ScI appear less important. It is plain that the inclusion or omission of G in the equations cannot make any difference in the underlying facts; the question is how are the facts to be interpreted, in the light of the equations and of what else is known or conjectured.

In this case it can be argued that G represents, more or less imperfectly, all the historical differences between the two groups of countries, that the large difference between the mean scores of the two groups are primarily due to these historical differences, that this applies alike to the scores at 10 and at 14, and that it is therefore best not only to include G in the analysis but also to let it account for as much of the variance as it can. If we take this line we must remember that the historical differences include the histories of the educational systems. If there were more countries in the survey it would be possible to replace G by a weighted sum of economic indicators and other variables; almost any economic indicator is highly correlated with G and with RCI, ScI, RCII and ScII. But with only 13 countries we have not enough degrees of freedom for this.

If we compare this analysis between countries with the analyses between-schools, or between-students, within countries we see that there is an analogy between G and the first group, of family variables, in the analyses for schools and students. Both represent past

Figure 7.1. *Path Diagrams corresponding to Table 7.2.*

(i) RCII=0.58RCI+0.36ScI   (R^2=0.85)

(ii) RCII=0.80G+0.18RCI   (R^2=0.93)

(iii) RCII=0.81G+0.18RCI−0.01 ScI   (R^2=0.93)

(iv) ScII=1.23ScI−0.40RCI   (R^2=0.78)

(v) ScII=0.49G+0.42ScI   (R^2=0.79)

(vi) ScII=0.92G+0.81ScI−0.86RCI   (R^2=0.88)

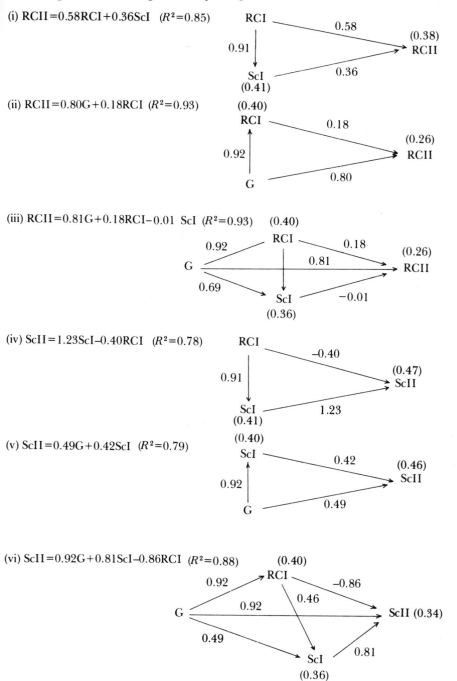

history, more or less imperfectly. The variables in the first group cover the facts so far as our measures permit, but it is clear that they do not cover them very well. For example, there are genetic differences between siblings which are not represented at all in the first group. There are differences in upbringing which are represented only to the extent that they are correlated with the measured variables, and these variations in upbringing may well affect motivation throughout schooling. If these hidden variables could be revealed the effect of bringing them into the equations would be similar, in kind at least though perhaps not in quantity, to the effect of bringing G into the equations between countries. There would be some increase in the total amount of variation accounted for, and some reduction in the amount hitherto attributed to the original measured variables.

Hidden variables are not peculiar to the social sciences. There can be no certainty in any branch of science that all the relevant variables have been considered, as may be seen from the fact that the laws are sometimes revised. What is peculiar to the social sciences is that we are often aware intuitively that there are variables that we would bring into the equations if we knew how to measure them. Two have been mentioned in the preceding paragraph. In *Inequality*, Jencks (1972) says that success in later life appears to be due mainly to luck. This remark has been much quoted. It is perhaps an unfortunate remark, since, as Jencks subsequently pointed out, it is more easily quoted than understood. "Luck" is a convenient portmanteau or catchword to cover all the relevant variables that are not brought into the equations, but this is not the connotation that most journalists and the general public attach to it. Taken in the more usual sense the word suggests a more chaotic view of life than Jencks and other reasonable men actually hold. In proclaiming that "I am the master of my fate" Henley no doubt overstated the case, though in justice to Henley it should be remembered that he was speaking not of the incidence of misfortune but of his response. But we have more command than is sometimes supposed. The fact that a variable cannot be, or at any rate has not yet been, assessed with enough accuracy to make its inclusion in a formal study worthwhile, need not imply that we do not recognize its existence or possible importance. It is reasonable to attribute a residual to luck if the phrase means, and is understood to mean, no more than that the residual exists after account has been taken of the measured variables, and that other variables, not yet brought into the equations, might account for much of it, and also change the estimate of the parts played by the original variables. Tables 7.3 (particularly the summary section) and Figure 7.1 illustrate both effects. Thus RCI and ScI alone leave RCII with a residual of no more than 15 %, but none the less G alone can account for 93 %, and taking G along with RCI and ScI changes the coefficients of the pair completely (Figure 7.1, (i) and (iii)). Even a small residual provides no guarantee that a new variable will not upset the apple cart.

Sir Karl Popper puts the point vigorously, in *The Logic of Scientific Discovery.* "We do not know" he says "we can only guess. And our guesses are guided by the unscientific, the metaphysical (though biologically explicable) faith in laws, in regularities which we can uncover—discover. Like Bacon, we might describe our own contemporary science—'the method of reasoning which men ordinarily apply to nature'—as consisting of 'anticipations, rash and premature' and of 'prejudices.'" Bad guesses are overthrown by new evidence. Good ones are those that have stood up to severe testing, and that therefore survive—on probation.[1] Severe testing is hardly practicable in the social sciences, where the best that can be done is to compare the conclusions tentatively reached in formal studies with each other and with the more general, but vaguer, evidence of common experience. As in Meredith's poem the quest for certainties will find a dusty answer, but critical discussion may make some answers appear more credible than others and so diminish the area of serious doubt.

How far can the IEA study be said to have contributed to this end? This is the main theme of the next, and final, chapter.

---

[1] There is an unresolved argument about this between Popper and Jeffreys. The latter maintains that hypotheses that have stood up to severe testing have thereby become more probable. Popper denies this. "Science" he says "never pursues the illusory aim of making its answers final, *or even probable."* The point at issue appears to relate to the meaning of probability; a recondite matter as to which the authorities are at variance. Since Popper, who has taught mainly in England after leaving Vienna, has also lectured in the United States, and in Australia, New Zealand, India and Japan, it is plain that he gives enough credence to the predictions of the *Nautical Almanac* to stake his life upon their accuracy. But in his view, or so it appears, credibility and probability are to be sharply distinguished.

Chapter 8

Retrospect

SOME SALIENT RESULTS

Looking back on the inquiry one sees that the more salient results may be briefly summarized as follows:

(1) What is taught is very much the same from country to country. There are no very striking differences from country to country in the curriculum, despite the differences in language[1] and history.

(2) Between the countries with long established universal educational systems there is not much variation in either the average or the range of achievement. In all these countries there are both children who have learnt a great deal and others who have learnt little. In the countries where the educational system is relatively new the standard of achievement is much lower.

(3) In all the countries where the educational system is well established there is ample evidence that parents and children vary much more than teachers and schools.

(4) Despite (3) the evidence supports what might be called the quantitative theory of teaching. Roughly speaking the more teaching the more learning.

(5) On the other hand the efforts made to subdivide the quantity of teaching into different aspects or elements were rather unrewarding, owing to intercorrelation. A great many variables were brought into the analyses, but most of them appeared to have little separable effect, and only the quantitative measure stood out in all countries.

(6) The quantitative theory is also supported by the very marked difference, noted in (2) above, between the countries where universal education has gone on for several generations and those where it is relatively new.

[1] Cf. "The adoption of rationalism implies, moreover, that there is a common medium of communication, a common language of reason; it establishes something like a moral obligation towards that language, the obligation to keep up its standards of clarity and to use it in such a way that it can retain its function as the vehicle of argument. That is to say, to use it plainly; to use it as an instrument of rational communication, of significant information, rather than as a means of 'self-expression' as the vicious romantic jargon of most of our educationists has it" --- "And it implies the recognition that mankind is united by the fact that our different mother tongues, so far as they are rational can be translated into one another. It recognises the unity of human reason." (Popper, 1949.)

THE ROOTS OF THE CURRICULUM

In the developed countries the educational systems have deep roots. In King Henry VI we read "Thou hast most traitorously corrupted the youth of the realm in erecting a grammar school, and whereas, before, our forefathers had no books but the score and the tally, thou hast caused printing to be used, and, contrary to the King, his crown and dignity, thou hast built a paper mill." It is five centuries since Jack Cade uttered these words, and nearly four since Shakespeare attributed them to him. During this interval the educational net has gradually been cast more widely. In Shakespeare's day the student was typically the lad of parts who was lucky enough to be able to go to school. He may not have been continuously conscious of his luck ("And then the whining schoolboy, with his satchel and shining morning face, creeping, like snail, unwillingly to school"), but usually he was capable of doing what was expected of him, by his parents and his schoolmaster. And what he was expected to do, and capable of doing, has been the foundation of the curriculum ever since, though school education is now compulsory for all. It is a hundred years since Robert Lowe introduced compulsory schooling to the English Parliament with the words "I believe that it will be absolutely necessary that you should prevail on our future masters to learn their letters" (often quoted as "We must educate our masters"), and the same step was taken at roughly the same time in other countries. During the ensuing century the upper limit of the age of compulsion has been gradually extended, and so has the curriculum, which in its upper reaches now includes much that was arcane, or even unheard of, in Shakespeare's day. This is one reason why the computer has now replaced the score and the tally. None the less there are still some students who leave school at the end of the compulsory period without having learned their letters in any but the most rudimentary meaning of that phrase. This is the case in all countries, as the IEA study reaffirms, and so far no country has been able to do very much about it.

THE CLIMATE OF OPINION

The continued existence of the backward child has been one of the causes of the present climate of educational opinion. This opinion is usually in a state of flux, for reasons which are not hard to find, and which can be summarized by saying that every reform has disappointed the hopes of some of its advocates. Before any reform can be put into effect it must command the support of a large body of opinion. In the nature of the case such bodies tend to be coalitions made up of people who support the reform for different reasons, so that in the upshot the hopes of some are gratified and those of others disappointed. Moreover the results of successful reforms soon come to be taken for granted. It may sometimes be the case that one good custom doth corrupt the world, but much more frequently when the good custom is once established its benefits cease to be noticed. The institution of junior scholarships in England at the beginning of the century provides a good example. Their purpose was to make it possible for the talented children of poor parents to continue their education beyond the statutory leaving age. In this they were extremely successful; they enabled many children to climb the educational ladder, to their own benefit and that of their country. The secondary schools to which the scholarship examination gave admission became grammar schools after the Education Act of 1944, and the examination became known as the "eleven plus," from the age at which it was held. The object of the new system was to provide secondary education for all, in schools of various types so that every child could receive an education suited to his "age, ability and aptitude." The eleven plus was to play its part in securing this end. But as time went on it was seen as a barrier rather than a ladder. Inevitably some of its decisions were mistaken, but the system of separate types of school made it rather difficult to correct these mistakes in the cases when they appeared later, and there was reason to think that some of them would not appear because of the tendency to conform to the usual pattern in the type of school to which the child was allocated. This led to the movement to replace the multitype system by the monotype or comprehensive system of schools.

So long as the multitype system prevailed its drawbacks could be plainly seen, while those of the comprehensive system were veiled in the future.[2] As always the body of opinion that supported the reform was a coalition made up of people who entertained different hopes. At one end of the spectrum were those who thought that the idea of suiting the education to the age, ability and aptitude of the child was

---

[2] Compare the remark of Tacitus about the Emperor Galba *"Omnium consensu capax imperii nisi imperasset,"* which might be roughly translated as "Every one thought he would make a good President. Unfortunately he was elected."

a good idea, and necessarily involved some kind of sorting or selection. Their objection to the multitype system was not that it involved selection *per se*, but that it involved it too soon and too irrevocably. At the other end were those who objected to selection altogether—at 11, at 15, at 18, or at any other age.

Initially the comprehensive schools tended to be an amalgamation of the preceding types, with the difference that the selection was now internal instead of external, and with the advantage, it was hoped, that mistakes would be more easily remediable. Children were sorted into fast and slow streams, with varied curricula, according to what was observed of their ability and aptitude. (Streams in the United Kingdom are tracks in the United States.) But this did not satisfy some of the reformers, who felt that new presbyter was but old priest writ large. Their target was not the career open to the talents, but equality *tout court*. Various modifications have been made in the system to meet these views, but they have not produced equality. Therefore, say the root and branch party, the system has proved a failure, and must be replaced. If working class children on the whole find it harder than middle class children to cope with the existing curriculum there must be something wrong with the curriculum. It must have a middle class bias. If we must have a bias, say these reformers, let it be a working class bias.

BIAS IN THE CURRICULUM

In one sense the curriculum certainly has a middle class bias. It grew up in Tudor times, as we have seen, to meet the need for a literate and numerate class of people who would be competent to manage the administration of the country. The later extension to science and technology is but a development of the same purpose. The competent class consists of people who have acquired some of these skills, and their continued acquisition by some people is needed if society as we know it is to survive. Despite modern discontents this view is still held by a majority of adults, but relatively few of them held it continuously as children. Children usually take shorter views, as Shakespeare remarked, and go unwillingly to school. None the less they tend to do what is expected of them if they have enough aptitude and parents and teachers are in agreement; trouble arises when this is not the case. Moreover, children are influenced by their companions, who may include some recalcitrants. Although what is meant by a curriculum with a working class bias is not altogether

175

clear it is possible that such a curriculum might suit some children better than the existing one, but it would raise the problem of selection in a new form; allocation to the new curriculum might be regarded by some children and their parents as a denial of educational opportunity. This would revive the questions raised by the multitype system.

A MORE EXTREME VIEW

Another group of reformers draws a different lesson from the fact that some children still leave school without having learned much from the current curriculum. The moral, they say, is that the attempt to make all children literate and numerate is mistaken. It should be abandoned, and attention should be concentrated on making children happy at school, without much regard to what they learn on the old pattern. Some go further, and say that children should do what they will, and that the government of schools should be in their hands.

Freedom or Anarchy

Time alone will show whether these movements of opinion will swell or subside. History appears to show that far-reaching revolutions, such as the French and the Russian, have tended to produce first anarchy and then reaction and the re-establishment of order. More moderate revolutions as those of 1688 and 1776 have avoided both the anarchy and the reaction.

STABILITY

Notwithstanding the tendencies to anarchy, and the corresponding reaction, that may be observed in some large conurbations it may be said that the educational systems of the developed countries taking part in the IEA project have not in fact been radically changed by the turbulent events that have occurred since the close of the Victorian era. This is remarkable, since these countries were all, except for Sweden and the Netherlands, belligerents in the first world war, and, except for Sweden and Eire, in the second, with some changes of sovereignty in between. In the second war, or immediately after it, all the belligerents apart from the English-speaking countries suffered enemy occupation, and during it all save Australia, New Zealand and the United States were devastated from the air. Despite all this there is still a strong resemblance between the systems of the developed countries, and the main contrast is between the developed countries taken together and the countries where the educational system is a comparatively recent growth. This suggests that educational systems are institutions with a certain toughness, and that the phenomena analysed in the IEA study may be less transitory than some fear and others hope.

The same phenomenon may inspire hope in some and fear in others, or both fear and hope in the same person at different times, or indeed at the same time. The history of the IQ provides a good example. Initially it was seen as a hopeful development, as an aid to providing courses of education suitable to the individual. Later it became feared as the means of cutting off some individuals from educational privileges. The hopeful were inclined to over-rate, and the fearful to under-rate, what it could accomplish in the way of prediction. A bottle that can optimistically be described as half full appears half empty to a pessimist. Many teachers adopted the more reasonable view that their duty was to attempt to confirm the prediction when it was favorable and to confound it when it was unfavorable.

Roughly speaking the doctrine of the IQ says (a) that those who begin as fast, or slow, learners tend to continue as fast or slow, because (b) of their innate capacity for learning. There is a wealth of evidence in favour of (a). The interpretation of the evidence on (b) has been a matter of hot dispute. There is general agreement that some part of the capacity to learn is innate; the dispute is about how much. But from the standpoint of the teacher the reason why a new student's rate of learning is what it is matters less than the question of whether it can be accelerated. To this question the IEA study gives a firmly positive but rather grudging answer—it is possible to accelerate the rate, but it is rather hard to do so, and even harder to give any prescription for doing so that is at once new and general. The variables in the short-term group in the IEA study can be regarded as descriptions of teaching. Taken together they can account for a modest proportion—perhaps not so modest when their short time of operation is allowed for—of the variation in achievement, but few of them except the Amount of study and homework stand out individually in many countries. But is this because teaching cannot do much to accelerate the rate of learning, or because the variables are not very good descriptions of teaching?

RESIDUALS

One way to examine this question lies through the residuals. In the advanced sciences progress has been made by attending to the residuals, one celebrated example being the discovery of Neptune through attention to hitherto unexplained planetary perturbations. In the IEA study the measured variables give predictions that are quite close for some pupils and for some schools, but for other pupils and other schools the gap, or residual, is considerable. Attention to the cases where the achievement of a school is much beyond expectation—i.e., beyond what is predicted by the measured variables— might be fruitful, and is being undertaken in some countries. The expectation may be high or low, but in either case the residual must stem from something that the measured variables have left out of account. Observation might suggest what that something is. There is an initial probability that it will be found to be unusually good teaching. If so, there is the further question of whether this unusually good teaching can be effectively described, or merely recognised. A comparison with acting, which teaching resembles in some ways, may make this point clearer. For acting there are some basic rules, which are necessary but not sufficient. Great actors (usually) follow the rules, but in addition they bring to their profession unique gifts, which can be recognised but not described in such a way that others can adopt them. This is merely one example of the baffling problem of the unique and the general that pervades the social sciences.

THE UNIQUE AND THE GENERAL

Science is a quest for general rules, and proceeds by abstraction. In the process of abstraction what is unique is necessarily lost. But what is too detailed, without being unique, is also lost. A map on the scale of 25 inches to the mile can show detail that cannot appear on the one inch map. Reducing the scale to 10 miles to the inch means that more detail must disappear, and the maps in an atlas of the world show very little in one sense, though they show the whole world in another. A map of a mountain range can indicate some general features. A map of a single peak can indicate the average steepness of the various slopes. A photograph can indicate whether a given slope is fairly uniform or consists of a sequence of cliffs and terraces. If part of the slope is above the snow line a photograph may also indicate the strike of the strata—that is whether the local texture is like a staircase or like the tiles on a roof. The staircase structure will support snow at a much steeper angle than the tiled. For a given angle it will also provide much better support for the climber, both when it is snow-covered and when it is not. All this information is helpful to the climber, but in the last resort he may be defeated by some smaller feature that has escaped observation, or by a change in the weather. The general rules abstracted from experience and information may be improved by more attention to detail, but even so they may sometimes fail.

The maps constructed by the social sciences must perforce omit not only what is unique but also what is too detailed for the scale. Thus it is plain that the net of the IEA variables necessarily omits much of both kinds. What is omitted from the net cannot play a direct part in the process of abstraction, but the recognition that it has been omitted need not be ignored in interpretation. In the interpretation advocated in this book the recognition comes into play at various levels. Thus the direct evidence of the study says nothing, about the ordering of the variables, though this is an essential part of the interpretation. The direct evidence does not compel the identification of the variables in the long-term and middle-term groups as partial surrogates for teaching, at home and at school, though this is part of the interpretation. Nor does it compel the identification of the Reading scores as partial surrogates for natural talent or ability, which again is part of the interpretation. On all this the author has been guided by the experience of a long life spent mostly in schools of many kinds. In other words he is interpreting the whole map by his experience of a small part of it on the ground, and he may be wrong in supposing that other parts of the wood look much the same. It is for the reader to say, and, if he wishes, to use the IEA data bank as the basis for a different interpretation.

USE OF THE DATA BANK

A small example may illustrate the kind of difficulty that may be encountered. Suppose that in Figure (i) of Table 6.8 it was decided to delete the direct paths from A to H and T. This involves recalculating the path coefficients as follows:

	Old	New		Old	New
HA	0.112	0.000	TA	0.093	0.000
HP	0.319	0.364	TP	0.521	0.553
HB	0.240	0.254	TB	0.151	0.160
			TH	0.208	0.219

and recalculating r_{AH} and r_{AT} as 0.266 and 0.380 to replace the obtained 0.352 and 0.469. It might be thought that in this case the difference between the obtained and the calculated values of r_{AH} and r_{AT} was too great to support the deletion, but even if this point is waived, or if, in another case, it did not arise, the justification for the deletion is finally a matter of interpretation. There seems to be no escape from the recognition that both the initial selection of variables from the bank and any subsequent manipulation and deletion must rest on interpretation, or in other words on theory. The adoption of a model is a declaration of a theory—this is how the thing works— based on some prior evidence. The immediate evidence may suggest that the theory could be modified without increasing the residuals by much—in this case by less than 0.01—but it does not compel a modification unless the residuals would be considerably reduced by making it.

In the competition between rival theories a theory can derive strength from two sources. On the one hand there is the external or prior evidence that led to its formulation. On the other there is the internal or immediate evidence which it fits more or less well, according to the size of the residuals. A theory that gave much larger residuals, on the immediate evidence, than a rival could be ruled out in favour of that rival. But if the residuals are roughly equal the decision can only be governed by the prior evidence, and if the prior evidence for the two theories seems equally strong (or weak) to a critic then he can only suspend judgment.

The relation of theory and observation is complicated, as may be seen from the most advanced of the sciences. "No doubt physics would like to forget its early history, which, like that of many established institutions, is not so creditable as could be wished ... The whole process is one of tinkering. If common-sense estimates of distance and size are roughly correct, then certain physical laws are roughly correct. If these laws are quite correct, the common-sense estimates must be slightly amended. If the various laws are not exactly compatible, they must be adjusted until the inconsistency ceases. Thus observation and theory interact; what, in scientific physics, is called an observation is usually something involving a considerable admixture of theory." (Russell, 1948.)

In the social sciences the tinkering process is at a very early stage, and the confusion of observation and theory is extremely perplexing. The IEA study illustrates this confusion, for example, by the vagueness of the definitions of the variables. This seems inevitable, since clear definitions are the goal rather than the starting point of inquiry. Progress has been made when the relevant questions become somewhat clearer. Notwithstanding these shortcomings the data bank is offered to the critic in the hope that he may be able to carry the tinkering forward by using it in conjunction with whatever theory or theories seem to him to have most initial support from all the evidence of which he is aware, whether in the shape of general experience, including his own, or of teacher opinion, or of formal studies. The choice of theory is not unlimited; there is no point in advancing a theory that is not supported by general experience, and this rules out from the beginning most of the theories that would be incompatible with the bank. It may be said with some confidence that any surviving theory would derive some support from the bank; the question is whether one would derive markedly more support, in the shape of smaller residuals, than others. If so something of what is now seen through a glass darkly would have become slightly clearer.

Appendix 1

The Development of the IEA Questionnaires and Attitudinal and Descriptive Scales

T. Neville Postlethwaite (International Institute for Educational Planning) and Bruce H. Choppin (National Foundation for Educational Research in England and Wales)

The general model of the IEA research was an input-process-output one. The cognitive output measures have been described in great detail in the six subject-matter volumes already published. Certain attitudes were measured and, in general, were used as independent variables in the multivariate analyses undertaken. The data for the bulk of the input and process variables were collected by means of a student questionnaire completed by each student tested, a teacher questionnaire completed by a sample of the relevant subject-matter teachers in each school, and a school questionnaire completed by the administrative representative for each school in the sample.

QUESTIONNAIRE DEVELOPMENT

For each questionnaire there was a set of questions of a general educational nature and a further set of questions specific to the subject-matter under consideration. The general questions were prepared by an international committee (B. S. Bloom, T. Husén, D. A. Pidgeon, T. N. Postlethwaite and R. M. Wolf) which was also responsible for the final editing of the subject-specific questions initially prepared by the subject-matter committees. The reasons for the subject-specific data collected by means of the questionnaires are set forth in the separate subject volumes.

As far as the general education data were concerned, the committee was able to profit from the Mathematics Study (Husén et al., 1967). At the completion of the Mathematics Study, IEA convened two meetings, the first at the Unesco Institute for Education, Hamburg, and the second at Lake Mohonk, New York, to which it invited educational economists, sociologists, psychologists, comparative educators etc., with a view to having suggestions concerning input and process variables from these different disciplines' points of view. The contributions of these social scientists are reported in a recent publication (Super et al., 1967). The major variables, different from those used in the Mathematics Study, which emerged in the Super report were considered at a Council meeting of IEA held in London in the spring of 1967. At that meeting some two thousand possible variables were suggested. Some were suggested together with proved measures and coding schemes. Others were vague, not to say ephemeral.

An initial sieving of the two thousand took place by eliminating those for which no immediate measure was possible, and by selecting only one variable out of a conceptual cluster which were known to be highly intercorrelated. The resultant number of variables were some two hundred to five hundred, dependent upon the subject area.

Since IEA was testing 10-year-olds for the first time, the possibility of obtaining valid responses to questionnaire items was queried. Therefore, a simple pilot study was undertaken to determine whether ten-year-olds could provide accurate responses to questionnaire items. Several classes of ten-year-olds in five countries were administered a short background questionnaire. Subsequently an interview was conducted with the mother of each student tested or a questionnaire was transmitted to the home to be completed by the mother. The results of this study were fairly clear (de Landsheere, 1968). Those questions which asked the student to describe some aspect of his present life situation showed a high degree of agreement with the responses given by his mother. There was considerably less agreement between mother and child on items which were retrospective and prospective in nature. Although the mother/child agreement is not proof of the truth of the response, it is sufficiently reassuring so that on the basis of the pilot study it was decided that a restricted questionnaire study of ten-year-olds was feasible.

The first set of questions was reviewed and edited by the Questionnaire committee and divided into questions of general interest and those of special interest to a single subject area which were

183

then reviewed by the Subject Area committees and the National Centers.

Some of the questions (such as one to determine Sex) were of a sort for which the options were obvious. There were others, however (such as one concerned with Hours of homework per week) for which it was difficult to tell in advance what range of responses would be received and how these should be divided into response categories in a precoded questionnaire. In order to guide the choice, a number of items were pretested in open-ended form. Frequency distributions of responses were prepared for the several countries in which the try-out had been conducted, and these were used as a basis for setting up response categories. For example, on a question asking about hours per week reading for pleasure, it appeared that a good spread of responses within and between-countries would result from choices as follows:

0 hours
Less than 1 hour
Between 1 and 2 hours
Between 2 and 3 hours
More than 3 hours

The same coding was used for all countries, and sometimes represented a compromise that was far from ideal for single countries in the study.

After review and preliminary try-out, the members of the Questionnaire committee carried out a final review and selection of questions. The review was designed to keep the questionnaires to manageable size in view of the demands upon student and teacher time, to phrase the questions so that they would be as clear and simple as possible, to provide suitable precoded response alternatives whenever this was possible, and to provide open-ended responses that would be easy to code in these few instances in which precoding was not practical.

These preliminary forms of the final questionnaires were circulated to National Centers for review and were revised on the basis of suggestions from this source. Final forms were then prepared and distributed for translation and use. As an example of the total number of independent variables used for a particular subject area, Table 1 presents the list of the names of the variables used in the study of French as a Foreign Language.

National Centers were encouraged to formulate other question-

Table 1. *Student, Teacher and School Variables in French Study.*

Student	Teacher	School
Age	French in Classroom	Class size
Grade	Teach other subjects in	Principal's degree
Father's occupation	French	Years as principal
Expected occupation	Hours instruction in	Years as principal of this
Father's language	French	school
Mother's language	Sex	Years teaching experience
First language of home	Age	Type of community served
Second language of home	Specialist teacher	by school
Sex	Full-time education	Museum available nearby
Father's education	Post-secondary education	Zoo available nearby
Mother's education	Teaching experience	Public library available
Expected education	Time teaching at this	nearby
Hours homework	school	Concert hall available nearby
Place of homework	Hours preparation of	Opera available nearby
Fixed time for homework	lessons	Foreign language societies
Help with homework	Hours marking papers	available nearby
Parents correct speech	Membership of teachers	Total amenities available
Parents check spelling	association	nearby score
Dictionary in home	Teaching journals read	Total enrollment, boys
Parents encourage reading	Subject journals read	Total enrollment, girls
Parents' interest in school	Attended conferences	Total enrollment
Parents encourage culture	Assessment, standardised	Lowest grade in school
Daily newspapers	tests	Highest grade in school
Books in home	Assessment, essay tests	Mean grade of school
Hours pleasure reading	Assessment, objective tests	Grade range of school
TV and radio	Assessment, homework	Enrollment of Pop. I
Size of family	Assessment, projects and	Enrollment of Pop. II
Position in family	papers	Enrollment of Pop. IV
Like/dislike of different	Assessment, variety and	Coeducation, Pop. I
subjects	extent	Coeducation, Pop. II
Interest in French	Importance of student	Coeducation, Pop. IV
French activities out of	needs	Day or boarding school
school	Importance of curriculum	Beginning French grade
Mother studied French	Importance of text books	Beginning English grade
Parents interest	Importance of examina-	Beginning Social Studies
Help with French home-	tions	Grade
work	Importance of next grade	Decision making, textbooks
Utility of French	Methods text books	Decision making, rules
Aspiration in French skills	Methods drill materials	Decision making, choosing
Grade beginning French	Methods individual ma-	teachers
Entry knowledge	terials	Decision making, conditions
Years studied French	Methods small group work	Decision making, student
Perception spoken French	Methods individual tutor-	selection
Perception listening	ing	Decision making, expendi-
French	Methods audio and visual	ture

Table 1 (continued).

Student	Teacher	School
Perception reading French	Methods field trips	Decision making, tuition fee
Perception writing French	Methods lectures	Decision making, administration
Opportunity to speak French	Methods questioning	
	Methods discussion	**Decision Making, syllabus**
Time in French country	Methods variety and extent of approaches	Decision making, methods
Ease/Difficulty French		**Decision making, syllabus and methods**
Perceived industry in French	Within class grouping	
French books in home	Teacher training institution	Inspection
Frequency of exposure to French books		Report to authorities
	Foreign language teaching load	Advice on school problems
		Advise teachers
	French in other subjects	Assess teachers
	Other foreign language	Role of inspection
	Grade range of French teaching	School operating costs
		Teacher salaries
	Number of groups taught	Non-teaching staff salaries
	Total time teaching French	Maintenance and repair
		Books and stationery
	Mother tongue	Purchase of equipment
	Age beginning French	Other (loan charges)
	Perceived listening skill	Total budget
	Perceived speaking skill	Total budget per pupil
	Perceived reading skill	Teacher salaries per pupil
	Perceived writing skill	Foreign language percentage budget
	Perceived pronunciation skill	
		Number full-time staff
	Residence French country	Pupil/teacher ratio
	Tertiary French in years	Teacher salaries per staff
	Method training	Number of teachers male
	Years teaching foreign language	Number of teachers in French
	Foreign language association member	Number of teachers in English
	Use of mother tongue, beginning	Number of teachers in Social Studies
	Use of mother tongue, intermediate	School librarian
	Use of mother tongue, advanced	**French foreign language assistant**
	Emphasis choices: listening comprehension	English foreign language assistant
	Emphasis choices: speaking fluency	Foreign language laboratory technician
	Emphasis choices: correct pronunciation	Total number of language auxiliaries
		Admission criteria, residence

Table 1 (continued).

Student	Teacher	School
	Emphasis choices: reading comprehension	Admission criteria, performance
	Emphasis choices: ability to write	Admission criteria, interview
	Order of spoken and written French	Admission criteria, examination
	Grammar teaching	Admission criteria, graduation
	Speaking emphasis	Admission criteria, membership
	Pronunciation methods	
	Teaching aids, blackboard	Streaming practices
	Teaching aids, pictures	School programme, variety
	Teaching aids, "props"	Type of course
	Teaching aids, film strips	Language of instruction
	Teaching aids, sound movies	Student decision making
	Teaching aids, phonograph records	Hours per week schooling, Pop. I
	Teaching aids, tape recorder	Hours per week schooling, Pop. II
	Teaching aids, language laboratory	Hours per week schooling, Pop. IV
	Teaching aids, variety and extent	Weeks per year schooling
		Hours per year schooling, Pop. I
		Hours per year schooling, Pop. II
		Hours per year schooling, Pop. IV
		When spoken French introduced
		When Reading and Writing French introduced
		Class conducted in French
		Selection of French students
		Percentage study French, Pop. I
		Percentage study French, Pop. II
		Percentage study French, Pop. IV
		Number of periods French, beginning
		Length of periods French, beginning
		Level present, beginning

Table 1 (continued).

Student	Teacher	School
		Number of periods French, intermediate
		Length of periods French, intermediate
		Number of periods French, advanced
		Length of periods French, advanced
		Total time French, beginning
		Total time French, intermediate
		Total time French, advanced
		Level present, advanced
		Native teachers French

naire items which were specific to particular aspects of their own national system which they wished to investigate. Such items were designated National Options and were to be used in national (as opposed to international) analyses only. For example, the NFER included questions to determine whether sample schools were using the new Nuffield Science curricula or not.

For certain variables, such as Father's Occupation, each National Center used a national set of occupational categories (up to 10 different categories were allowed). In some cases, these were research proved schemes but in other cases, were developed from previous work especially for this study. However, criterion scaling was used to form the categories into a linear variable. This technique proved to be satisfactory in estimating the contribution of such a variable in the regression analyses.

Each National Center was allowed to restructure questions to make them easily answerable by the respondents, but the collected data had always to be recorded according to the internationally agreed scheme.

The sampling errors and design effects for selected variables have been given in Chapter 2 of this report.

In some cases (e.g., teachers' salaries in some countries) it was not possible to collect data. Typically where there were more than 20 percent missing data for a particular variable, that variable was dropped from any multivariate analyses. In many cases the variables had to be transformed (either in terms of direction or values). There were certain scoring errors (e.g., School motivation scale for Populations II and IV which resulted in the scale being omitted from further analysis).

By early 1975, a Data Bank of all IEA data will have been created and a series of Data Bank manuals and code books will be available. Detailed information will be given in these concerning the amount of missing data for each variable and the coding schemes used. The scoring of mis-scored scales will be corrected before the Data Bank is made available.

In 1975 the questionnaires together with all the cognitive and affective instruments will be avilable on microfilm from the ERIC Processing and Reference Facility.

ATTITUDE, INTEREST, ACTIVITIES AND DESCRIPTIVE SCALES

The bulk of the Civic Education output measures consisted of attitude measures and those have been reported in detail in the Civic Education Reports (Oppenheim & Torney, 1974 and Torney, Oppenheim and Farnen, 1975). However, the scales produced for the other subjects are reported here.

The *attitude, interest* and *activity* scales were intended to measure the following:

1. *Like/Dislike school*—12 items
The extent to which a student reported liking or disliking school.

2. *School motivation*—12 items
The extent to which doing well at school was important to a student and the satisfaction he obtained from doing well at school. (There is previous evidence to indicate that this type of motivation is strongly associated with student performance.)

3. *Interest in science (Science)*—16 items
The extent to which a student was interested in science as a subject. This was measured partly by asking about participation in Science-related activities, e.g. photography, building a radio set, visiting a Science museum etc., and partly by expressed liking for studying Science in school. (It was assumed that there would be a strong

association between this type of interest and student performance in Science.)

4. *Attitudes towards school science (Science)*—6 items
The extent to which a student felt Science to be a difficult or easy subject for him to learn.

5. *Attitudes towards science and the world (Science)*—6 items (Populations II and IV only)
The extent to which the student felt Science to be a force for good (in that Science solves certain world problems, e.g. makes life more pleasant through technical advancement) or evil (in that, at the same time, it destroys the environment and human values).

6. *Literary transfer (Literature)*—10 items
The extent to which a student brought his literary experiences to his life and involved himself personally in the books he read and films he saw.

7. *Literature interest (Literature)*—10 items
The extent to which a student voluntarily indulged in reading literary works.

8. *Interest in French (French)*—10 items
The extent to which a student was interested in French and felt French to be important.

9. *Perceived utility of French (French)*—12 items
The extent to which the study of French was felt to be useful both for a future career and in itself.

10. *Activities in French outside school (French)*—6 items
The extent to which a student was involved in French-related activities, e.g. reading French newspapers, corresponding with pen pal, visiting a French-speaking country etc.

11. *Interest in English (English)*—10 items
The extent to which a student was interested in English and felt English to be important.

12. *Perceived utility of English (English)*—12 items
The extent to which the study of English was felt to be useful both for future study and career and in itself.

13. *Activities in English outside school (English)*—6 items
The extent to which a student was involved in English-related

activities outside the school situation (e.g. reading English newspapers, corresponding with pen pal, visiting an English-speaking country etc.).

The descriptive scales were:

14. *School environment (sometimes called School behavior)*—12 items
The extent to which, through the perceptions of the students, the school tended to have rigid rules on one hand or on the other a flexible and permissive ambiance.

15. *Science teaching (Science)*—12 items (Populations II and IV only)
The extent to which the students in a school reported that Science teaching was largely from textbooks or from practical experience.

16. *Science laboratory teaching (Science)*—3 items (Populations II and IV only)
The extent to which the students reported their laboratory work to be structured or unstructured.

The scales are given in detail at the end of this appendix. However, it should be noted that the items from two scales were often scrambled when presented in the actual testing situation, to the students.

Whereas the attitude scales were meant to measure between-student differences in attitudes (and were mostly Likert type scales) the descriptive scales (of a Pace-Stern type) were meant to measure between-school differences. Although these two sets of measures are conceptually separate, the development and piloting were conducted simultaneously.

In general, a three-step development was foreseen:

1. A preliminary trial of a pool of items in one or two countries only to give some item statistics.
2. A trial of draft scales in two or three countries to check the dimensions and reliabilities.
3. A full-scale pretest of scales in all relevant countries.

Work on the actual construction of the scales started in September 1967. Unfortunately, the need to produce scales by December 1968, together with the considerable variation of school schedules (and therefore of possible testing occasions) in the different countries, made it impossible to carry out the full series of steps outlined above in all cases. The basic shortage of time was aggravated in some countries by school strikes, committees of revolutionary students, unexplained postal losses, and the like. It was necessary, therefore, to take certain short cuts, particularly with regard to step 2. Step 3 was, in general, replaced by a full-scale rehearsal in all countries. No scales were included in this that had not been pretested in at least 3 countries. The statistical analyses of the pretest data for the scales were carried out by the IEA Data Processing Unit which, at that time, was stationed in London. The analyses performed were of two different types: (1) a factor analysis to investigate the dimensionality of the attitude space concerned, and (2) a standard item analysis giving response distributions for each variable together with internal consistency data.

Initially, a large pool of items (over twice the number eventually retained for use) was collected from various sources.

Many of the items employed in the Mathematics Study attitude scales were of use. The international subject-matter committees indicated to Dr Choppin the types of measures they required. Discussions were held concerning the constituent items. The School Motivation scale benefitted from items in already existing measures in the United States and England. Finally, interviews were conducted with school children in order to identify the sorts of statements they themselves made about some of the major attitudinal dimensions mentioned above.

National Centers expressed themselves as experiencing more difficulty with the translation of attitudinal items than with questionnaire or cognitive test items. Discussions were held at international meetings with the research officers responsible for the translation of the items and a detailed explanation of the intention and connotation of nearly every item was drawn up and circulated to all National Centers.

Typically, preliminary testing was conducted in two or three countries on samples of 100–150 students per population. In addition, comments on the original form of the instruments were recieved from National Centers, schools, teachers and students, and these were taken into account in producing revised versions. In some cases, the revised versions were given a further pretesting and in other cases had to be used as they stood in the dry run. Some changes then took place between the dry-run and main testing.

The reliabilities for the attitude scales were estimated by means of alpha coefficients (Cronbach, 1951) (9) and the descriptive scale reliabilities *were to be calculated* in a different way. These measures were of the school, as perceived by the students in the school, rather than measures of individual students. Whereas it is recognised that there will be differences between individual students perceptions of what goes on in the school, it was expected that such measures, when pooled, would give a reliable estimate of the mean for any one school. The intention was to calculate the reliability for each *item* by comparing the variance on that item within and between-schools. The reason for this was because not *all* items were expected to work in *all* countries. Indeed, some National Centers (e.g., Hungary) omitted some items. The formula (Hoyt and Krishnaiah, 1966) for calculating this reliability was:

$$r = \frac{\sigma_B^2}{\sigma_B^2 + \sigma_W^2}$$

where σ_B^2 and σ_W^2 are respectively the estimates of between and within school variance. At the same time, correlations between the school mean values of the items in a scale were calculated and in the development of the scales any item not correlating highly with the rest of the items was dropped.

The reliability for the descriptive scale was meant to be calculated using the same formula as for items, only in this case using school scale means.

Unfortunately, in the processing of the final testing data, the difference in the modes of calculating between-student and between-school reliabilities was overlooked and all reliabilities were therefore calculated on a between-student basis. It is to be expected that if the descriptive scales reliabilities had been correctly calculated, the reliability coefficients would have been higher.

It is interesting to note that the reliability coefficients from pre-testing and the full-scale rehearsal were consistently higher than in the main testing. This may be due to the different composition of the samples or to fatigue since the attitude scales were administered at the end of several hours of testing.

Tables 2–6 present the reliabilities for each scale given at each population level in each country. Where no reliability coefficient is given, the country did not use this scale in its testing programme. The general scales were also given in the second set of testing, namely French, English and Civics and the coefficients were much the same as those reported for the first set of testing. As might have been expected, reliabilities were lower in countries where students had difficulty with reading and, in general, the reliabilities were some-

Table 2. *Reliabilities (α coefficients) of Scale by Population and Country—Population I.*

Country	Like School (1)	School (2) Motivation	School (14) Behavior	Interest in Science (3)	Science (15) Teaching
Belgium (Fl)	.686	.523	.002	.705	.415
Belgium (Fr)	.716	.455	−.236	.684	.281
Chile	.578	.482	−.205	.708	.523
England	.776	.481	−.027	.688	.575
FRG	.723	.257	.069	.731	.614
Finland	.785	.413	.057	.670	.571
Hungary	.732	.472	−.009	.675	.516
India	.511	.489	−.308	.763	.629
Iran	.666	.365	.117	.826	.540
Israel	.651	.427	−.008	–	–
Italy	.702	.322	.063	.660	.540
Japan	.670	.370	.042	.759	.306
Netherlands	.679	.242	−.006	.686	.478
Scotland	.793	.506	−.005	.689	.570
Sweden	.703	.372	−.064	.630	.499
Thailand	.491	.181	−.089	.713	.407
United States	.763	.463	−.037	.726	.344

what higher for older populations. There was an error in scoring the School motivation scales for Populations II and IV and these scales were not used in the multivariate analyses. The School behaviour scale reliabilities presented in the table would appear to be about zero, but it is impossible to know what the real reliabilities of this and the other descriptive scales are until the reliabilities are computed according to the formula presented above. On the other hand, the School behaviour scale correlates highly with certain achievement measures which reinforces the argument above that the alpha coefficients do not reflect the true reliability.

The Literature scales, in particular, proved to be more reliable than had been expected with the notable exceptions of the Transfer scale in Finland and Iran.

It should, perhaps, also be pointed out that attempts were made to develop scales measuring "self-esteem," "authoritarianism" and "ethnocentrism." It proved impossible within the time constraints to develop suitable cross-cultural items for "self-esteem." There was lack of agreement, particularly by European members, on the ac-

Table 3. *Reliabilities (α coefficients) of Scales by Population and Country—Population II.*

Country	Like School (1)	School Behavior (14)	Interest in Science (3)	Science in the World (5)	Science Teaching (15)	Science Lab. Teaching (16)	Literary transfer (6)	Literary Interest (7)
Australia	.769	.117	.758	.645	.073	.083	–	–
Belgium (Fl)	.679	.133	.720	.642	.043	–.060	.316	.584
Belgium (Fr)	.670	.103	.717	.653	.095	.057	.655	.660
Chile	.542	.025	.724	.486	.127	.081	.658	.703
England	.767	.175	.758	.652	.177	.011	.676	.670
FRG	.710	.294	.723	.383	.183	.146	–	–
Finland	.771	.067	.718	.606	.127	.305	.098	.699
Hungary	.653	.145	.687	.649	.322	.100	–	–
India	.513	–.124	.771	.259	.409	–.097	–	–
Iran	.463	.001	.800	.557	.397	–.096	.007	.610
Israel	.583	.143	–	–	–	–	–	–
Italy	.695	.047	.722	.561	.396	–.005	.623	.622
Japan	.636	–.104	.767	.591	.315	.066	–	–
Netherlands	.693	.076	.712	.549	.292	.138	.704	.676
New Zealand	.779	.190	.728	.653	.060	–.035	–	–
Scotland	.781	.262	.789	.657	.150	.062	.699	–
Sweden	.699	.058	.716	.575	.126	.188	.699	.675
Thailand	.534	.141	.681	.462	.386	.185	–	–
United States	.754	.216	.755	.686	.567	.286	.666	.684

Table 4. Reliabilities (α coefficients) of Scale by Population and Country—Population IV.

Country	Like School (1)	School Behavior (14)	Interest in Science (3)	Science in the World (5)	Science Teaching (15)	Science Lab. Teaching (16)	Literary Transfer (6)	Literary Interest (7)
Australia	.750	.124	.763	.710	.297	.059	–	–
Belgium (Fl)	.614	.165	.723	.753	-.030	.419	.355	.698
Belgium (Fr)	.688	.163	.757	.747	.300	-.063	.687	.722
Chile	.652	.183	.752	.608	.441	.135	.694	.716
England	.695	.129	.765	.759	.303	.170	.758	.759
FRG	.684	.323	.722	.397	.373	.101	–	–
Finland	.706	.238	.764	.646	.249	.257	.128	.738
France	.659	–	.726	.755	.180	-.081	–	–
Hungary	.613	.158	.697	.643	.315	.090	–	–
India	.491	.003	.841	.461	.453	-.002	–	–
Iran	.591	.004	.806	.582	.328	-.066	.000	.597
Israel	.641	.157	–	–	–	–	–	–
Italy	.667	.150	.737	.549	.453	.196	.687	.677
Netherlands	.652	.133	.731	.725	.302	.275	–	–
New Zealand	.704	.194	.773	.742	.227	.253	.736	.719
Scotland	.737	.091	.776	.766	.251	.195	–	–
Sweden	.662	.237	.771	.692	.114	.245	.716	.703
Thailand	.573	.202	.703	.504	.486	.157	–	–
United States	.765	.298	.774	.743	.501	.370	.732	.733

Table 5. *Reliabilities (α coefficients) for Like School and School Behavior Scales—Populations II and IV.*

Country		Like School English	French	Civics	School Behavior English	French	Civics
Belgium (Fr)	Pop. II	.702			.261		
	Pop. IV	.654			.350		
Chile	Pop. IV	.627	.630		.413	.385	
England	Pop. II		.751			.381	
	Pop. IV		.655			.341	
FRG	Pop. II	.706		.660	.390		.361
	Pop. IV	.694		.655	.408		.422
Finland	Pop. II	.742		.686	.282		.343
	Pop. IV	.723			.442		.441
Hungary	Pop. IV	.669			.326		
Ireland	Pop. II		.694				.356
	Pop. IV		.710				.418
Israel	Pop. II	.601		.509	.299		.231
	Pop. IV	.553			.182		
Italy	Pop. II	.678		.639	.353		.335
	Pop. IV	.656			.441		
Netherlands	Pop. II	.616	.637	.618	.235	.220	.274
	Pop. IV	.631	.635	.622	.337	.310	.259
New Zealand	Pop. II		.735	.698		.289	.309
	Pop. IV		.730	.662		.327	.375
Rumania	Pop. II		.488			.078	
	Pop. IV		.583			.243	
Scotland	Pop. II		.817			.326	
	Pop. IV		.788			.383	
Sweden	Pop. II	.609			.323		
	Pop. IV	.602	.598	.637	.405	.317	.342
Thailand	Pop. II	.604			.570		
	Pop. IV	.169			.168		
United States	Pop. II		.744	.726		.368	.352
	Pop. IV		.746	.730		.408	.420

Table 6. *Reliabilities (α coefficients) for all English and French scales—Populations II and IV.*

Country		Interest in French (8)	Utility of French (9)	French activities (10)	Interest in English (11)	Utility of English (12)	English activities (13)
Belgium (Fr)	Pop. II				.70	.64	.52
	Pop. IV				.70	.87	.61
Chile	Pop. IV	.77	.78	.59	.75	.90	.63
England	Pop. II	.75	.75	.43			
	Pop. IV	.60	.69	.52			
FRG	Pop. II				.64	.70	.40
	Pop. IV				.57	.88	.58
Finland	Pop. II				.81	.72	.52
	Pop. IV				.60	.84	.51
Hungary	Pop. IV				.72	.86	.60
Israel	Pop. II				.62	.66	.55
	Pop. IV				.61	.85	.53
Italy	Pop. II				.71	.70	.53
	Pop. IV				.67	.89	.58
Netherlands	Pop. II	.70	.61	.50	.63	.55	.49
	Pop. IV	.70	.63	.57	.60	.83	.55
New Zealand	Pop. II	.79	.76	.41			
	Pop. IV	.76	.74	.54			
Rumania	Pop. II	.62	.61	.54			
	Pop. IV	.71	.64	.55			
Scotland	Pop. II	.80	.74	.47			
	Pop. IV	.73	.73	.67			
Sweden	Pop. II				.68	.62	.46
	Pop. IV	.70	.72	.67	.60	.88	.58
Thailand	Pop. II				.56	.64	.52
	Pop. IV				.63	.88	.57
United States	Pop. II	.77	.78	.45			
	Pop. IV	.73	.78	.55			

ceptability of items in the "authoritarianism" scale and, therefore, these two scales were dropped. In the case of "ethnocentrism," no agreement whatsoever could be reached.

IEA SCALE ITEMS

1. Like/Dislike School

1. The most enjoyable part of my life is the time I spend in school
   A. Agree
   B. Disagree

2. I generally dislike my school work
   A. Agree
   B. Disagree

3. There are many school subjects I don't like
   A. Agree
   B. Disagree

4. I want as much education as I can get
   A. Agree
   B. Disagree

5. I enjoy everything about school
   A. Agree
   B. Disagree

6. I find school challenging
   A. Agree
   B. Disagree

7. School is not very enjoyable
   A. Agree
   B. Disagree

8. The only thing I look forward to in school are weekends and holidays
   A. Agree
   B. Disagree

9. The only thing I like about school is the opportunity to meet my friends
   A. Agree
   B. Disagree

10. I hope eventually to study at a College or University
    A. Agree
    B. Disagree

11. I agree with people who say, "school days are the happiest days"
    A. Agree
    B. Disagree

12. I would rather do more homework and spend less time at school
    A. Agree
    B. Disagree

2. School Motivation

1. Is it important to you to do well at school?
    A. Yes
    B. No

2. Does your mind often wander off the subject during lessons?
    A. Yes
    B. No

3. Do you think school is rather a waste of time?
    A. Yes
    B. No

4. Do your teachers think that you misbehave too much?
    A. Yes
    B. No

5. Do you worry about not doing well in class?
    A. Yes
    B. No

6. Do you find it difficult to keep your mind on your work?
    A. Yes
    B. No

7. Do you work hard most of the time?
    A. Yes
    B. No

8. Have you ever invented a new game?
    A. Yes
    B. No

9. Have you ever entered a competition?
    A. Yes
    B. No

10. Have you ever made something as a present for somebody?
    A. Yes
    B. No

11. Are you more interested in games than school work?
  A. Yes
  B. No

12. If you were given lower marks than usual in a test, would this make you unhappy?
  A. Yes
  B. No

3. Interest in Science

1. The marks I get in Science are usually . . .
  A. Better than in most other subjects
  B. About average compared with other subjects
  C. Worse than in most other subjects

2. I like Science . . .
  A. More than most other subjects
  B. About the same as other subjects
  C. Less than most other subjects

3. I would like to study Science after the end of this school year
  A. Yes
  B. Not sure
  C. No

4. I hope that in my career I will be able to make use of some of the Science I learned at school
  A. Yes
  B. Not sure
  C. No

Below is a list of things you might do outside school. Look at each one and if it is something you do very often or used to do very often, mark A. If you have ever done it at all, mark B. If you have never done it, mark C.

5. Visit a Science museum
  A. Often
  B. Sometimes
  C. Never

6. Go to meetings of a scientific club
  A. Often
  B. Sometimes
  C. Never

7. Build working models of ships, cars or aeroplanes
  A. Often
  B. Sometimes
  C. Never

8. Build a radio set or other piece of electronic apparatus
    A. Often
    B. Sometimes
    C. Never

9. Visit an airfield to watch the planes
    A. Often
    B. Sometimes
    C. Never

10. Visit a harbour to watch the ships
    A. Often
    B. Sometimes
    C. Never

11. Read a science fiction book
    A. Often
    B. Sometimes
    C. Never

12. Look at the moon or the planets through a telescope
    A. Often
    B. Sometimes
    C. Never

13. Do Chemistry experiments with your own equipment
    A. Often
    B. Sometimes
    C. Never

Below is a list of things you may do. If you do, mark A. If you do not, but would like to, mark B. If out are not interested in doing it, mark C.

14. Make a hobby of studying or collecting flowers or leaves
    A. I do it
    B. I would like to
    C. I am not interested

15. Make a hobby of studying or collecting insects
    A. I do it
    B. I would like to
    C. I am not interested

16. Make a hobby of studying or collecting rocks or fossils
    A. I do it
    B. I would like to
    C. I am not interested

4. Attitudes towards School Science

1. I like reading about Science
   - A. I strongly agree
   - B. I agree
   - C. I am uncertain
   - D. I disagree
   - E. I strongly disagree

2. Science has many technical terms which are hard to remember
   - A. I strongly agree
   - B. I agree
   - C. I am uncertain
   - D. I disagree
   - E. I strongly disagree

3. Science is a very difficult subject
   - A. I strongly agree
   - B. I agree
   - C. I am uncertain
   - D. I disagree
   - E. I strongly disagree

4. I enjoy watching (listening to) Science programmes on TV (radio)
   - A. I strongly agree
   - B. I agree
   - C. I am uncertain
   - D. I disagree
   - E. I strongly disagree

5. There are too many facts to learn in Science
   - A. I strongly agree
   - B. I agree
   - C. I am uncertain
   - D. I disagree
   - E. I strongly disagree

6. I am very interested to learn all I can about Science
   - A. I strongly agree
   - B. I agree
   - C. I am uncertain
   - D. I disagree
   - E. I strongly disagree

5. Attitudes towards Science and the World (Science)

1. Science is steadily destroying the world
   - A. I strongly agree
   - B. I agree

C. I am uncertain
D. I disagree
E. I strongly disagree

2. Science helps to make the world a better place to live in
    A. I strongly agree
    B. I agree
    C. I am uncertain
    D. I disagree
    E. I strongly disagree

3. Science is no good for people
    A. I strongly agree
    B. I agree
    C. I am uncertain
    D. I disagree
    E. I strongly disagree

4. Science makes life more pleasant
    A. I strongly agree
    B. I agree
    C. I am uncertain
    D. I disagree
    E. I strongly disagree

5. Scientific discoveries will eventually lead to people not thinking for themselves
    A. I strongly agree
    B. I agree
    C. I am uncertain
    D. I disagree
    E. I strongly disagree

6. Science is making us slaves to machines
    A. I strongly agree
    B. I agree
    C. I am uncertain
    D. I disagree
    E. I strongly disagree

6. Literary Transfer

1. Have you done something you would not ordinarily have done because you read about it in a story, poem or play? (For example, when you were younger have you dressed up as a pirate because you read a story about pirates?)
    A. Often
    B. Occasionally
    C. Once or twice
    D. Never

2. While you were reading a book, have you thought of yourself as one of the people in it?
   A. Often
   B. Occasionally
   C. Once or twice
   D. Never

3. Have you compared a person you meet in real life with people you have read about? (For instance, have you ever called a strong person Samson?)
   A. Often
   B. Occasionally
   C. Once or twice
   D. Never

4. Have you been in a situation and asked yourself what some person in a story you read would have done in that situation?
   A. Often
   B. Occasionally
   C. Once or twice
   D. Never

5. When you read a novel or a story, do you imagine that what is happening in the story takes place in some town or city that you have seen?
   A. Never
   B. Once or twice
   C. Occasionally
   D. Often

6. Have you done someting or gone somewhere, felt that this has happened before, and then realized that in fact it happened in a book you read?
   A. Never
   B. Once or twice
   C. Occasionally
   D. Often

7. When you read a story, how often do you imagine that the people in the story look like people you know?
   A. Often
   B. Occasionally
   C. Seldom
   D. Never

8. When you meet a new person, how often do you compare the person to someone you saw in a movie?
   A. Often
   B. Occasionally
   C. Seldom
   D. Never

9. How often do you think that the people you are reading about in a story are real people and not simply people in a story?
   A. Often
   B. Once or twice
   C. Occasionally
   D. Never

10. When you read a story or a play, do you try to remember something that happened to you that is like what you are reading about? Do you say to yourself "Something like this happened to me once"?
    A. Never
    B. Once or twice
    C. Occasionally
    D. Often

7. Literary Interest

1. How many books have you read for your own pleasure in the past year?
   A. None
   B. Fewer than 5
   C. 5 to 10
   D. More than 10

2. During the past year, how many plays have you read for your own pleasure?
   A. None
   B. One or two
   C. 3 to 5
   D. More than 5

3. During the past year, how many novels have you read for your own pleasure?
   A. None
   B. One or two
   C. 3 to 5
   D. More than 5

4. During the past year, how many biographies have you read for your own pleasure?
   A. None
   B. One or two
   C. 3 to 5
   D. More than 5

5. When you choose a story or novel to read, which one of the following is most likely to be the reason for your choice?
   A. Friends or parents recommend it
   B. I have read other books by the same author

C. The title attracts me

D. I just choose any

6. How often do you re-read novels, stories or plays?

   A. Never
   B. Once or twice
   C. Occasionally
   D. Frequently

7. Have you ever gone to a movie because you read the story in a book?

   A. Often
   B. Occasionally
   C. Once or twice
   D. Never

8. Have you ever read a book because you saw the story in a movie?

   A. Never
   B. Once or twice
   C. Occasionally
   D. Frequently

9. Have you ever read a book because you saw the story on television or heard the story on the radio?

   A. Often
   B. Occasionally
   C. Once or twice
   D. Never

10. After you have seen a play or movie, would you want to read a criticism of the work?

   A. Often
   B. Occasionally
   C. Once or twice
   D. Never

8. Interest in French

1. The marks I get in French are usually

   A. Better than in most other subjects
   B. About average compared with other subjects
   C. Worse than in most other subjects

2. I like French

   A. More than most other subjects
   B. About the same as other subjects
   C. Less than most other subjects

3. I would like to study French after the end of this school year
   A. Yes
   B. Not sure
   C. No

4. French gets more interesting all the time
   A. Yes
   B. Not sure
   C. No

5. I would like to be able to speak more languages than (mother tongue)
   A. Yes
   B. Not sure
   C. No

6. I hope that in my career I will be able to make some use of the French I learned at school
   A. Yes
   B. Not sure
   C. No

7. I cannot profit from learning French because it is too difficult for me
   A. Yes
   B. Not sure
   C. No

8. I think that everyone would benefit from learning French
   A. Yes
   B. Not sure
   C. No

9. There are many subjects more important to learn at school than French
   A. Yes
   B. Not sure
   C. No

10. It is important to learn French while still at school
    A. Yes
    B. Not sure
    C. No

9. Perceived Utility of French

1. Studying French may someday help me to get a good job
   A. Strongly agree
   B. Agree
   C. Uncertain
   D. Disagree
   E. Strongly disagree

2. I need to study French because a foreign language is required in the school curriculum or to be admitted to a higher school
   A. Strongly agree
   B. Agree
   C. Uncertain
   D. Disagree
   E. Strongly disagree

3. I need to study French because it is used in school in the higher grades
   A. Strongly agree
   B. Agree
   C. Uncertain
   D. Disagree
   E. Strongly disagree

4. I need to study French in order to read books, newspapers or magazines that I want to read
   A. Strongly agree
   B. Agree
   C. Uncertain
   D. Disagree
   E. Strongly disagree

5. Studying French will help me if I need to study another foreign language later on
   A. Strongly agree
   B. Agree
   C. Uncertain
   D. Disagree
   E. Strongly disagree

6. Studying French will allow me to make friends more easily with French-speaking people
   A. Strongly agree
   B. Agree
   C. Uncertain
   D. Disagree
   E. Strongly disagree

7. Studying French will enable me to meet, talk or correspond with a greater variety of people
   A. Strongly agree
   B. Agree
   C. Uncertain
   D. Disagree
   E. Strongly disagree

8. One is well educated only if he knows at least one foreign language
   A. Strongly agree
   B. Agree
   C. Uncertain
   D. Disagree
   E. Strongly disagree

9. I am studying French because I enjoy it
   A. Strongly agree
   B. Agree
   C. Uncertain
   D. Disagree
   E. Strongly disagree

10. I am studying French because I was given no choice in the matter
    A. Strongly agree
    B. Agree
    C. Uncertain
    D. Disagree
    E. Strongly disagree

11. Studying French will help me to understand my own language better
    A. Strongly agree
    B. Agree
    C. Uncertain
    D. Disagree
    E. Strongly disagree

12. Studying French will help me to know and appreciate the way of life of people who speak French
    A. Strongly agree
    B. Agree
    C. Uncertain
    D. Disagree
    E. Strongly disagree

10. Activities Outside School (French)

1. Read French newspapers or magazines
   A. Often
   B. Sometimes
   C. Rarely or never

2. Listen to French language radio programs or watch French language films or French language TV programs
   A. Often
   B. Sometimes
   C. Rarely or never

3. Talk with French-speaking children or adults
   A. Often
   B. Sometimes
   C. Rarely or never

4. Correspond in French with a pen pal
   A. Often
   B. Sometimes
   C. Rarely or never

5. Attend meetings of French language societies or other French language cultural organizations
   A. Often
   B. Sometimes
   C. Rarely or never

6. Have visited a French-speaking country
   A. More than a month
   B. One month or less
   C. Never

11. Interest in English

1. The marks I get in English are usually
   A. Better than in most other subjects
   B. About average compared with other subjects
   C. Worse than in most other subjects

2. I like English
   A. More than most other subjects
   B. About the same as other subjects
   C. Less than most other subjects

3. I would like to study English after the end of this school year
   A. Yes
   B. Not sure
   C. No

4. English gets more interesting all the time
   A. Yes
   B. Not sure
   C. No

5. I would like to be able to speak more languages than (mother tongue)
   A. Yes
   B. Not sure
   C. No

6. I hope that in my career I will be able to make some use of the English I learned at school
    A. Yes
    B. Not sure
    C. No

7. I cannot profit from learning English because it is too difficult for me
    A. Yes
    B. Not sure
    C. No

8. I think that everyone would benefit from learning English
    A. Yes
    B. Not sure
    C. No

9. There are many subjects more important to learn at school than English
    A. Yes
    B. Not sure
    C. No

10. It is important to learn English while still at school
    A. Yes
    B. Not sure
    C. No

12. Perceived Utility of English

1. Studying English may someday help me to get a good job
    A. Strongly agree
    B. Agree
    C. Uncertain
    D. Disagree
    E. Strongly disagree

2. I need to study English because a foreign language is required in the school curriculum or to be admitted to a higher school
    A. Strongly agree
    B. Agree
    C. Uncertain
    D. Disagree
    E. Strongly disagree

3. I need to study English because it is used in school in the higher grades
    A. Strongly agree
    B. Agree
    C. Uncertain
    D. Disagree
    E. Strongly disagree

4. I need to study English in order to read books, newspapers or magazines that I want to read
   A. Strongly agree
   B. Agree
   C. Uncertain
   D. Disagree
   E. Strongly disagree

5. Studying English will help me if I need to study another foreign language later on
   A. Strongly agree
   B. Agree
   C. Uncertain
   D. Disagree
   E. Strongly disagree

6. Studying English will allow me to make friends more easily with English-speaking people
   A. Strongly agree
   B. Agree
   C. Uncertain
   D. Disagree
   E. Strongly disagree

7. Studying English will enable me to meet, talk or correspond with a greater variety of people
   A. Strongly agree
   B. Agree
   C. Uncertain
   D. Disagree
   E. Strongly disagree

8. One is well educated only if he knows at least one foreign language
   A. Strongly agree
   B. Agree
   C. Uncertain
   D. Disagree
   E. Strongly disagree

9. I am studying English because I enjoy it
   A. Strongly agree
   B. Agree
   C. Uncertain
   D. Disagree
   E. Strongly disagree

10. I am studying English because I was given no choice in the matter
    A. Strongly agree
    B. Agree

C. Uncertain
D. Disagree
E. Strongly disagree

11. Studying English will help me to understand my own language better
    A. Strongly agree
    B. Agree
    C. Uncertain
    D. Disagree
    E. Strongly disagree

12. Studying English will help me to know and appreciate the way of life of people who speak English
    A. Strongly agree
    B. Agree
    C. Uncertain
    D. Disagree
    E. Strongly disagree

13. Activities Outside School (English)

1. Read English newspapers or magazines
    A. Often
    B. Sometimes
    C. Rarely or never

2. Listen to English language radio programs or watch English language films or English language TV programs
    A. Often
    B. Sometimes
    C. Rarely or never

3. Talk with English-speaking children or adults
    A. Often
    B. Sometimes
    C. Rarely or never

4. Correspond in English with a pen pal
    A. Often
    B. Sometimes
    C. Rarely or never

5. Attend meetings of English language societies or other English language cultural organizations
    A. Often
    B. Sometimes
    C. Rarely or never

6. Have visited an English-speaking country
    A. More than a month
    B. One month or less
    C. Never

14. School Behavior

1. Students rarely express opinions which differ from the teacher's
    A. Agree
    B. Disagree

2. We are now allowed to sit in our classrooms during break
    A. Agree
    B. Disagree

3. The teachers often make you feel small
    A. Agree
    B. Disagree

4. Students can enter the school buildings as they arrive, without waiting to be lined up by the teachers
    A. Agree
    B. Disagree

5. The students decide for themselves where they will sit in the classroom
    A. Agree
    B. Disagree

6. In our school good behavior is more important than good grades
    A. Agree
    B. Disagree

7. The teachers always seem to criticize our best ideas
    A. Agree
    B. Disagree

8. Most teachers expect us to stand up when they come into the classroom
    A. Agree
    B. Disagree

9. We are allowed a free choice of some of the subjects we study
    A. Agree
    B. Disagree

10. Most of our teachers are very strict about homework
    A. Agree
    B. Disagree

11. The teachers do not usually punish a student who admits at the beginning of a lesson that he has not done his homework
    A. Agree
    B. Disagree

12. There is a clear distinction made in our school between students who are lazy and those who are less talented
    A. Agree
    B. Disagree

15. Science Teaching

1. We learn most of our Science through practical work and experiments
    A. Always
    B. Sometimes
    C. Never

2. Our Science teacher tests us only on what is in the textbook
    A. Always
    B. Sometimes
    C. Never

3. Students are encouraged to read Science magazines and reference books to become familiar with all aspects of Science
    A. Always
    B. Sometimes
    C. Never

4. We have a textbook for Science
    A. Always
    B. Sometimes
    C. Never

5. For Science homework we write up our laboratory and practical work
    A. Always
    B. Sometimes
    C. Never

6. Our Science classes contain more theoretical work than practical work
    A. Always
    B. Sometimes
    C. Never

7. During our Science lessons the amount of time we spend reading our textbooks is about
    A. 1/4 or less
    B. Half
    C. 3/4 or more

8. The main aim of our Science lessons is to understand our textbooks
   A. Always
   B. Sometimes
   C. Never

9. We are encouraged to take part in fieldwork and scientific research outside school
   A. Always
   B. Sometimes
   C. Never

10. Our Science lessons include laboratory experiments in which we all take part
    A. Always
    B. Sometimes
    C. Never

11. Our Science homework requires using a textbook
    A. Always
    B. Sometimes
    C. Never

12. We make observations and do experiments during our Science lessons
    A. Always
    B. Sometimes
    C. Never

16. Science Laboratory Teaching

1. When we work in the laboratory we are given complete instructions from the teacher as to what to do
   A. Always
   B. Sometimes
   C. Never

2. We use a book which tells us how to do our experiments in the laboratory
   A. Always
   B. Sometimes
   C. Never

3. We usually make up our own problems and then the teacher helps us to solve them experimentally
   A. Always
   B. Sometimes
   C. Never

4. In class we are encouraged to devise our own projects and experiments, either individually or in groups
   A. Always
   B. Sometimes
   C. Never

5. Our Science teacher demonstrates how to carry out the experiments before we do them
   A. Always
   B. Sometimes
   C. Never

6. In our practical work our teacher gives us certain problems to solve and then leaves us to find our own methods and solutions
   A. Always
   B. Sometimes
   C. Never

7. The teacher gives us questions to answer while we do our experiments
   A. Always
   B. Sometimes
   C. Never

8. We do our practical work from laboratory cards or instructions which tell us how to carry out the experiment
   A. Always
   B. Sometimes
   C. Never

REFERENCES

Acland, H. *The Impact of Schooling in the Elementary Grades*. Educational Policy Research Center, Harvard University, 1972.

Carroll, J. B. *The Teaching of French as a Foreign Language in Eight Countries*. Stockholm; Almqvist and Wiksell International and New York: John Wiley, 1975.

Coleman, J. S. et al. *Equality of Educational Opportunity, Vol. I and II.* Washington, D.C.: U.S. Government Printing Office, 1966.

Coleman, J. S. "Effects of School on Learning: The IEA Findings," Paper presented at the Harvard–IEA Conference, Harvard University, November, 1973.

Coleman, J. S. "Addendum and Corrections to 'Effects of School on Learning: The IEA Findings'" Paper presented at the Harward–IEA Conference, Harvard University, November, 1973.

Comber, L. C. and Keeves, J. P. *Science Education in Nineteen Countries: An Empirical Study*. Stockholm: Almqvist and Wiksell, and New York: John Wiley, 1973.

Crombach, L. J. Coefficient alpha and the internal structure of tests. *Psychometrika*, 16, 1951, pp. 297–334.

Flanagan, F. C. et al. *The American High School Student*. New York: United States Office of Education, 1964.

Hoyt, C. G. and Krishnaiah, P. R. Estimation of Test Reliability by Analysis of Variance Techniques. *Journal of Experimental Education*. Vol. 28, 1960, pp. 257–259.

Husén, T. (Ed.). *International Study of Achievement in Mathematics: A comparison of Twelve Countries, Vol. I and II.* Stockholm: Almqvist and Wiksell, and New York: John Wiley, 1967.

Jeffreys, Sir H. *Theory of Probability*. Oxford: Clarendon Press, 1939.

Jeffreys, Sir H. Scientific Inference. Cambridge: Cambridge University Press, 1957.

Jencks, C. et al. *Inequality: A Reappraisal of the Effect of Family and Schooling in America*. New York: Basic Books, 1972.

Kish, Leslie. *Survey Sampling*. New York: John Wiley (Halsted Press), 1964.

de Landsheere, G. Des enfants de 10 ans et leurs parents répondent à un questionnaire sur le milieu familial. *Education*, mai 1968, pp. 17–21.

Lewis, E. G. and Massad, C. E. *The Teaching of English as a Foreign Language in Ten Countries*. Stockholm: Almqvist and Wiksell International and New York: John Wiley, 1975.

Likert, R. "A Technique for the Measurement of Attitudes." *Archives of Psychology*, 140, 1932.

Mayeske, G. W. et al. *A Study of Our Nation's Schools*. Washington, D.C.: U.S. Government Printing Office, 1969.

Mosteller, F. and Tukey, J. W. "Data Analysis, Including Statistics." In G. Lindzey and E. Aronson (eds.), *The Handbook of Social Psychology*. Reading, Mass.: Addison-Wesley, 1968, Vol. II, pp. 80–203.

Newton, R. G. and Spurrell, D. J. "A Development of Multiple Regression for the Analysis of Routine Data." *Applied Statistics* XVI(1): 51–64, 1967.

Oppenheim, A. N. and Torney, Judith. *The Measurement of Children's Civic*

Attitudes in Different Nations. Stockholm: Almqvist and Wiksell and New York: John Wiley, 1974.

Pace, C. R. and Stern, G. G. An approach to the Measurement of Psychological Characteristics of College Environments. *Journal of Educational Psychology,* 49, 1958, pp. 269–277.

Peaker, G. F. "The Regression Analyses of The National Survey" in *Children and Their Primary Schools (The Plowden Report),* Vol. II. London: HMSO, 1971.

Peaker, G. F. "Statistics and Experimental Design." A mimeographed paper issued by the International Association for the Evaluation of Educational Achievement (IEA/TR/74), 1967.

Peaker, G. F. *The Plowden Children Four Years Later.* London: National Foundation for Educational Research in England and Wales, 1971.

Peaker, G. F. "Increments through Intervals." Paper presented at the Harvard–IEA Conference, Harvard University, November, 1973.

Peaker, G. F. "The Principles of 'Effects of School on Learning: The IEA Findings' Applied to an Example." Paper presented at the Harvard–IEA Conference, Harvard University, November, 1973.

Purves, A. C. *Literature Education in Ten Countries: An Empirical Study.* Stockholm: Almqvist and Wiksell and New York: John Wiley, 1973.

Popper, Sir K. R. *The Logic of Scientific Discovery.* London: Routledge and Kegan Paul, 1949.

Popper, Sir K. R. *The Open Society and its Enemies.* London: Routledge and Kegan Paul, 1945.

Russell, B. *Human Knowledge: Its Scope and Limits.* London: George Allen and Unwin, 1948.

Super, D. E. (editor). *Toward a Cross-National Model of Educational Achievement in a National Economy.* ERIC ED 040969.

Thorndike, R. L. *Reading Comprehension Education in Fifteen Countries: An Empirical Study.* Stockholm: Almqvist and Wiksell and New York: John Wiley, 1973.

Thorndike, R. L. "Reading as Reasoning." *Reading Research Quarterly,* Vol. IX, No. 2, pp. 135–147, 1973–4.

Torney, J. V., Oppenheim, A. N. and Farnen, R. F. *Civic Education in Ten Countries: An Empirical Study.* Stockholm: Almqvist and Wiksell International and New York: John Wiley, 1975.

IEA Data Processing

Roy W. Phillipps (IEA International and Department of Education, New Zealand)

The task of collecting, editing and processing the data from the IEA Six Subject Survey was a formidable task. Although it is hoped to report in detail on the Data Processing operation in a separate publication, it is appropriate here to outline the basic organization used throughout the study.

PRETEST DATA

During the instrument development stage of the project, the National Centers and an IEA Data Processing Unit shared the data processing. Each National Center concerned undertook the responsibility for scoring the cognitive instruments and producing an item analysis of the pretest forms. These item analyses were collated in IEA International for use by the International Subject Committees. The Data Processing Unit established at the National Foundation for Education Research in England and Wales (NFER) under Dr. Buce H. Choppin carried out the factor and item analyses of the attitudinal scale data. At the same time the initial planning and programming for the file development of the main data were commenced in this Unit.

DATA COLLECTION

Answer Cards

In preference to having National Centers punch all their data onto cards, IEA decided to make extensive use of answer cards for optical scanning. (Four countries, India, Iran, Israel and Japan, elected not to use answer cards and their data was punched at the National Centers and the card images were entered onto magnetic tape.) The cards selected were the same size as ordinary punch cards but had the special feature of pre-designated positions where respondents

221

could make marks on the card in pencil which were directly machine readable. An added attraction was that these cards, known in the survey as MRC cards, could carry responses on both sides. The answer cards were designed to match the instruments in the study and for both stages some 23 different cards were designed and over 2 500 000 single cards were printed (see Figure 1). The printing of answer cards which is a specialized process was undertaken for Stage 2 in Sweden and for Stage 3 in the USA.

Pre-Identification of Answer Cards

Each student was expected to complete more than one answer card. In order to avoid having to instruct the students how to mark up the code numbers for student, school and country it was decided to pre-punch identifications into the cards before they were distributed. This was undertaken at NFER by Miss Doreen Trinder using a computer program control. The time sequence proved to be too tight for most countries to be able to supply accurate numbers for their sample before the pre-identification process commenced. As a consequence, an estimated number of cards had to be used which meant that more answer cards than were ultimately used were ordered. Provision also had to be made for a supply of blank cards on which the National Centers could hand mark the identifications if the actual number of cards supplied was less than their estimated numbers or should cards be lost or damaged.

Processing

There were few optical scanners suitable and available for reading answer cards. After early trials with a machine in Stockholm the operation was transferred to the Measurement Research Center in Iowa City, USA. Apart from two systematic errors detected from a quality control process, the reading performance of the optical scanner proved highly satisfactory. The machine had to cope with marks having a wide range of densities, yet through the process it continued to produce near perfect correspondence with human scrutiny of the marks. The costs of the operation suggested that using MRC cards effected a saving of some four to eight times the cost of using punched cards as well as a tremendous saving in time.

Figure 1. *Specimen MRC cards*
Science Achievement Test Card

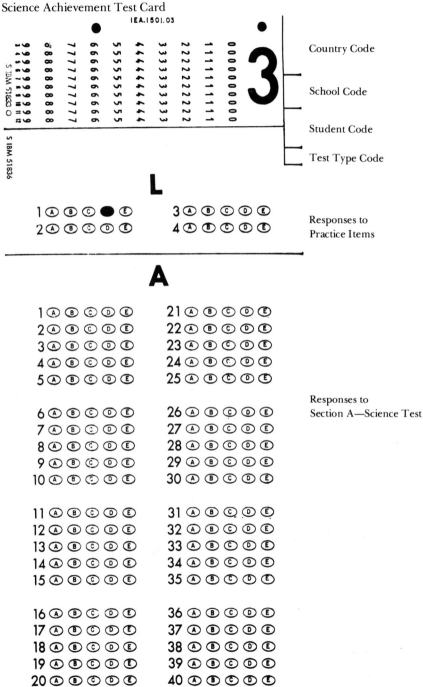

Country Code

School Code

Student Code

Test Type Code

Responses to
Practice Items

Responses to
Section A—Science Test

S IBM 51836 B

B

1 Ⓐ Ⓑ Ⓒ Ⓓ Ⓔ		21 Ⓐ Ⓑ Ⓒ Ⓓ Ⓔ
2 Ⓐ Ⓑ Ⓒ Ⓓ Ⓔ		22 Ⓐ Ⓑ Ⓒ Ⓓ Ⓔ
3 Ⓐ Ⓑ Ⓒ Ⓓ Ⓔ		23 Ⓐ Ⓑ Ⓒ Ⓓ Ⓔ
4 Ⓐ Ⓑ Ⓒ Ⓓ Ⓔ		24 Ⓐ Ⓑ Ⓒ Ⓓ Ⓔ
5 Ⓐ Ⓑ Ⓒ Ⓓ Ⓔ		25 Ⓐ Ⓑ Ⓒ Ⓓ Ⓔ
6 Ⓐ Ⓑ Ⓒ Ⓓ Ⓔ		26 Ⓐ Ⓑ Ⓒ Ⓓ Ⓔ
7 Ⓐ Ⓑ Ⓒ Ⓓ Ⓔ		27 Ⓐ Ⓑ Ⓒ Ⓓ Ⓔ
8 Ⓐ Ⓑ Ⓒ Ⓓ Ⓔ		28 Ⓐ Ⓑ Ⓒ Ⓓ Ⓔ
9 Ⓐ Ⓑ Ⓒ Ⓓ Ⓔ		29 Ⓐ Ⓑ Ⓒ Ⓓ Ⓔ
10 Ⓐ Ⓑ Ⓒ Ⓓ Ⓔ		30 Ⓐ Ⓑ Ⓒ Ⓓ Ⓔ
11 Ⓐ Ⓑ Ⓒ Ⓓ Ⓔ		31 Ⓐ Ⓑ Ⓒ Ⓓ Ⓔ
12 Ⓐ Ⓑ Ⓒ Ⓓ Ⓔ		32 Ⓐ Ⓑ Ⓒ Ⓓ Ⓔ
13 Ⓐ Ⓑ Ⓒ Ⓓ Ⓔ		33 Ⓐ Ⓑ Ⓒ Ⓓ Ⓔ
14 Ⓐ Ⓑ Ⓒ Ⓓ Ⓔ		34 Ⓐ Ⓑ Ⓒ Ⓓ Ⓔ
15 Ⓐ Ⓑ Ⓒ Ⓓ Ⓔ		35 Ⓐ Ⓑ Ⓒ Ⓓ Ⓔ
16 Ⓐ Ⓑ Ⓒ Ⓓ Ⓔ		36 Ⓐ Ⓑ Ⓒ Ⓓ Ⓔ
17 Ⓐ Ⓑ Ⓒ Ⓓ Ⓔ		37 Ⓐ Ⓑ Ⓒ Ⓓ Ⓔ
18 Ⓐ Ⓑ Ⓒ Ⓓ Ⓔ		38 Ⓐ Ⓑ Ⓒ Ⓓ Ⓔ
19 Ⓐ Ⓑ Ⓒ Ⓓ Ⓔ		39 Ⓐ Ⓑ Ⓒ Ⓓ Ⓔ
20 Ⓐ Ⓑ Ⓒ Ⓓ Ⓔ		40 Ⓐ Ⓑ Ⓒ Ⓓ Ⓔ

Responses to
Section B—Science Test

World Knowledge and General
Questionnaire Response Card

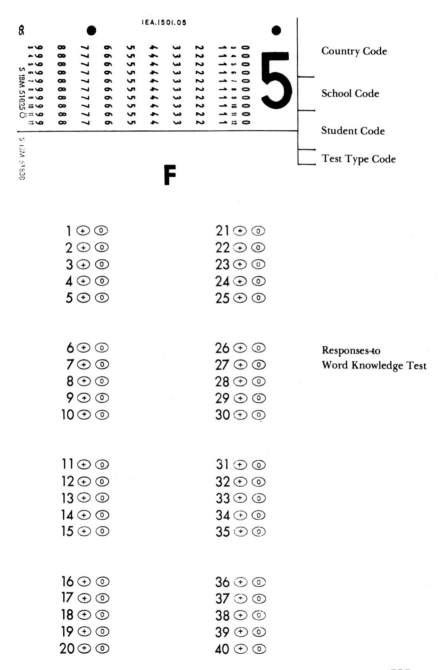

IEA.I5OI.05

5

Country Code

School Code

Student Code

Test Type Code

F

1 ⊕ ⊙	21 ⊕ ⊙
2 ⊕ ⊙	22 ⊕ ⊙
3 ⊕ ⊙	23 ⊕ ⊙
4 ⊕ ⊙	24 ⊕ ⊙
5 ⊕ ⊙	25 ⊕ ⊙

6 ⊕ ⊙	26 ⊕ ⊙
7 ⊕ ⊙	27 ⊕ ⊙
8 ⊕ ⊙	28 ⊕ ⊙
9 ⊕ ⊙	29 ⊕ ⊙
10 ⊕ ⊙	30 ⊕ ⊙

Responses to
Word Knowledge Test

11 ⊕ ⊙	31 ⊕ ⊙
12 ⊕ ⊙	32 ⊕ ⊙
13 ⊕ ⊙	33 ⊕ ⊙
14 ⊕ ⊙	34 ⊕ ⊙
15 ⊕ ⊙	35 ⊕ ⊙

16 ⊕ ⊙	36 ⊕ ⊙
17 ⊕ ⊙	37 ⊕ ⊙
18 ⊕ ⊙	38 ⊕ ⊙
19 ⊕ ⊙	39 ⊕ ⊙
20 ⊕ ⊙	40 ⊕ ⊙

Word Knowledge and General
Questionnaire Response Card—
Reverse Side

S IBM 51838 B

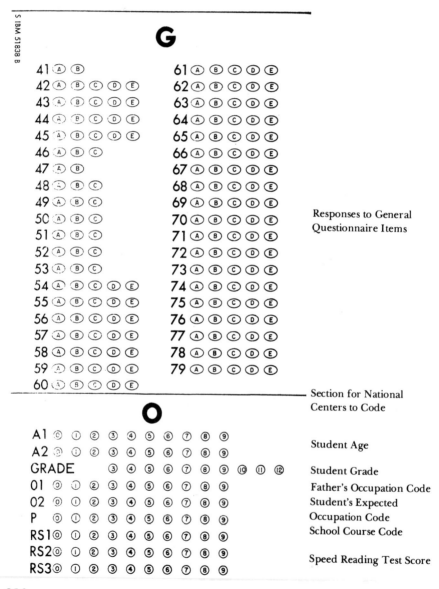

G

41 Ⓐ Ⓑ	61 Ⓐ Ⓑ Ⓒ Ⓓ Ⓔ
42 Ⓐ Ⓑ Ⓒ Ⓓ Ⓔ	62 Ⓐ Ⓑ Ⓒ Ⓓ Ⓔ
43 Ⓐ Ⓑ Ⓒ Ⓓ Ⓔ	63 Ⓐ Ⓑ Ⓒ Ⓓ Ⓔ
44 Ⓐ Ⓑ Ⓒ Ⓓ Ⓔ	64 Ⓐ Ⓑ Ⓒ Ⓓ Ⓔ
45 Ⓐ Ⓑ Ⓒ Ⓓ Ⓔ	65 Ⓐ Ⓑ Ⓒ Ⓓ Ⓔ
46 Ⓐ Ⓑ Ⓒ	66 Ⓐ Ⓑ Ⓒ Ⓓ Ⓔ
47 Ⓐ Ⓑ	67 Ⓐ Ⓑ Ⓒ Ⓓ Ⓔ
48 Ⓐ Ⓑ Ⓒ	68 Ⓐ Ⓑ Ⓒ Ⓓ Ⓔ
49 Ⓐ Ⓑ Ⓒ	69 Ⓐ Ⓑ Ⓒ Ⓓ Ⓔ
50 Ⓐ Ⓑ Ⓒ	70 Ⓐ Ⓑ Ⓒ Ⓓ Ⓔ
51 Ⓐ Ⓑ Ⓒ	71 Ⓐ Ⓑ Ⓒ Ⓓ Ⓔ
52 Ⓐ Ⓑ Ⓒ	72 Ⓐ Ⓑ Ⓒ Ⓓ Ⓔ
53 Ⓐ Ⓑ Ⓒ	73 Ⓐ Ⓑ Ⓒ Ⓓ Ⓔ
54 Ⓐ Ⓑ Ⓒ Ⓓ Ⓔ	74 Ⓐ Ⓑ Ⓒ Ⓓ Ⓔ
55 Ⓐ Ⓑ Ⓒ Ⓓ Ⓔ	75 Ⓐ Ⓑ Ⓒ Ⓓ Ⓔ
56 Ⓐ Ⓑ Ⓒ Ⓓ Ⓔ	76 Ⓐ Ⓑ Ⓒ Ⓓ Ⓔ
57 Ⓐ Ⓑ Ⓒ Ⓓ Ⓔ	77 Ⓐ Ⓑ Ⓒ Ⓓ Ⓔ
58 Ⓐ Ⓑ Ⓒ Ⓓ Ⓔ	78 Ⓐ Ⓑ Ⓒ Ⓓ Ⓔ
59 Ⓐ Ⓑ Ⓒ Ⓓ Ⓔ	79 Ⓐ Ⓑ Ⓒ Ⓓ Ⓔ
60 Ⓐ Ⓑ Ⓒ Ⓓ Ⓔ	

Responses to General
Questionnaire Items

Section for National
Centers to Code

O

A1 ⓪ ① ② ③ ④ ⑤ ⑥ ⑦ ⑧ ⑨
A2 ⓪ ① ② ③ ④ ⑤ ⑥ ⑦ ⑧ ⑨
GRADE ③ ④ ⑤ ⑥ ⑦ ⑧ ⑨ ⑩ ⑪ ⑫
01 ⓪ ① ② ③ ④ ⑤ ⑥ ⑦ ⑧ ⑨
02 ⓪ ① ② ③ ④ ⑤ ⑥ ⑦ ⑧ ⑨
P ⓪ ① ② ③ ④ ⑤ ⑥ ⑦ ⑧ ⑨
RS1 ⓪ ① ② ③ ④ ⑤ ⑥ ⑦ ⑧ ⑨
RS2 ⓪ ① ② ③ ④ ⑤ ⑥ ⑦ ⑧ ⑨
RS3 ⓪ ① ② ③ ④ ⑤ ⑥ ⑦ ⑧ ⑨

Student Age

Student Grade
Father's Occupation Code
Student's Expected
Occupation Code
School Course Code

Speed Reading Test Score

NEW YORK DATA PROCESSING UNIT

Although the initial file building programming took place at NFER, it was planned that the bulk of the data processing would take place in New York where the computation facilities at Columbia University were considered to be advantageous. In 1969 Dr Choppin moved to Teachers College, Columbia, New York to establish the IEA New York Data Processing Unit (NYDPU), together with Mr John Hall and Mr Dick Russell. During 1969 countries had undertaken a trial run, known as the "dry run," of the procedures connected with the Stage 2 testing. This involved the use of a small judgment sample of schools in each country. Apart from providing National Centers with an opportunity to evaluate their own national arrangements, it gave the New York Data Processing Unit (NYDPU) an opportunity to test its programs for file building and the production of univariate and item analyses. Ideally, this should have provided an opportunity for further feedback to IEA and the International Committees before the instruments were used in the main testing. In the event, time and financial constraints limited the amount of review that was possible and in consequence the scheduled data processing was not completely programmed and tested by the time the first Stage 2 data arrived in late 1970.

File Building

The raw data arrived at the NYDPU as:

1. Card images on magnetic tape
2. Punched cards

Not all the IEA data was planned for answer cards. As mentioned above, four countries had opted to use punch cards for all their data. Each country had to punch the responses to the School Questionnaires. These were forwarded to New York either as punch cards or as card images on magnetic tape. The raw records were then compounded into the records belonging to the same unit, e.g., student, teacher or school. At the same time an extensive operation of detection and correction of errors had to be undertaken. These simple statements do not convey the tremendous difficulties inherent in file building. A single file of all a country's data is not necessarily the most convenient form for the envisaged future processing. At Stage 2, where it was largely true that the same students were tested for all three subjects, each country's record was split up by populations and then further divided according to whether the data was based on student, teacher or school, making in all 165 files. At Stage 3 the data had to be organized by subjects as well.

Statistical Analyses

As a first step, weights were assigned to the samples to compensate for imbalances in the sampling plan or for loss of data (see Chapter 2). This was followed by the scoring of all cognitive tests and attitudinal scale measures culminating in the production of comprehensive univariates for each population in a country. Univariate printouts for students, teachers and schools were at this stage made available to the International Committees and to the respective National Centers. It had always been the policy of IEA to report back to the schools which took part in the survey. The National Centers were therefore supplied with information for each school on how their students performed, together with information for other similar schools and for the country as a whole. Programs were also written which enabled printouts of a full item and scale analysis to be produced for the International Subject Committees and the National Centers.

The New York Data Processing Unit continued its operations until mid 1973, when the remaining tasks were transferred to the Stockholm Data Processing Unit which had been established in 1969. During its existence the NYDPU operated under very difficult conditions due mainly to the tight time-table but also to unforeseen technical problems. Throughout its life the Unit was under the general supervision of Professor Robert Thorndike and Dr Richard Wolf, Teachers College, Columbia, New York. A number of changes in key staff members added to the already complex difficulties of handling such a vast amount of data. Mr John Hall replaced Dr Bruce Choppin as leader of the Unit at the end of 1969. Mr Hall left the project towards the completion of the Stage 2 analyses and he was succeeded by Mr Paul Barbuto and Mr Kevin Doyle who carried the brunt of the Stage 3 processing. IEA worked to very rigid deadlines which were determined by the time limits of the grants received from funding agencies. That the data were organized and analyzed by and large within the time-table testified to the competence and ingenuity of the NYDPU members.

STOCKHOLM DATA PROCESSING UNIT

Late in 1969 it became evident that additional data processing resources would be required if all the planned analyses were to be completed in time. A second Data Processing Unit was therefore established in Stockholm (SDPU) to undertake among other things the analyses associated with the regressions reported in Chapter 4 *et seq.* and to produce the bivariates needed for these analyses. The core staff consisted of Mr Mats Carlid, Miss Birgit Cedheim and Mr Krister Widén, assisted at various times by Miss Zenia Hellström and consultant Mr Bo Jansson.

For both stages the same technical procedures were followed. Once cleaned and scored tapes were received from New York for students, teachers and schools a merged file was produced. Zero order correlation matrices were produced using a set of selected student variables which included contenders for the criteria variables. This enabled the authors of the reports to select the criterion variables that were to be entered into the next step—a partial "scrubbing" run where an extended list of student, teacher and school variables were used as predictors against the selected criteria once the Home Background Variable (SHS) had been partialled out. By plotting the partial regression co-efficients by countries for each variable on a single scale the process of selecting the variables to enter the regression equation was simplified. For Stage 2 both between-students and between-schools regressions were produced. At Stage 3 a between-school regression was not possible for reasons of both time and finance.

Concurrent with the production of the regression analyses the SDPU created imaginative programs for the Newton and Spurrell analyses as well as many special analyses requested by authors of the reports. The resourcefulness and dedication of the SDPU staff has played a very significant part in the success of the IEA Six Subject Survey. It would be fair to say that without the creativity of Mr Carlid in designing programs that were not only time saving but economical as well, the project could not have been completed within the time span available.

DATA BANK

Through the generosity of the Ford Foundation, the Bank of Sweden Tercentenary Fund and the University of Stockholm, IEA has been able during 1973–1974 to undertake further editing of the Six Subject Survey data. These data have now been assembled on to 10 different merged files each supported by code books, as outlined in the Foreword to this Report. It is hoped that research workers in the field of education and allied disciplines will make use of this rich and unique source of data for further analyses.

CONCLUSION

Although IEA had previous experience with the data processing from the Mathematics Survey to support the organization and processing of the Six Subject Survey data, it soon became evident that dealing with six subjects did not simply mean repeating the prior experience six times. The sheer magnitude ot the data assembled from the 21 countries, together with the international nature of the enterprise, posed special problems. It is a tribute to international cooperation that most member countries were able to keep to the deadlines for testing and dispatch of their data. That IEA International, based in Stockholm since 1969, was able to collate the work of the satellite Data Processing Units and have the analyses completed before the project officially ended in May 1973, in spite of major processing difficulties, exemplifies the spirit of cooperation which permeated the whole project. However, as the project progressed, two recommendations for future surveys became abundantly clear. First, in the interests of efficiency of communication between IEA and the data processors it would be wise to consolidate all the data processing facilities at the same center as the international headquarters. Second, closer collaboration with the data programmer at the instrument construction stage would possibly anticipate a number of coding and data problems that arose during the processing of the survey data.